Spur
of the
Moment
Cook

ALSO BY PERLA MEYERS

The Seasonal Kitchen

The Peasant Kitchen

From Market to Kitchen

Perla Meyers' Art of Seasonal Cooking

Spur of the Moment Cook

Perla Meyers

William Morrow and Company, Inc. • New York

It is the policy of William Morrow and Company, Inc., and its imprints and affiliates,
recognizing the importance of preserving what has been written, to print the books
we publish on acid-free paper, and we exert our best efforts to that end.

Library of Congress Cataloging-in-Publication Data

Meyers, Perla.
    Spur of the moment cook / Perla Meyers.
       p.   cm.
    Includes index.
    ISBN 0-688-11009-6
    1. Cookery.   I. Title.
TX652.M475   1994
641.5—dc20   93-33690
                                                                 CIP

Printed in the United States of America

2 3 4 5 6 7 8 9 10

To My Family

for enthusiastically tasting every type of "spur of the moment" food and
putting up with my preoccupation with this project for so long

And to Michael

in appreciation for eighteen years of unfailing friendship that would be
hard to match in and out of the family

Contents

Spur
of the
Moment
Cook

Introduction

This book IS FOR EVERY PERSON IN AMERICA WHO HAS EVER SAID EVEN ONE OF THESE PHRASES: "I LOVE TO COOK, BUT WHO HAS THE TIME?" "IT'S NO FUN COOKING WHEN I COME HOME EXHAUSTED," "COOKING USED TO BE A PLEASURE—NOW IT'S JUST ANOTHER CHORE," OR "I ONLY COOK ON WEEKENDS WHEN I HAVE MORE TIME." FRANKLY, EVEN THOUGH I LOVE TO COOK, AND THAT'S WHAT I DO FOR A LIVING, I'VE OFTEN FELT THE SAME WAY!

THE PROBLEM IS WE'RE ALL OVERBOOKED AND OVERWHELMED THESE DAYS. BUT I DON'T THINK THE SOLUTION HAS TO BE A LIFETIME SENTENCE OF TAKE-OUT PIZZA, NOISY RESTAURANTS SERVING FOOD YOU COULD PROB-

ably make better at home, tasteless frozen dinners, or a charge account at the local Chinese restaurant. I think the answer is a different kind of cooking for the way we live today: cooking that allows for our busy schedules and our desire to spend less time in the kitchen but that still embraces our desire for simple, satisfying home cooking.

And this is what *Spur of the Moment Cook* is all about: recipes that rely on a combination of basic ingredients and the best of what's fresh and seasonal, cooked with ease and pleasure; recipes that balance organization with spontaneity; recipes that are helpful guides rather than strict formulas; recipes that result in meals that are spirited and flavorful, that nourish us both emotionally and physically. Recipes for a robust roasted vegetable soup, a creamy chèvre omelette with fresh tarragon, a last-minute brochette of grilled shrimp with a sesame marinade, or a luscious gratin of peaches with a creamy pecan crumble: What all of these recipes have in common is my firm belief that the only thing more satisfying than a home-cooked meal is being able to cook it with enthusiasm and pleasure — to feel that the only restraint is your imagination, to know that you can sacrifice time without sacrificing taste, to enjoy the process as much as you delight in the result.

If what makes Spur of the Moment cooking necessary is our need to find a way to cook at home when we're not home all day, what makes this kind of cooking possible is a wonderful wealth of options that we've never had before.

We now have both lots of help in the kitchen — everything from food processors and microwaves to cut down on prep work and speed up the process — and excellent time-saving ingredients like quick-cooking polenta and ready-made pasta, both fresh and dried.

As a nation, we now have, I think, a much more enlightened sensibility about championing and promoting the best of what's local and regional, with a huge variety and abundance to inspire us. Just think of what we see in the market these days: twelve kinds of apples in the fall; yellow corn, white corn, and butter and sugar corn in August; local melons and squashes; tomatoes that range from antique yellow cherry varieties to enormous red-and-green-streaked Big Boys; purple potatoes, sweet potatoes, red potatoes, and fingerlings; and fresh chives, parsley, and scallions to go with them!

Because there's so much available, I find that food shopping is more pleasurable than ever. As a transplanted European living in New York City, I'm lucky enough to have here what I grew up with: a butcher I trust, a bakery where I know I'll get the freshest bread, a fish store where I can find the smallest scallops, the sweetest lobster, and, of course, the best gossip. Growing up in Europe, I learned at an early age that the sociability and camaraderie of the neighborhood food merchant can be every bit as satisfying as the food!

Because of my background I have never been a big proponent of American supermarkets, but I'm happy to report that as I've traveled across the country teaching cooking classes, I've noticed a huge change. Supermarkets from Denver to Danbury have become more focused, more experienced, more specialized. They're looking at food more as a delicacy and less as a commodity. They don't just have shelves filled with meat—they have a butcher in the back to give you advice. They know that no one's going to race in after a long, exhausting day just to experience the thrill of iceberg lettuce, all-too-familiar Red Delicious apples, and boiled ham at the deli counter, so they offer arugula, radicchio, and mesclun, Rome Beauties, Cortlands, and Pippins, honey-baked ham, imported prosciutto, and hickory-smoked turkey.

And supermarkets, reflecting the diversity of their neighborhoods, are much more multicultural these days, stocking the kinds of ethnic foods and spices that can add a new dimension to Spur of the Moment cooking. Not so long ago in New York City, I would have had to go to Little Italy for good Parmesan, to Chinatown for lemon grass and fresh cilantro, to four or five neighborhood fruit stands for mangoes and papayas. Now I can usually find everything from Greek olives to Arborio rice to chanterelle mushrooms on my local supermarket shelf.

Clearly, the "no time to cook" refrain makes Spur of the Moment cooking a good idea. The abundance of fresh ingredients and the convenience of modern kitchens make Spur of the Moment cooking possible. But there are two other important components. One is spontaneity and the other is organization. At the risk of creating a new cooking oxymoron, Spur of the Moment cooking means a kind of prepared spontaneity.

Spontaneity is the willingness to be open to new ideas, to know that being impulsive can help you be more creative, to throw away a list you made at 9:00 A.M. and give in to what you're in the mood to cook at 5:00 P.M., to being so curious about the purple Peruvian potatoes at the farmer's market that you just have to buy a pound or two to try. Spontaneity is not finding a fish worthy enough to be the main course you had in mind for dinner that night but cooking two seafood pasta side dishes instead.

The joy of being spontaneous is finding that cooking can be liberating, creative, and exciting. You can experiment, use your judgment, make up your own rules, do everything different from the way your mother taught you, and still produce great dishes and dinners!

The other essential ingredient of Spur of the Moment cooking is organization. You can't have spontaneity without organization. You can't, for example, impulsively whip up a fragrant summer risotto with the pattypan squash and fresh basil you found at the farm stand unless you've got Arborio rice, a good green olive oil, and a chunk of Parmesan already on hand. You must have a well-organized kitchen and a well-stocked pantry. You must make sure your vegetable bin is filled with basics, that your pantry has at least three kinds of dried pastas, that your jarred spices haven't dried out or lost their punch.

If being organized is the key to spontaneity, then careful shopping for even basic ingredients is the key to organization. To shop for a Spur of the Moment dinner, you have to be focused. Go with a list that will be your basic plan, but then ask yourself: What's fresh today? What haven't I served for a while? What would be fun to cook? The key is to use your eyes, nose, and taste buds. They'll tell you what to buy—and what to stay away from! If you're buying what's fresh and fragile, buy only what you'll use in the next few days.

I usually shop once or twice a week for fresh greens and seasonal fruits and vegetables. I do a monthly supermarket run to stock up on staples like carrots, celery, and baking potatoes. When I'm selecting meat, fish, and poultry, I let whatever is the most fresh sway me. I may have planned to buy salmon, for example, only to discover that tender Maryland soft-shell crabs, available for only a short time, have just arrived in town. The salmon can wait; I buy the crab knowing that once I get home and my imagination takes over, I'll be able to create a fresh, spirited Spur of the Moment meal. (To be perfectly frank, the downside of this open-ended spontaneity has occasionally resulted in some dishes that I would call Noble Failures, but I believe that's why God invented pizza delivery.)

Ultimately, Spur of the Moment cooking is all about pleasure. It is food of mood, spirit, and season. It is cooking that mirrors the way we live. Which is to say, I don't know anybody whose social life revolves around fancy, formal dinner parties, four-course meals, or the perfect wine. We'd rather have food that tastes good than something that looks as if it were sculpted by a food stylist for the cover of *Gourmet*. We want to try new tastes, to be surprised, to cook Thai on Tuesday and Italian on Wednesday. We want to be able to buy a great take-out grilled chicken and use all our time baking a fabulous dessert. We are sophisticated enough to know that just because something is quick and easy doesn't mean it won't produce complex and captivating results. We have figured out that spending hours slaving over something really complicated in the kitchen doesn't mean it's going to taste better than something ridiculously simple. As some wise cook once said, "Life is too short to stuff a mushroom."

Spur of the Moment cooking is at heart more about ease than time. So while some of the recipes in the book take just minutes to prepare and serve, others are quick to put together but require a longer time in the oven, giving you some time to do other things. The Spur of the Moment cook is one who can enjoy being in the kitchen nibbling on bread or cheese, sipping a glass of wine, while creating the kind of richly textured meal you can get only at home. To achieve that, you'll find I've included more stove-top preparation than oven cooking, more pasta than beef, more creative quick dishes like skillet salads and main-dish polentas than long-cooking roasts and stews, more flavor-infused skillet roasting and oven braising of vegetables than boiling and steaming, more ripe fruit compotes and sabayons than traditional cakes and pies.

In short, Spur of the Moment cooking is a fresh and timely way to enjoy the timeless tradition of home cooking.

The $\mathscr{P}$antry

If you really WANT TO KNOW WHO I AM, HOW I LIVE, WHERE I'VE TRAVELED, WHAT MAKES ME HAPPY, IT'S EASY TO FIND OUT: JUST LOOK IN MY PANTRY. THE TRUTH IS, PANTRIES ARE EXTREMELY REVEALING ABOUT PEOPLE'S EATING AND COOKING HABITS, PASSIONS, AND PERSONALITIES.

BECAUSE THEY ARE A REFLECTION OF OUR OWN UNIQUE PREFERENCES, WHIMS, AND HABITS, NO TWO PANTRIES WILL (OR SHOULD) LOOK EXACTLY THE SAME. THE HOISIN SAUCE AND RICE VINEGAR ONE PERSON CAN'T LIVE WITHOUT ARE INGREDIENTS THAT WOULD ONLY GATHER DUST FOR SOMEONE WHO RARELY COOKS CHINESE FOOD. THREE TYPES OF BREAD FLOUR, FOUR KINDS OF SUGAR, WHEAT BERRIES, AND DRIED FRUITS ARE ALL STAPLES TO

the serious baker but of little use to the rest of us.

A well-stocked pantry is the key to successful Spur of the Moment cooking. Your pantry should contain all the everyday ingredients you need to create good, flavorful food, but exactly what it should be

stocked with has more to do with good sense and personal preference than with strict rules and edicts.

So while my pantry may always have porcini mushrooms, at least five kinds of dried pasta, oil-cured olives, sun-dried–tomato paste, and Arborio rice for the Italian (and Italian-inspired) dishes I make all the time, your pantry may reflect a recent fascination with Thai cooking, your penchant for soup making, your husband's peanut butter obsession. Neither one of us will get in trouble with the Pantry Police.

There are, I believe, certain guidelines that can help all of us shop wisely for the kinds of basics we are most likely to need for Spur of the Moment cooking. These guidelines can help us steer clear of trendy, overpriced, exotic goodies we'll never use, the cute little jars we're likely to pick up in airports and fine gourmet stores on our travels. And with any luck, we won't experience the searing headache that comes when you have all the items you need for the dish you're dying to make for dinner except one essential ingredient — and it's 7:15 and the nearest store that stocks it is ten miles away and closes at 7:30! It goes without saying that real basics like dried herbs, spices, jams and syrups, powdered bouillon and canned broth, cooking oils, condiments, potatoes, garlic, and onions are the backbone of everyday cooking. But because our repertoire has expanded to include a wide variety of ethnic and regional dishes, what used to be considered an "exotic" ingredient can now be considered a pantry staple. So, depending on

your favorite cuisine and cookbooks, make sure you have an assortment of ingredients like green and red chili paste, quick couscous, polenta, toasted sesame seed oil, lemon grass, and mirin.

In addition to a basic shelf and an ethnic shelf, I often use what I've got on what I call my gourmet shelf. This is where I store the really special ingredients, like truffles, canned snails, red salmon caviar, and saffron, that help turn a simple Spur of the Moment dish into a truly exciting, memorable meal. The other shelf I would recommend is a basic baker's shelf, with flour, sugar, cocoa, and vanilla beans.

You're not finished yet! If you're really going to be organized, you have to extend your concept of the pantry into your refrigerator, where the vegetable bin needs stocking at least twice a week and the dairy shelf should include fresh milk, sour cream, yogurt, butter, and eggs. Think of your freezer as part of the pantry, too, and use it for supplies like soup, stock, fruit concentrates, nuts, ice cream, and pastry dough.

And remember, if it's out of style, out of date, or out of taste, throw it out! Admit to yourself that you'll never, ever use those pink and green peppercorns you bought during that food fad. Ask yourself why you seem to have an irrational emotional attachment to half a tin of flavorless curry powder and a can of flat paprika. Confess that there is probably no recipe you'll ever use that will call for the jalapeño chutney mint sauce you bought on a trip to Santa Fe. Be vigilant, be organized, be sensible, be prepared. (And if you look in my pantry, ask me what I'm doing with that enormous jar of fancy French brandied cherries soaked in kirsch, the tiny bottles of fruit extract with pretty hand-painted labels, and the homemade jar of Jerusalem artichoke chutney that's turned an unappetizing shade of chartreuse!)

To help you keep a well-stocked pantry, I have devised a quick checklist. Personally, I follow no set schedule for restocking. Whenever I am out shopping for a Spur of the Moment meal, I may pick up something for any one of my pantry shelves.

The Cupboard

Canned Ingredients

ANCHOVIES

Anchovies are an important basic. When used properly, their taste is not "fishy" at all. Instead it is a bit like adding MSG to a dressing, a quick tomato sauce, a green mayonnaise, or pasta. I like the Duet brand best of all, but it is usually available only in specialty stores. If you are supermarket shopping, look for brands that are packed in olive oil, from Portugal or Spain. These anchovies are usually tastier, "meatier," and less salty than others. If you do find Duet, buy several extra cans and store them, unopened, in the refrigerator, where they will last for several months.

BEETS

Canned or jarred beets are an excellent pantry basic. They do not have the texture of freshly cooked beets but can nevertheless give a nice taste to, for example, an endive and potato salad. Tip: One beet pureed with a balsamic vinegar dressing will produce a wonderful deeply red vinaigrette that is lovely with fresh steamed asparagus or poached leeks.

BOUILLON

I prefer dehydrated bouillon to canned, and usually opt for MBT or Knorr, since they have the best taste and are far less salty than other brands. If you cannot find either, then a canned broth such as Swanson's or College Inn will give you pretty good results.

CORN NIBLETS

Canned corn has nothing to do with fresh corn, but I like the flavor of this canned vegetable and in fact prefer it over frozen corn, which I find rather tasteless. I often use canned corn for additional texture in soups, legume salads, and quick salsas.

LEGUMES

Canned pinto beans, chick peas, Great Northern beans, black beans, and kidney beans are all pantry basics. As an addition to a chili, a salad, a soup, or a stew, they are quite acceptable. Certain brands are better than others; I usually opt for either Goya or Progresso since they are less mushy and are available in most supermarkets.

SARDINES

Sardines are one of my favorite pantry basics. I like them packed in olive oil, with bones and skins. Dressed in a dill, olive oil, and lemon juice vinaigrette, they make for a quick and delicious appetizer. Of course, sardines mashed with cream cheese with a dicing of red onion is one of those delicious snacks that you can also use as a filling for large roasted mushrooms to serve as a quick starter.

TINY PEAS

I have a personal liking for Le Sueur tiny canned peas. Heated with a touch of butter and some minced fresh mint, they make a perfectly acceptable side dish. Of course, they do not resemble fresh or even frozen peas in any way, but they are a vegetable in their own right.

TOMATOES

Canned tomatoes are probably my premier pantry basic and I keep at least four two-pound cans on hand at all times. I buy only whole plum tomatoes, preferably those imported from the San Marzano area of Italy. They are usually sweeter and juicier than the American varieties, though more pricey. Good American brands are Montini, Sclafani, Cento, Pastene, and Muir Glen (an organic round tomato from California).

TOMATO PASTE

I prefer to buy tomato paste in tubes, which keep a long time—although this may require a stop at a specialty store. Most of the time you do not need more than two to three teaspoons of tomato paste in any given recipe, and opening a can is truly a waste since, once opened, it has a relatively short shelf life.

TUNA

Even people who never cook and whose "pantry" consists of less than a dozen items include canned tuna in their selection of "must haves." I use canned tuna in pasta dishes, as a topping to peasant salads, as a stuffing for roasted peppers, and of course as the main ingredient in a salad. I far prefer light tuna packed in olive oil or vegetable oil over white tuna, which tends to be not only more expensive but also usually dry and rather tasteless. Good brands are Progresso, Genova, and Pastene, all of which offer tuna packed in olive oil. Tuna packed in spring water also works well in many preparations, so if fat content is a consideration, it would be a good choice.

Jarred Ingredients

CAPERS

There are usually at least three or four brands of capers available in every supermarket. The biggest and "meatiest" are those grown in Sicily, and they come either pickled or salted. These capers are good in pasta sauces or ground together with basil, parsley, and anchovies into a tapenade, the Mediterranean paste used as a dip and as an accompaniment to grilled fish and boiled meats. My favorite capers are the small nonpareil type imported from France. There is a great difference in taste between brands, so try a few to find your favorite. A good caper should not be mushy, briny, or too salty.

HONEY

See page 17.

HORSERADISH

Horseradish, like anchovy and tomato paste, is available in tubes in many specialty stores. Sour cream or crème fraîche with a dash of horseradish is a delicious accompaniment to a piece of pan-seared or grilled fish.

MAYONNAISE

Along with canned tuna, a jar of mayonnaise is considered "the" basic by just about everyone. I like to make my own, but I also keep a couple of jars of Kraft Real mayonnaise on hand. I find it less sweet than the others. If it is not available, good old Hellmann's will do. Depending on the region, Kraft is also sold under the Best Food's label.

MUSTARD

See page 14.

PICKLES

I always keep jars of baby dill gherkins and cornichons in my pantry, mainly for potato, tuna, and egg salads. A mincing of cornichons together with a minced garlic clove and finely chopped fresh parsley is delicious added to the pan juices of pan-seared pork tenderloins or a chicken fricassee.

PIMIENTOS

Pimientos are good for a quick garnish and to add a touch of color to potato or tuna salads. They are not a substitute for roasted red peppers, since they are peeled by a different process and therefore lack the distinct "roasted" flavor. They are the traditional garnish to a paella, and that is the way I most often use them.

R O A S T E D   R E D   P E P P E R S

Jarred roasted peppers are a quick substitute for fresh roasted peppers in many dishes. I like to marinate these peppers in some virgin olive oil and sliced garlic, which takes away their "jarred" taste. They are a good addition to salads, pasta dishes, and many dressings. I usually choose Progresso or Goya, but there are good brands available in most supermarkets.

T A B A S C O

Although there are many variations of hot sauces available in supermarkets, true Tabasco sauce is made of just chilies and vinegar and has a pure, slightly tangy, hot flavor. It is excellent used sparingly in egg batters, a quick tomato sauce, a gazpacho, and a variety of marinades.

Oils, Vinegars, and Mustards

E X T R A - V I R G I N   O L I V E   O I L

Extra-virgin oils should not be used in cooking but rather saved to dress fresh and roasted vegetables and greens. Combined with balsamic or sherry vinegar, they produce an emulsion you cannot get from other oils. I rely more heavily on the French extra-virgin oils, which are always available—Old Monk, Plagniol, Hilare Fabrè, and St. Regis are consistently excellent.

The shelf life of olive oil is limited. If you don't cook with it often, store it in the refrigerator. It will congeal but will clear when brought back to room temperature.

P U R E   O L I V E   O I L

This oil has an affinity for sunny vegetables like tomatoes, eggplant, peppers, and garlic. Basic supermarket brands such as Berio, Sasso, Bertolli, and Colavita are good for sautéing or for making assertive mustard and garlic dressings.

C O R N   O I L   A N D   P E A N U T   O I L

These are light, almost tasteless oils. Their high smoking point makes both of them excellent for deep-frying, but peanut oil is also good in salad dressings.

Peanut oil has a short shelf life, and I usually taste it before using. Of all oils, corn oil has the longest shelf life when stored in a cool, dark place.

TOASTED OR CHINESE SESAME SEED OIL

This is a tasty, distinctive oil that has made the move from Asian cooking into the everyday kitchen. Combined with other oils, it is excellent for sautéing. Buy it in small quantities, as a little goes a long way. It has a short shelf life and goes rancid rather quickly, so store it in the fridge.

WALNUT OIL

With a rich aroma redolent of walnuts, this oil makes wonderful salad dressing. Be sure to refrigerate it once opened. Even then, it will last only two or three months.

BALSAMIC VINEGAR

Aged and imported from Italy, this has become the "in" vinegar because good balsamic vinegar is fabulous in just about any preparation, whether part of a vinaigrette or added as a finishing touch to grilled seafood and vegetables.

CHAMPAGNE VINEGAR

Wonderful in many salads and some shallot and butter sauces, champagne vinegar is also a good addition to a court bouillon for poaching fish. It is usually available in specialty stores; La Marne is a reliable brand.

RED WINE VINEGAR

Buy a brand that has fermented naturally; it will have a mellow and pleasant flavor. Both Dessaux Fils and Témèraire are dependable.

SHERRY VINEGAR

Aged and imported from Spain, sherry vinegar is to me the most important vinegar in the pantry. It's the only one to cook with, since it leaves a mellow taste after the vinegar has evaporated. The best brands are La Posada, Santa Maria, Bodega, and Romate.

MUSTARDS

All mustards have a short shelf life. While refrigerating them once they are opened does help prolong their vibrancy, it is best to consume them shortly after they have been purchased.

The single most important mustard to have in the pantry is Dijon. Grey Poupon is a domestic brand made according to the Dijon formula, but to me it lacks punch. I prefer the imported varieties that are now widely available, such as Maille, Dessaux, and Témèraire. I also keep grainy and herb-flavored mustards on hand. They are good in some dressings, and I add them to the pan juices of lamb, veal, and beef dishes for interesting flavor.

SALAD CHART

Oil	Vinegar and Citrus	Flavorings	Greens
Pure Olive Oil, Peanut Oil, and Avocado Oil	Red Wine, Champagne, and Herb Vinegars, Lemon and Lime Juices	Mustards, Garlic, Scallions, Cumin, and Curry	Bibb, Romaine, Red and Green Leaf, and Boston
Extra-virgin Olive Oil	Sherry Vinegar, Balsamic Vinegar, Lemon and Lime Juices	Shallots, Red Onions, Garlic, Basil, Cilantro, Fresh Ginger, and Honey	Arugula, Dandelions, Bibb, Radicchio, Mâche, Curly Endive, Belgian Endives, and Mustard Greens
Walnut and Hazelnut Oils	Sherry Vinegar, Herb Vinegars, and Fruit Vinegars	Chives, Chervil, Shallots, Pureed Beets, Port, and Roasted Red Peppers	Red Leaf, Bibb, Mâche, Boston, Watercress, Belgian Endives, and Arugula

Grains, Pastas, and Legumes

ARBORIO RICE

When I think of rice, I think of Arborio or Spanish rice. I find its flavor incomparable to any other rice. It can be used in everything from a risotto or rice pudding to a quick skillet paella or a pilaf. It is relatively pricey and often requires a stop at a specialty store. The best Arborio rice is labeled "superfino" and is sold in cloth bags under the Amore label, but Baretta is almost as good and much less expensive. During the warm-weather months, Arborio rice has a tendency to attract tiny bugs so I store it in the refrigerator.

LONG-GRAIN RICE

A box of long-grain rice is always a good pantry basic for making a quick parsley or other fresh herb pilaf. I prefer River Brand or Texmati rice, which actually is a cross between long-grain and basmati rice grown in Texas.

BULGUR

The bulgur I use is similar in texture to couscous and prepared in the same way, but the flavor is quite different, more nutty and more intense. In many parts of the country, bulgur is still available only in health food stores or specialty stores, but I have recently seen it sold in bulk in Colorado and California and packed in small boxes in supermarkets on the East Coast. Be sure to get the quick-cooking grain rather than cracked wheat (which is often confused with bulgur and requires hours of cooking). For a change of flavor, you can substitute bulgur in any preparation calling for couscous. The grain only needs swelling or a ten-minute simmer in liquid over low heat.

CORNMEAL AND POLENTA

Polenta is basically the Italian word for cornmeal mush. The best cormeal for preparing polenta is stone-ground and can be made from either white or yellow corn. I keep some of both on hand. Now that you can find quick-cooking polenta in many specialty stores, I usually opt for it since it requires shorter cooking and does not lump.

COUSCOUS

Couscous is sold both boxed and in bulk. The loose variety can be found in health food stores, while the boxed varieties, both domestic and imported, are available in supermarkets everywhere. When buying boxed couscous, make sure that it is labeled "quick cooking" or "instant," which means that the grain

does not even need cooking but will fluff up in hot broth in ten to fifteen
minutes.

....

DRIED LEGUMES

Your pantry should include one pound each of pinto beans, chick peas, Great
Northern beans, black beans, cranberry beans, red lentils, and the tiny green
lentils imported from France called *lentilles de Puy.*

DRIED PASTAS

I like to have a variety of dried pastas on hand, including penne, fusilli, ziti,
rigatoni, spaghettini, cappellini, linguine, fettuccine, and orecchiette. Buy pasta
imported from Italy; preferably De Cecco. Orzo, a rice-shaped pasta, is one of
my favorite "grains." Simply boiled and tossed in butter and a mincing of fresh
herbs, it goes well with almost any main course—and takes just minutes to
prepare. Orzo is available in supermarkets, but the best brands are those imported from Greece and Italy; you may have to seek these out in specialty or
health food stores.

Sweeteners

HONEY

Like good olive oil, honey can make all the difference in a dish. I prefer clover,
Acadia, and, occasionally, thyme honey.

MAPLE SYRUP

Canadian brands are good quality and less expensive than domestic varieties.
Use the dark syrup for cooking. For toppings, use the medium- to amber-
colored.

PRESERVES AND JELLIES

Buy quality jams and jellies. Apple and red currant jelly in particular should
be top quality, as these are used often in cooking.

The Ethnic Pantry

Today's cook can choose a quick Thai, Chinese, or Vietnamese stir-fry for the evening or weekend meal. Now that so many types of cuisines have worked their way into the American cooking repertoire, it makes sense to stock up on some key ethnic items that can make that a Spur of the Moment decision.

Aside from the purely ethnic, so many "new American" dishes call for Eastern ingredients, such as fresh ginger, soy sauce, toasted sesame seed oil, rice vinegar, and garam masala, to mention just a few, that our pantries have become eclectic and highly personal. Here is a list of some special ingredients I like to keep in my pantry at all times.

ASSORTED DRIED CHILI PEPPERS

Chili peppers come in various sizes, but the general rule is, the smaller, the hotter. I always look for the very small Thai or African Devil, both of which are very spicy; you will usually need to use only one in most dishes. The new vogue of dried chili peppers can be rather confusing for anyone not familiar with Southwestern cooking. The best thing to do is to try one or two of the many different dried chili peppers now available, such as ancho, habanero, and pasilla, and work your way through until you have decided which ones you really prefer. Store dried chili peppers in a screw-top jar and they will keep indefinitely.

DRIED MUSHROOMS

Dried mushrooms such as porcini, Chilean, and shiitake have a more intense flavor than fresh and make for a fabulous pantry basic. I reserve true porcini for very delicate preparations because they are quite pricey. For an excellent substitute, use the imported Chilean mushrooms, available in many supermarkets, which are inexpensive and extremely flavorful. The best ones are sold in small clear plastic containers marked "imported by Kirsch." Choose those that are very large and dark and avoid those that are small and light in color. Dried shiitakes are also wonderful to have on hand. Once reconstituted in a little water, they make a flavorful addition to a stir-fry of peppers or snow peas or to a roast.

HARISSA

Harissa is Moroccan hot sauce available in cans or tubes. It is great for giving instantaneous punch to marinades and tomato-based preparations.

Mirin

This syrupy rice wine is usually available in the Oriental section of specialty stores and many produce markets. Its sweet flavor is a good addition to a quick stir-fry of vegetables, shrimp, or scallops.

Rice vinegar

Made from sake, this is an assertive vinegar, excellent with grilled vegetables or as a substitute for lemon juice in vinaigrettes.

Smoked chipotle peppers

These smoked chilies are available dried or in cans, packed in adobo sauce. I personally prefer the ones packed in cans. They are extremely spicy but, used with care, can give a robust, smoky zest to many dishes.

Soy sauce

I find myself using soy sauce in many dishes, although I rarely prepare Chinese or Japanese food. Now you can be selective in your choice of soy sauces. I usually opt for tamari or other Japanese or Chinese light (*not* lite!) or thin soy sauce, basically because of texture rather than taste. Light or thin soy sauce is thinner but saltier than dark soy sauce. It does not burn as quickly in cooking and works well in marinades and as an addition to a quick vegetable stir-fry.

Not Essential but Nice to Have

Anchovy paste

The advantage of stocking a tube of anchovy paste in your fridge is that you do not have to open a whole can of anchovies when all you need is a taste. I usually add some anchovy paste to a green mayonnaise or use it as a flavoring, together with mashed garlic, when seasoning a leg of lamb.

Candied ginger

Candied ginger is available imported from either China or Austria. Austrian candied ginger is superb and a dicing of this pungent sweet root is a wonderful addition to a fruit salad or a sabayon.

Garam masala

This is an aromatic ground spice mixture used extensively in Indian dishes. It is traditionally added to foods at the end of their cooking period. I like using it in marinades and as part of my flavoring for roast lamb or grilled chicken. Prepared garam masala is available in many specialty stores.

OLIVADA

Olivada is a delicious black oil-cured olive paste that is imported from Italy packed in jars. It can be used as a flavorful topping for grilled fish or on its own as a dip with raw vegetables. I like to use it as a snack with some hard-boiled eggs and crispy radishes.

THAI FISH SAUCE

A thin soy-like sauce, this is a salted fish extract, usually made from anchovies. I use it to give a boost of flavor to many fish preparations.

WASABI

This pungent Japanese condiment, similar in taste to horseradish, comes either powdered in cans or as a paste in tubes. A teaspoon or so of powdered wasabi combined with several tablespoons of soy sauce is a traditional accompaniment to Japanese fish preparations. It works equally well with any grilled fish steaks.

The Baker's Shelf

Even with baking ingredients that have a long shelf life, there are certain rules that should be followed.

BAKING POWDER

Always buy baking powder in small cans since it goes flat rather quickly. Keep it in a cool dry place, because moisture will cause it to spoil. The best baking powder is aluminum-free. You can get it in health food stores and some supermarkets.

BAKING SODA

Keep fresh by replacing it twice a year.

CHOCOLATE

When it comes to chocolate, you really do get what you pay for. Good chocolate is expensive but well worth it, since the taste of inferior chocolate cannot be masked and its consistency can make or break a dessert. I personally prefer Swiss or French chocolate and usually buy Tobler bittersweet, Lindt extra-bittersweet, or Valrhona bittersweet chocolate. These are found in the candy section of the supermarket and in specialty stores. Keep chocolate in a cool dry place or in the butter compartment of your refrigerator, away from moisture and strong odors.

COCOA

I use only Droste or Dutch-processed cocoas, which are unsweetened and can be stored successfully for months. Be sure to keep in a tightly closed container.

FLOUR

Unless you are a bread baker, you need only unbleached all-purpose flour, which can be used for cakes, pastries, and breads. Choose a brand you like and stick with it. If you like to bake, you will want to keep cake flour (not self-rising) on hand. This flour is milled the finest; as it is light, it produces more tender cakes and quick breads. Do not use it for making tart shells.

GELATIN

I usually keep only unflavored gelatin on hand. Stored in a cool dry place, it will last for three years. One teaspoon dissolved gelatin added to a bowl of whipped cream will keep the cream from watering down.

INSTANT COFFEE

Instant coffee is a terrific basic for making coffee-flavored whipped cream or adding to a mousse or custard. I prefer instant espresso to other instant coffees. Keep it tightly closed in a cool place.

SUGAR

Confectioner's: Store in an airtight container; if it cakes, try processing it with a little cornstarch.

Dark brown: I prefer dark brown to light brown sugar because of its more pronounced molasses flavor. Store in a heavy-duty plastic bag with a piece of the heel of a loaf of bread to help absorb moisture and keep the sugar from caking. Tip: Dissolve hopelessly caked brown sugar in orange juice flavored with orange rind over low heat for a delicious syrup for sliced bananas or ice cream.

Granulated: Store in an airtight container to prevent caking.

VANILLA BEANS

I prefer the Tahitian vanilla beans, but you may opt for Mexican vanilla beans, which are somewhat sweeter and more pungent. Store in a tightly closed jar. You can make your own vanilla sugar by putting a split vanilla bean in a jar of granulated sugar. It will keep for months.

VANILLA EXTRACT

Buy only pure vanilla extract in dark glass bottles. You can now get excellent quality Nielsen-Massey vanilla in many specialty stores as well as supermarkets. You can make your own extract by combining a pint of Cognac or brandy with two or three vanilla beans in a jar. In three to four weeks, you will have a terrific extract that you can use in many quick desserts and homemade sorbets and ice creams.

Herbs and Spices

Dried herbs and spices are essential basics in the everyday kitchen, and their proper selection and storage is of great importance. Herbs are the leaves, and sometimes soft stems, of annual plants; they are at their best used fresh but are also effective when dried. Spices come from the roots, barks, and seeds of tropical or subtropical plants and are always used dried. Dried herbs and spices are sold in every supermarket, but there are great differences in flavor.

Herbs

Do not buy dried herbs indiscriminately; look for the very best quality herbs, which are very fragrant. For starters, I never buy herbs packaged in cans or boxes, or the "gourmet" type sold in small cellophane or plastic bags. I am also quite suspicious of herbs sold in bulk, unless the store has great turnover. The bulk herbs are exposed to light and often are left open to the air for months on end, with the result that their delicate aromas have usually evaporated. Besides Spice Island and Vann's Spices (a small herb and spice company located in Baltimore), there are a number of small regional companies, in particular Pocket Creek in the Northwest, that produce excellent dried herbs. But even the very best dried herbs have a short shelf life and will lose their punch and flavor after six months, at which time it is best to replace them.

To check the freshness of a dried herb, put a little of it on the palm of your hand and rub it with your fingers: If the herb is fresh, you will smell it immediately and distinctly; if not, it is time to replace it.

For those recipes in which a fresh herb is a must, and you have only the dried, it is best to omit the herb entirely—or move on to another recipe. Fortunately, over the past few years, a variety of fresh herbs have become available practically year-round in many supermarkets. Although these are grown in hothouses and lack the punch of the garden variety, they have opened up a vast repertoire of dishes that were once exclusively in the domain of the gardening and truly seasonal cook.

Herbs are divided into two distinct categories:

Character herbs, which can be used either fresh or dried. They are added to a dish at the beginning of cooking. They include bay leaves, marjoram, oregano, rosemary, sage, tarragon, and thyme.

Accent herbs, which are delicate herbs that should be used only fresh and should be added to dishes just before serving. They include basil, chervil, chives, cilantro, dill, mint, and parsley (both curly and flat-leaf).

Spices

Most cooks, especially the Spur of the Moment cook, prefer using ground spices, but in some cases the spice in its whole or seed form is so much better that I highly recommend it. The advantage of those spices that come whole is that they have a far longer shelf life and that when freshly ground, they exude a far more delicious and pungent aroma than their ground counterparts.

The two most important pantry basic spices are salt and pepper. Fortunately, gone are the days when the choice was limited to table salt and ground pepper. Now you can buy a variety of both, and looking for quality and understanding the importance of it in these two ingredients can make a real difference in your cooking.

I am often asked about the difference between fine salt and coarse (kosher) salt. The only difference is texture, as both are made from rock salt. I prefer using coarse salt, however, since fine salt penetrates foods quickly, making them lose their natural juices. Coarse salt is particularly good for roasts, giving them a crisper crust or topping. My favorite salt by far is sea salt imported from Europe. It is high in natural minerals and is both tastier and less salty than rock salt. Sea salt is becoming increasingly available in supermarkets both fine and in crystal form, for which you have to use a salt mill.

The number-one spice to have on hand in good quality is whole black peppercorns, preferably Tellicherry, Lampong, Malabar, or Sarawak, which are available packed in tubes in many specialty stores. If these are difficult to find, look for black peppercorns that are marked Java, which means that they are imported from Indonesia rather than from South America. What you are looking for in a peppercorn, be it white or black, is a sharp, fresh, full-bodied flavor—but not one that will make you sneeze or will interfere with food rather than complement it. Besides a mill for black pepper, you should have one for whole white peppercorns. These are usually sold under the name of Muntok. White pepper is better than black in white sauces and with seafood and poultry. All peppercorns have a long shelf life, so it makes sense to stock up on them.

The accompanying chart is a checklist of the herbs and spices that I feel are essential for a well-stocked pantry, along with a few optional choices.

HERB AND SPICE CHECKLIST

Essential Dried Herbs	Essential Fresh Herbs	Essential Ground Spices	Essential Whole Spices	Optional Spices and Herbs
Bay Leaves	Basil	Arrowroot	Black Pepper	Dried Mustard
Marjoram	Bay Leaves	Black Pepper (medium grind)	Caraway Seeds	Mustard Seeds
Oregano	Chervil	Cardamom	Cardamom Pods	Lemon Peel
Rosemary	Chives	Cayenne Pepper	Chili Peppers (dried)	Ground Allspice
Sage	Cilantro	Chili Powder	Cinnamon Sticks	Ground Ginger
Tarragon	Dill	Cinnamon	Cloves	Red Pepper Flakes
Thyme	Marjoram	Cloves	Coriander Seeds	Crystallized Ginger
	Mint	Coriander	Cumin Seeds	Garam Masala
	Oregano	Cumin	Fennel Seeds	Ground Saffron
	Parsley (curly and flat-leaf)	Curry Powder	Nutmeg	Green Peppercorns
	Rosemary	Paprika	Saffron Threads	Pink Peppercorns
	Sage	Turmeric	Vanilla Beans	Szechwan Peppercorns
	Tarragon		White Pepper	
	Thyme			

VEGETABLE AND FRUIT CHECKLIST

Essential Vegetable and Fruit Bin	Optional Vegetable and Fruit Bin	Vegetable Basket and Fruit Bowl
VEGETABLES	**VEGETABLES**	**VEGETABLES**
Bell Peppers	Artichokes	Onions:
Carrots	Asparagus	All-purpose
Celery	Bagged Spinach	Red
Cucumbers	Belgian Endives	Spanish
Garlic*	Broccoli	Potatoes:
Ginger	Cabbage	All-purpose
Jalapeño Peppers	Fennel	Baking
Leeks	Mushrooms	Red
Lettuces	Scallions	Sweet
Radishes	Tomatoes	Rutabagas (optional)
Shallots*		
FRUIT	**FRUIT**	**FRUIT**
Dried Fruits	Grapefruit	Bananas
Granny Smith Apples	Navel Oranges	
Lemons		
Limes	**HERBS**	
Oranges	Basil	
Red Delicious Apples	Cilantro	
	Dill	
	Mint	
	Oregano	
	Tarragon	
	Thyme	

*Can also be stored in the vegetable basket.

The Refrigerator

The Vegetable Bin

It is in the hydrator, the vegetable container(s) at the bottom of the refrigerator, that a good cook stores the basic fresh ingredients that are so important to Spur of the Moment dishes. Keeping the bin well stocked requires almost daily attention.

Unfortunately, shopping for fresh vegetables and fruits is easier than storing them properly. How many times have you come home from the market and, because you are in a hurry, dumped all the fresh produce into the bin? In go the carrots, celery, leeks, lemons, limes, and radishes. Close the drawer and voilà!—it's done. If, per chance, you don't have time to cook in the next couple of days but then decide to make a soup, it's likely that when you open the bin you will be surprised to see that everything has wilted or died.

Proper storage is the key to having a fresh vegetable bin. Most vegetables should go into plastic bags. Remove the greens from carrots, radishes, turnips, and any other vegetable with tops, and cut off two inches of scallion and leek greens. But don't store tomatoes, cucumbers, onions, eggplants, or peppers in plastic bags—this will make them spoil faster. Garlic will remain fresh longer if kept loose in the refrigerator rather than out in a bowl, and shallots also do well in an open plastic bag in the refrigerator.

Once you have the vegetables ready to store, try some kind of organization. For example, keep citrus fruits with vegetables that don't need to be bagged. Keep herbs and bagged vegetables in another bin.

BELL PEPPERS

Now that red, yellow, and orange peppers are available year-round in almost every market, peppers have become one of my vegetable basics. Be sure to buy peppers that are firm and crisp, with thick, glossy, unblemished skins. Store them loose in the vegetable bin for up to a week or more.

CARROTS

I far prefer buying carrots with their tops rather than the trimmed packaged carrots. As soon as you purchase carrots, remove their tops, leaving about one inch of stem. Store them in a plastic bag, never loose, and wash them just before peeling. There are lots of vitamins in the carrot peel, so for stocks, I just rinse the carrots and add them to the water unpeeled. (Once tender, they make a delicious snack.)

CELERY

Celery usually comes either in packages with two "hearts" per package or in large bunches with most of the leaves attached—the best way to purchase celery, since so much of the assertive taste is in the leaves. Use the leaves as an addition to stocks or in a quick celery soup. If you want to prolong the shelf life of celery, cut off two inches of the tops.

CUCUMBERS

Although cucumbers are at their best in the summer, you can get the long gourmet or seedless cucumbers year-round. Cucumbers can be stored in the vegetable bin for up to ten days. Be sure to buy cucumbers that are uniformly firm. Always examine the tips, and avoid those that are soft or shriveled.

GARLIC

I usually keep garlic in a ceramic garlic jar in the refrigerator, but when I have a lot of it, I simply drop it into my vegetable bin. You can also store it for months in a cool place, such as a cold bin or cellar. I keep four to six heads of garlic on hand at all times since it is essential in so many preparations.

GINGER

This light brown, knobby root has become one of my favorite basics. I often have to stop myself from using it in too many dishes. When buying ginger, look for taut skin, not wrinkled—a sure sign of age. If you use ginger only infrequently, you can peel and slice it and place it in a jar with white wine or dry sherry to cover by one inch. Stored in the fridge, it will keep for months.

JALAPEÑO PEPPERS

A few fresh hot peppers are good to have on hand for spicing up marinades, vinaigrettes, and tomato-based preparations, such as pastas, soups, and shellfish dishes.

LEEKS

Leeks are great in stocks, soups, and ragoûts and as a vegetable on their own. I can't think of any member of the onion family that I prefer. Two factors are important when purchasing leeks: size and freshness. The best leeks are not too fat; look for bunches of leeks of uniform size, which is an important consideration when serving them poached as a vegetable. Fresh leeks have deep greens and snowy white tops. Although leeks are available year-round, they are at their best and least expensive in the fall, at which time you should consider them a versatile vegetable and prepare them with creativity. At other times, have them on hand to enhance a soup or stock.

Always cut off at least two inches of the greens, and store the leeks in a plastic bag. Rinse them just before using. If you have left the leeks for a week or two and they look a little slimy, simply remove the outer leaves and rinse the leeks under warm water. Dry well and use as soon as possible.

LETTUCES

With the ever-growing popularity of salads both as starters and light meals, lettuces are an important vegetable bin basic. The lettuces with the longest shelf life are romaine and iceberg. I prefer Romaine, and I keep a head or two of this good-natured lettuce on hand at all times. Other lettuces that do well for a fairly long stay in the fridge—and provide you with the possibility of making a more interesting salad—are Belgian endives, curly endive, Bibb, and radicchio.

PARSLEY

Parsley has an incredibly long shelf life provided it is kept unwashed and dry in a plastic bag in the vegetable bin. I like to use Italian flat-leaf parsley in cooking since it is so flavorful. I add the stems to chicken stock and often sprinkle a dish with the tiny whole leaves rather than chopping them, which diminishes the flavor. Curly parsley has an even longer shelf life and I use it a lot, minced, for garnishing finished dishes. Wash parsley just before using and dry thoroughly before chopping.

RADISHES

I love radishes, either as a snack with a piece of cheese before dinner or sliced into a green salad, so I keep them on hand at all times. If you buy radishes with their tops, remove the tops as soon as you get home. Store radishes in a perforated plastic bag. They will keep for at least ten days; if they start to shrivel up, simply trim them and immerse in a bowl of cold water. They will perk right up.

SHALLOTS

Most books and cooks recommend that you store shallots at room temperature or at least in a cool space, but I find that storing shallots in the vegetable bin works very well. They will keep for several months.

The Dairy Shelf

In spite of the current concern about fat in general, certain dairy products are an important basic in the everyday kitchen. Whether you opt for whole milk, 2% milk, or another low-fat variety to be used with your cereal or breakfast coffee, you will still need to keep some heavy cream, crème fraîche, and, sometimes, sour cream and yogurt on hand. Today's dairy products have quite a long shelf life, making them well worthwhile stocking—at least in small quantities, which are all you need most times for enrichment of a sauce or for giving that extra flavor to a soup.

HEAVY CREAM

Not long ago, the heavy cream available was just pasteurized. Unfortunately, in most parts of the country, you can now get only ultrapasteurized heavy cream, which contains stabilizers to give it a longer shelf life. This cream does not whip as well as pasteurized heavy cream and has a rather strange aftertaste. Fortunately, heavy cream is still widely available in the Northeast, and it's the only type I use, because of its delicious flavor.

I often get asked if light cream or half-and-half can be substituted for heavy cream. The answer usually is yes to light cream, but always no to half-and-half. Light cream has only 18 percent fat content compared to the 36 percent of heavy cream. It is a good choice for certain desserts such as crème brûlée or mousse, but it does not whip well.

BUTTER

I use only unsalted butter in cooking. Make sure that it is always labeled both "sweet" and "unsalted." In many parts of the country, unsalted butter is only available frozen. I prefer butter that has not been frozen, since frozen butter will naturally have absorbed moisture, which makes it burn at a lower temperature. However, I do keep at least one pound of butter in the freezer for emergencies.

Storing butter properly is a must. Once you unwrap it, it is best to drop the butter into small Ziploc baggies, which will keep it fresher longer.

Clarified butter, which is called for in a number of the recipes in this book, is another important basic to have on hand. Clarified butter will keep for several weeks or even longer. To clarify butter, see page 103.

YOGURT

Whether yogurt is a basic or not depends on individual taste. I find myself stocking up on yogurt mostly during the warm-weather months, when I use it for marinades and vinaigrettes and in cold soups. American yogurt tends to be somewhat watery, unlike the creamier European varieties, so I drain it of its excess liquid. To do this, place yogurt in a strainer lined with a coffee filter or cheesecloth set over a bowl, cover, and refrigerate. Overnight, the yogurt will become as thick as sour cream and develop a delicious consistency.

SOUR CREAM

Sour cream is a basic that I always keep on hand because there is simply no end to its many uses. It is extremely versatile and good-natured: Put a dollop on a bowl of spicy chili, stir two or three tablespoons into a broccoli or potato puree, or add a couple of tablespoons to the batter of a quick bread.

Look for sour cream that does not have any added ingredients, such as sweeteners. Sour cream will keep for a good ten days beyond the sell-by date on the carton.

Remember that sour cream will curdle or separate if it gets too hot: So add it to cooked foods only after you have taken them off the heat. When reheating foods that have sour cream in them, be sure to do so over the lowest possible heat and stir constantly.

CRÈME FRAÎCHE

Unlike sour cream, crème fraîche does not curdle in cooking; it can be used at high heat, and reduced just like cream. With its slightly sour taste, it is one of the most important dairy basics. My favorite commercial crème fraîche is Vermont Crème Fraîche, but homemade crème fraîche is far cheaper than the store-bought variety, and it takes only minutes to put together.

To make Crème Fraîche: Combine 2 cups *non*-ultrapasteurized heavy cream and 3 tablespoons buttermilk in a glass jar and whisk until well blended. Cover the jar loosely and set aside in a warm, draft-free place until the cream becomes very thick, about twenty-four to thirty-six hours. Then stir it thoroughly, cover, and refrigerate. It will keep from ten days to two weeks.

EGGS

In spite of their high cholesterol content, eggs are still a very important basic. I usually use only extra-large eggs (the size used in testing the recipes for this book). I prefer brown eggs since they tend to have a harder shell, making them easier to separate. Unfortunately, the grade of an egg is an indication but no real guarantee of how fresh it is. Eggs take anywhere from two days to three weeks to get to your local market—and the dating on the carton is also misleading, since it indicates the date the eggs were packaged rather than laid.

I use only very fresh eggs for frying, poaching, and omelettes. I keep older eggs for hard-boiling and baking. Tip 1: The whites of old eggs will not whip as well as those of fresh eggs, so I usually keep some extra whites in a jar in the refrigerator, where they keep well for two weeks, or in the freezer, or both. Tip 2: When freezing extra whites, always do so in a "set" of four or six, as this is what most recipes call for. Since many dishes call for yolks only, you are bound to have extra whites in your fridge or freezer.

The Freezer

FROZEN FRUITS

Frozen strawberries, blueberries, and raspberries are among the Spur of the Moment cook's best friends. I use them for quick berry sauces, sorbets, and fruit soups, or pureed and folded into whipped cream for a delicious "berry fool."

FROZEN CONCENTRATES

I stock up on pineapple and grapefruit concentrates for a Spur of the Moment sabayon, to be served either by itself as a warm flavorful dessert or as a cool topping to fresh fruit.

STOCK

Chicken stock, which takes only minutes of actual preparation time, is one of those freezer basics I personally cannot be without. Although you can easily substitute a bouillon cube or canned bouillon for chicken stock in any recipe, there is always a difference in the final result, especially soups, roasts, or sauces, made with the real stuff. If you find yourself with a few extra trimmings, some wings or pieces of chicken you did not get to use on your grill, it is well worth the time to make a flavorful stock and freeze it. To make a stock, see page 145.

NUTS

I store all nuts in the freezer to keep them from turning rancid. Be sure to toast them lightly in a low oven before using.

FROZEN VEGETABLES

Frozen vegetables such as peas, corn, and spinach are good to have on hand for additions to soups, purees, salads, and fritters.

ICE CREAMS

I always keep good-quality vanilla or chocolate ice cream in the freezer since a topping of ice cream can be just the right Spur of the Moment touch for a quick sauté of apples, a bowl of fresh berries, or sautéed bananas.

The Vegetable Basket

ALL-PURPOSE ONIONS

Most of the year, I just keep two to three pounds of simple yellow onions on hand. I choose them small, about one and a half inches in diameter. Three or four onions of this size can be cut in half crosswise and placed unpeeled around a whole chicken, a leg of lamb, or a loin of pork while it is roasting to add great taste. And the cooked onions can be served as an accompaniment.

RED ONIONS

For salads, onion jams, and roasted onions, I prefer red onions. These are at their best in late summer and early fall, at which time I usually buy several pounds and store them in a cool dark place or the vegetable bin. In the cold-weather months, most supermarkets carry only Texas red onions, which I find are too large and lack the sweetness of the imported Italian variety.

SPANISH ONIONS

These very large onions, similar to what we used to call Bermuda onions, are great for onion jams or when you need three or four cups of chopped or diced onions. Since they have a rather short shelf life, I keep only two or three in my vegetable basket and buy more as I need them.

POTATOES

Only a short time ago, the choice of potatoes was limited to baking, all-purpose, and the seasonal Red Bliss potatoes. Now things have changed for the better, and buying potatoes is becoming an art, with fingerlings, Yellow Finns, new baking potatoes, and many other varieties around. Although all the new varieties may not yet be available in supermarkets throughout the country, they are well worth seeking out and tasting.

Still, the mainstay of potato cooking is the baking potato, which is good for baking whole, mashing, and deep-frying. The all-purpose potato is best for mashing or in soups and stews. The large red potato is best when cooked in the skin, left to cool, and then used shredded in individual pancakes, such as the delicious Swiss rösti. Use the small Red Bliss for potato salads. Cubed but left unpeeled, they will keep their shape during cooking without the skin coming off. They are also suitable for roasting with herbs and olive oil.

Whatever potatoes you buy, don't just grab a bag at the supermarket. Look through the plastic or the netting and check each potato in the sack. As with apples, one bad potato will contaminate the whole lot. If you want your potatoes to last, I suggest you buy them loose, choosing each one carefully. Potatoes should be firm and have tight-fitting skins. Avoid potatoes with cracks, those that have a green tinge, and those that are sprouting and soft.

Storing potatoes is not an easy matter since they like best to be stored at 45° to 50°F, and that means a cellar. The refrigerator is not the answer, because the starch in potatoes converts to sugar in cold temperatures. The best solution is not to buy too many and to shop for potatoes often.

A word of warning: Although onions and potatoes do best under the same storing conditions, do not mix them in the same basket. Each exudes a different gas that will make the other vegetable decay faster.

SWEET POTATOES

Sweet potatoes are a great Spur of the Moment basic. Cooked sweet potatoes are terrific used in pancakes and soups or pureed with carrots. Buy sweet potatoes loose and look for smooth, unbroken skins. The skins should be dry and the flesh firm. In general, sweet potatoes like the same storing conditions as regular potatoes (45° to 50°F), but they can be refrigerated successfully for up to ten days as long as they stay dry and are not given the chance to get moldy.

The Fruit Bowl

FRESH FRUIT

Lemons, limes, and oranges all are good basics since they lend their delicious flavor to both savory and sweet preparations. Of the three, limes have the shortest shelf life. If you use only half a lime or lemon, store the remainder unwrapped in the vegetable bin. The next time you use it, cut off a thin slice and the fruit will be as good as fresh.

Of all apples, Granny Smith and Red Delicious are particularly good vegetable bin basics. The Red Delicious are good for quick fruit salads, and Granny Smith are best for sautéing.

DRIED FRUIT

Dried fruits are wonderful, intensely sweet, chewy, and delicious. They are great on their own as a snack or as an addition to many dishes, both sweet and savory. I buy Sultana raisins, currants, and golden raisins in the supermarket, but I prefer to buy apricots, prunes, figs, and dates in bulk in health food stores, where the quality is usually superior to the packaged fruit. Although dried fruits are supposed to have a long shelf life, this is the case only under ideal circumstances. In order for the fruit to stay soft and springy, it must be kept well sealed in the refrigerator or in a cool place—where it can be stored up to a year. If the fruit becomes hard, it can be brought back to life by poaching it in a sugar syrup.

The chart on page 25 is a checklist of essential vegetables and fruit, along with some optional choices. And be sure to be on the lookout for seasonal produce, which is the key to spontaneous and fresh cooking.

A pot of

*S*oup

While some FOODS COME WITH EXACT RECIPES AND COOKING TIPS, SOUP COMES WITH LIFE LESSONS, PHILOSOPHIES, AND MORE MEMORIES THAN PROUST HAD. THERE ARE FEW FOODS AS SATISFYING AND TIMELESS, FEW COOKING AROMAS AS WARMING AND SOOTHING. SOUP IS THE ULTIMATE COMFORT FOOD, AND FOR THE SPUR OF THE MOMENT COOK, IT IS ESPECIALLY COMFORTING TO KNOW THAT THERE ARE DOZENS OF FLAVORFUL, MEMORABLE SOUPS THAT CAN BE MADE WITH A RELATIVELY SMALL AMOUNT OF TIME AND EFFORT.

ONE OF MY EARLIEST MEMORIES IS OF MY VIENNESE GRANDMOTHER STIRRING A THICK PEA SOUP OR PEASANT LEEK AND POTATO SOUP IN HER CAST-

iron Le Creuset pot, chipped from years of almost daily use. I don't think my grandmother ever started out with a specific soup in mind. Rather, she considered her mood, her inclination, the weather, and, most of all, the season before she decided on the menu.

For my grandmother, spring meant "apron greens," and soups incorporating the vast array of wild greens she would toss into her apron as she walked through the fields near our house in Spain. With summer came the ripe bounty from her garden and the local market. Tomatoes, tomatoes, and still more to-matoes were the basis for endless soup variations—some cool, some hot, some thickened with rice, others with pastina.

In the fall, her cooking became a more serious and time-consuming affair. Fall was colors: orange, rust, pumpkin, the sharp yellow of early winter squash, the pale green of celery and fennel, the rosy hues of turnips and beets. Winter brought the hearty and soul-nourishing richness of potatoes and root vegetables—parsnips, leeks, onions, kohlrabi—simmered together for hours until their flavors harmonized and blended. And there were rich chowders thickened with sweet cream too.

Some things haven't changed since my grandmother's time. The best soups still fit the season, the best ingredients are still those that are fresh and plentiful, the best flavors a combination of what's intense and interesting. We're still guided by basic logic and experience. For example, asparagus is best combined with spring greens—it has so much personality that it dominates any other ingredient. Corn is wonderful but almost never the main ingredient. And, as my mother used to say, "The best soup du jour is yesterday's soup," where the flavors have had a whole day to sit and get to know each other.

Some things have changed, however, and they are a boon for the Spur of the Moment cook. Because we've acquired a taste for somewhat undercooked vegetables, there's no need to cook a soup forever and a day. Instead, it's very nice when the carrots, green beans, or turnips still retain a certain texture and character. We define our meals less rigidly today: Add some homemade croutons and smoked ham to your vegetable soup and turn it into a satisfying main course.

Soup making is easier now: There are excellent commercial broths and bouillons available to cut down on prep time. Soup making is more fun: We can experiment with exuberant ethnic ingredients like fresh ginger and chilies, unexpected flavorings like Thai fish sauce, lemon grass, and soy sauce. And it's less timid: Bolder herbs and spices like curry, cumin, cilantro, and chili powder can give soup a whole different dimension. Now, at the end of the day, what we sit down to and savor is a pot of soup that respects tradition, thrives on creativity, delights the stomach, and nourishes the soul. While it may have been made quickly, it will not be soon forgotten.

Vine-Ripened Tomato and Mint Soup

To prepare: 15 minutes
To cook: 55 minutes
Serves 6

....

3 tablespoons olive oil

1 large onion, peeled and finely minced

1 large garlic clove, peeled and finely minced

2 tablespoons all-purpose flour

6 to 8 large ripe tomatoes, peeled, seeded, and chopped

4 cups Chicken Stock (page 145) or chicken bouillon

1 tablespoon finely minced fresh thyme

2 sprigs fresh mint plus 3 to 4 tablespoons finely minced mint

Salt and freshly ground black pepper

Optional: ⅓ cup heavy cream

T i p

....

You can skip the step of peeling and seeding the tomatoes by passing the entire soup through a food mill, giving it a perfect texture.

I a d m i t that it is hard to improve on an old-fashioned fresh tomato soup. There are probably as many ways to make it as there are cooks who enjoy using the farm stand ripe fruit in its rather short season. Still, this Moroccan version, which combines the wonderful taste of tomatoes with the delicate yet assertive taste of mint, is well worth a try. Other herbs, particularly basil and dill, have an equal affinity to tomatoes but the marriage is more predictable. An interesting Middle Eastern variation is the addition of cubed cooked potatoes and diced feta cheese, turning the soup almost into a stew. I often serve this version as a main course, followed by a salad, an interesting cheese, and a spicy salami to complete an easy and informal supper.

....

1. Heat the oil in a large casserole over low heat. Add the onion and garlic and cook, covered, until very soft but not browned, about 10 minutes. Add the flour and cook for 1 minute longer. Add the tomatoes, stock or bouillon, thyme, and mint sprigs, season with salt and pepper, and simmer, partially covered, for 30 to 40 minutes, stirring often.

2. Puree the soup in a food processor and return to the casserole. Add the optional cream and the minced mint and just heat through. Correct the seasoning and serve warm, accompanied by crusty French bread or garlic croutons.

Cream of Roasted Vegetable Soup

To prepare: 15 minutes
To cook: 45 to 50
minutes
Serves 5

....

3 tablespoons olive oil

2 large garlic cloves, peeled and
thickly sliced

1 medium eggplant (about 1
pound), trimmed and cut
crosswise into ½-inch slices

1 medium yellow squash,
trimmed and cut crosswise
into ½-inch slices

1 medium zucchini, trimmed and
cut crosswise into ½-inch
slices

2 large red bell peppers, cored,
seeded, and cut into eighths

1 medium onion, peeled and
quartered

Salt and freshly ground black
pepper

2 tablespoons unsalted butter

2½ tablespoons all-purpose flour

5 cups Chicken Stock (page 145)
or chicken bouillon

¼ cup heavy cream

T i p

....

*Vegetables roasted in this manner
make for a wonderful starter salad
topped with thinly sliced red onion
and drizzled with a balsamic vinaigrette (see page 90). They also
make a terrific omelette filling.*

I am always searching for new soup ideas, and here is one that happened one day when I had some leftover roasted vegetables and good chicken stock. The result became a new favorite. Whenever possible I like to add a few caramelized or double-poached garlic cloves, which give the soup additional texture and punch. Another interesting variation is a topping of thin slices of young goat cheese and a sprinkling of fresh thyme. This soup keeps well and is equally good served at room temperature or slightly chilled.

....

1. Preheat the oven to 425°F.

2. Heat 2 tablespoons of the oil in a heavy flame-proof baking dish over low heat. Add the garlic and cook for 30 seconds. Add the vegetables, season with salt and pepper, and drizzle with the remaining 1 tablespoon oil. Roast in the oven for 30 to 35 minutes, or until the vegetables are tender and nicely browned; turn them often during roasting.

3. While the vegetables are roasting, melt the butter in a 4-quart casserole over low heat. Whisk in the flour and cook for 1 minute. Whisk in the stock or bouillon, season with salt and pepper, and simmer for 15 minutes.

4. Puree the vegetables in a food processor. Whisk the puree into the broth and simmer for 10 minutes. Add the heavy cream and just heat through. Correct the seasoning and serve hot.

Double-Poached Garlic and Broccoli Soup

To prepare: 10 minutes
To cook: 35 minutes
Serves 5

....

1½ pounds broccoli, trimmed

4 tablespoons unsalted butter

1 large onion, peeled and finely minced

2 tablespoons all-purpose flour

5 cups Chicken Stock (page 145) or chicken bouillon

12 large garlic cloves, double-poached (see Tip)

Optional: ⅓ cup heavy cream

GARNISH
Optional: garlic croutons

Freshly grated Parmesan cheese

T h e combination of mild garlic and broccoli in a velvety soup is a winner, and it is a great soup to have in your repertoire since it calls for ingredients that are available fresh year-round. In the fall I often substitute fresh farm stand cauliflower or the more flavorful purple broccoli.

If you have the time, drop a crusty garlic crouton into each soup bowl. This is simple enough to do: Just rub slices of French bread with the cut side of a garlic clove, brush with olive oil, and run under the broiler until golden brown. Follow the soup with a sauté of chicken or a pasta dish such as Mussels and Tomatoes alla Romagnola with Linguine (page 126) or Linguine with Spicy Shrimp al'Ajillo (page 124).

....

1.   Separate the broccoli florets from the stalks. Peel the stalks with a vegetable peeler, dice, and set aside. Reserve 2 cups of the florets separately.

2.   Melt the butter in a large casserole over medium heat, add the onion, and cook until soft. Add the flour and cook for 1 minute. Whisk in the stock or bouillon and simmer for 5 minutes. Add the diced broccoli stalks and remaining florets and simmer for 20 minutes, or until very tender.

3. Strain the soup and return the broth to the casserole. Puree the vegetables together with the garlic and cream in a food processor. Add to the broth and whisk until well blended. Add the reserved 2 cups florets and simmer until tender. Correct the seasoning and serve hot, with optional garlic croutons and a sprinkling of Parmesan.

T i p

To double-poach garlic, place the desired number of peeled garlic cloves in a saucepan with water to cover. Bring to a boil and cook for 1 minute. Drain and discard the poaching liquid. Return the garlic to the saucepan with fresh water to cover and simmer for 15 to 20 minutes, or until tender. Drain again. The garlic may be double-poached days in advance. To keep, place in a jar, cover with olive oil, seal tightly, and store in the refrigerator until needed. The garlic will keep for up to 3 months.

Sausage, Spinach, and Pastina Soup

To prepare: 15 minutes
To cook: 20 minutes
Serves 4 to 5

....

1 tablespoon olive oil

¾ pound sweet Italian fennel
   sausage, casings removed

2 large onions, peeled and
   coarsely chopped

2 large garlic cloves, peeled and
   finely minced

½ teaspoon fennel seeds

6 cups chicken bouillon

½ cup pastina, tiny pasta shells,
   or tubettini

¾ pound spinach, stemmed and
   rinsed

Salt and freshly ground black
   pepper

GARNISH
Freshly grated Parmesan cheese

T i p
....

*Your best bet is to buy spinach in
10-ounce bags, as bagged spinach
is quite clean and requires only a
quick rinse. Squeeze the bag to
test for crispness.*

**He r e is a gutsy soup reminiscent of the Central
European goulash soup. Be creative with your selection
of greens, and go with what you see fresh in your market. Kale, Swiss chard, and escarole are all good and
inexpensive choices. Serve this for supper, preceded by
either cooked globe artichokes (see page 76) or a plateful of steamed asparagus accompanied by a mustardy
dill vinaigrette. Peasant bread, a ripe piece of Brie, and
a juicy pear would complete this simple and quick meal.**

....

1. Heat the oil in a large casserole over medium
heat. Add the sausage and sauté until nicely
browned, breaking it up with a fork. Transfer to a
colander and drain.

2. Discard all but 2 tablespoons of the fat from the
casserole. Add the onions, garlic, and fennel seeds
and cook until the vegetables are soft and lightly
browned. Return the sausage to the casserole together with the bouillon and pasta and simmer for
6 to 8 minutes, or until the pasta is tender; skim off
the fat often. Add the spinach and cook until just
wilted. Taste and correct the seasoning. Serve hot,
with a grating of Parmesan.

Spicy Lime and Lemon Grass Bouillon with Shrimp and Avocado

To prepare: 15 minutes
To cook: 20 minutes
Serves 6

3 tablespoons unsalted butter

2 stalks fresh lemon grass, cut into 1½-inch pieces and crushed

2 tablespoons finely minced shallots

1 tablespoon finely minced fresh ginger

2 large garlic cloves, peeled and finely minced

1 tablespoon finely minced jalapeño pepper

2½ tablespoons all-purpose flour

6 cups Chicken Stock (page 145)

1 fish bouillon cube

Juice of 1 lime

½ pound medium shrimp, peeled and cubed

Optional: ½ pound large sea scallops, each cut crosswise into 3 slices

1 ripe avocado, peeled, pitted, and cubed

Salt and freshly ground black pepper

GARNISH

2 to 3 tablespoons tiny fresh cilantro leaves or julienne of fresh basil

1 large ripe tomato, seeded and finely diced

Lemon grass, the key ingredient in this dish, is becoming increasingly available, and its unique taste adds a special zest to the light soup. If you cannot get it, use the juice of two to three limes; the result will still be delicious. I often make this soup using chicken breasts instead of the shellfish, for a less expensive variation. If you try it, omit the fish bouillon cube and add one or two more vegetables for texture, such as snow peas and a few sliced all-purpose mushrooms.

1. Melt the butter in a 4-quart casserole over medium heat. Add the lemon grass, shallots, ginger, garlic, and jalapeño pepper and cook for 2 minutes. Add the flour and mix thoroughly. Add the stock and whisk until well blended. Add the bouillon cube and simmer for 15 minutes.

2. Remove the lemon grass and discard. Add the lime juice, shrimp, and optional scallops and simmer for 1 minute longer; do not overcook, or the shellfish will be tough. Add the avocado, season with salt and pepper, and just heat through. Serve hot, garnished with a sprinkling of cilantro or basil and diced tomato.

Tip

If your lemon grass is very fresh, you can mince it very finely and avoid having to remove it from the finished soup. It will also give the soup a more intense flavor.

Grilled Eggplant, Tomato, and Basil Soup

To prepare: 20 minutes
To cook: 50 minutes
Serves 4 to 5

....

2 medium eggplants (about 1 to
1¼ pounds each)

5 to 7 tablespoons extra-virgin
olive oil

1 medium onion, peeled and
finely minced

2 large garlic cloves, peeled and
finely minced, plus 1 large
clove, peeled and mashed

1 tablespoon finely minced fresh
oregano

6 to 8 large ripe Italian plum tomatoes, peeled, seeded, and
chopped

3 cups Chicken Stock (page 145)
or chicken bouillon

Salt and freshly ground black
pepper

Pinch of cayenne pepper

2 cups packed fresh basil leaves,
well washed and dried

Optional: 4 ounces mild goat
cheese, such as Montrachet

GARNISH
Tiny leaves of fresh basil

Th e best way to get the wonderful taste of grilled eggplant is by placing them on hot coals, or a gas flame; still you can get excellent results by putting the egg-plant directly on the medium-hot coils of an electric stove.

Combine the smoky eggplant with tomatoes and good chicken broth and you have the makings of a ter-rific and uniquely flavored soup. A dollop of yogurt and a sprinkling of cilantro or mint is an elegant touch. If you do cook the eggplant on a grill, plan to continue to use the grill for Pepper-and-Sage Grilled Pork Tender-loins (page 172) or Grilled Chicken in Lemon-Cumin Marinade (page 165).

....

1.   Place the eggplants directly over a medium-high flame on a gas stove or on medium-hot coils of an electric stove and "grill" until they are completely charred on all sides and tender. (To grill over a char-coal fire, see page 183.) Transfer to a cutting board, cut in half lengthwise, and scoop out the pulp, dis-carding the charred skin.

2.   Heat 2 tablespoons of the oil in a large casserole over medium-low heat. Add the onion, minced gar-lic, and oregano and cook until the onion is soft. Add the eggplant pulp, tomatoes, and stock or bouillon, season with salt, pepper, and the cayenne, and sim-mer, partially covered, for 35 minutes.

3. While the soup is simmering, prepare the garnish: Puree the 2 cups basil in a food processor with enough of the remaining oil to make a smooth paste. Add the optional goat cheese and the mashed garlic and process until smooth. Set aside.

4. When the soup is done, puree in the food processor and return to the casserole. Correct the seasoning and just heat through. Spoon into individual shallow soup bowls and garnish with a dollop of the basil paste and basil leaves. Serve hot, accompanied by crusty French bread.

Remarks: I often serve this soup at room temperature rather than hot. A nice cool garnish is a tomato concassée made of diced unpeeled tomatoes, tossed with a drop or so of extra-virgin olive oil, a touch of sherry vinegar, and minced basil. If you use this garnish, omit the basil paste.

T i p

When purchasing eggplants, remember that the lighter the eggplant in weight, the fewer seeds. Also, the longer, thinner eggplants are less seedy than the shorter, fatter ones.

Lemon Split Pea Soup

To prepare: 20 minutes
To cook: 55 minutes
Serves 6 to 8

....

1 cup sour cream

3 tablespoons finely minced fresh
  cilantro or dill

1 tablespoon finely grated lemon
  zest

2 tablespoons unsalted butter

1 tablespoon olive oil

2 large onions, peeled and finely
  diced

2 teaspoons finely minced jalapeño pepper

1 large carrot, peeled and finely
  diced

2 large celery stalks, trimmed and
  finely diced

Optional: 1 parsley root, peeled
  and finely diced

2 teaspoons ground cumin

1½ cups split peas, well rinsed

8 to 10 cups Chicken Stock
  (page 145) or chicken bouillon

Salt and freshly ground white
  pepper

¼ cup heavy cream

OPTIONAL GARNISH
1 cup snow peas, cut into very
  fine julienne and steamed

T h e classic Dutch split pea soup, made with smoked pigs' knuckles or bacon, is hard to improve upon, and I rarely come across other ways of preparing this delicious legume. But, one day, I found myself without either bacon or smoked pork butt and through improvisation came up with this soup that I find somewhat lighter but equally as satisfying as the classic.

....

1. Combine the sour cream, cilantro or dill, and lemon zest in a small bowl and set aside.

2. Melt the butter together with the oil in a 4-quart casserole over medium-low heat. Add the onions, jalapeño pepper, carrot, celery, and optional parsley root and cook until soft, about 4 to 5 minutes.

3. Add the cumin and cook for 1 minute. Add the split peas and 8 cups of the stock or bouillon, season with salt and white pepper, and simmer, covered, for 45 minutes, or until the peas are very soft.

4. Puree the soup in a food processor and return to the casserole. If the soup seems too thick, add additional stock or bouillon. Add the cream and just heat through. Correct the seasoning and serve in individual shallow bowls, garnished with a dollop of the sour cream mixture and the optional julienne of snow peas.

Remarks: Snow peas cut into a fine julienne are an interesting and easy garnish. You can steam them for 1 minute well ahead of time and keep them in a small bowl of cold water. When ready to serve, drain the snow peas and either sauté quickly in a touch of butter to heat through or reheat in the microwave.

Other herbs, such as dill or tarragon, can be substituted for the cilantro.

T i p

Split peas and lentils are the only legumes that do not require presoaking, making them interchangeable in this recipe. For the curious cook, substitute some of the many different lentils that are available in Indian markets and specialty stores for the split peas.

Butternut Squash and Sweet Potato Soup with Indian Spices

To prepare: 10 minutes
To cook: 35 minutes
Serves 4 to 5

....

1 tablespoon unsalted butter

2 tablespoons corn or peanut oil

1 large onion, peeled and diced

1 teaspoon ground cumin

¼ teaspoon ground coriander

1 medium to large butternut
squash, peeled, seeded, and
cubed

2 medium sweet potatoes, peeled
and cubed

6 cups Chicken Stock (page 145)
or chicken bouillon

Optional: ½ cup heavy cream

Salt and freshly ground black
pepper

Small pinch of cayenne pepper

Large pinch of freshly grated
nutmeg

GARNISH
Small fresh cilantro or mint leaves

T h e r e is no question that fall and winter are the soup seasons, and this one is a winner. The spice combination adds complexity to this soup, making it an ideal starter for a simple roast turkey or roast pork. It is at its best when given time to develop flavor, so I like to double the recipe and refrigerate the leftovers for two to three days. My favorite garnish is a dollop of crème fraîche and a sprinkling of diced ripe pear.

....

1.   Melt the butter with the oil in a large heavy casserole over medium heat. Add the onion and cook until soft but not browned. Add the cumin and coriander and stir for 1 minute. Add the squash, sweet potatoes, and stock or bouillon and simmer for 25 minutes, or until the vegetables are very soft.

2.   Strain the broth and return it to the casserole. Puree the vegetables in a food processor, whisk the puree into the broth, and simmer for 2 to 3 minutes. Add the optional cream and just heat through. Season carefully with salt and black pepper, cayenne pepper, and nutmeg and serve hot, garnished with cilantro or mint leaves.

T i p

....

All winter squashes are similar in texture and flavor. Try acorn squash, pumpkin, or any other winter squash (except spaghetti squash) you may find at your local farm stand or supermarket during late harvest season.

Arborio Rice Soup with Spring Vegetables

To prepare: 10 minutes
To cook: 15 minutes
Serves 4 to 5

....

5½ cups Chicken Stock (page 145) or chicken bouillon

2 cups diced leeks, well rinsed

1½ cups diced asparagus

¼ cup Italian rice, preferably Arborio

½ cup fresh peas

Salt and freshly ground black pepper

2 cups tightly packed spinach, stemmed and rinsed

GARNISH
Freshly grated Parmesan cheese

T i p

....

Arborio rice can be used either lightly rinsed or as is. Rinsing removes some of the starch, creating a less creamy soup, which is more suitable in combination with a homemade stock, and reduces the cooking time by 5 minutes.

N o t h i n g is simpler and more delicious than a rice soup. Although you can't beat Italian Arborio rice for flavor, you can also use a medium-grain California rice or a Spanish paella rice here. This soup is good in every season—just change the greens, using whatever is fresh in your market. I especially like escarole, curly endive, beet tops, kale, and mustard greens, which add both texture and taste.

....

1. Combine the stock or bouillon, leeks, asparagus, rice, and peas in a 4-quart casserole. Season with salt and pepper and simmer, uncovered, until the rice is tender, about 10 to 12 minutes.

2. Add the spinach and simmer until just wilted. Correct the seasoning and serve hot with a grating of Parmesan.

Remarks: You can use frozen peas: Thaw and add to the soup along with the spinach.

Mediterranean Zucchini and Orzo Soup with Pesto

To prepare: 10 minutes
To cook: 25 to 30 minutes
Serves 6

....

1 cup fresh basil leaves

2 large garlic cloves, peeled and finely minced

3 tablespoons freshly grated Parmesan cheese

2 to 3 tablespoons olive oil

3 tablespoons unsalted butter

2 tablespoons all-purpose flour

6 to 7 cups Chicken Stock (page 145) or chicken bouillon

½ cup orzo

2 small zucchini, trimmed and cut into ½-inch dice

Salt and freshly ground white pepper

T i p

....

Whenever possible, use imported Greek orzo rather than the ordinary supermarket brand. It will take about 5 minutes longer to cook but has a much better texture and flavor.

I never tire of the subtle taste of zucchini and find use for it in many spring and summer preparations. We tend to take the vegetable for granted because it is available fresh almost year-round. But zucchini deserves to be treated with creativity and this soup does just that. Here it is simply blended with good chicken stock and a mild garlicky basil paste, one that does not overwhelm the taste of this good-natured vegetable. You can substitute tiny pastina or broken spaghettini for the orzo. The soup is best served at room temperature and keeps well for several days. Be sure to make enough for leftovers.

....

1. Combine the basil, garlic, and Parmesan in a food processor. With the machine running, add enough oil to form a smooth paste. Set aside.

2. Melt the butter in a large casserole over medium heat. Add the flour and cook for 1 minute. Whisk in 6 cups stock or bouillon and simmer for 15 minutes. Add the orzo and simmer for 5 minutes, or until barely tender. Add the zucchini and simmer for 5 to 7 minutes longer, or until tender.

3. Whisk in the basil paste and season with salt and white pepper. If the soup seems too thick, add additional stock or bouillon.

Green Chili, Crab, and Bacon Chowder

To prepare: 15 minutes
To cook: 30 minutes
Serves 5

....

3 tablespoons unsalted butter

5 ounces slab bacon, blanched and diced, about 1 cup (see Tip)

2 medium onions, peeled and finely minced

1 large green bell pepper, cored, seeded, and finely diced

2 teaspoons finely minced jalapeño pepper or 1 teaspoon red pepper flakes

2 tablespoons all-purpose flour

4 cups fish bouillon or chicken bouillon

1 cup half-and-half

¼ cup orzo

½ pound fresh lump crabmeat, picked over

3 tablespoons finely minced fresh parsley

Salt and freshly ground black pepper

Tip

....

Whenever possible, look for meaty slab bacon. Be sure to blanch the bacon whole, not cubed or diced. Drain well and dry in a kitchen towel.

You can substitute diced smoked turkey for the bacon.

As is the case with so many old-fashioned dishes these days, all kinds of chowders are popping up on restaurant menus and in food magazines. I have always liked the creamy New England fish and clam chowders but find them somewhat too heavy. Here is a version that is good practically year-round. Although it calls for little flour, the soup is nice and creamy and allows great room for Spur of the Moment creative touches. You can substitute shrimp for the crab and add both a red and a yellow diced pepper to the mixture. In the summer I usually include fresh corn, diced zucchini, and a julienne of fresh basil; in the cool-weather months a sprinkling of Indian spices such as curry and cumin add a lively accent.

....

1. Melt the butter in a heavy 3½-quart casserole over medium heat. Add the bacon and cook until lightly browned. Add the onions, green pepper, and jalapeño pepper or pepper flakes and cook for 5 minutes.

2. Stir in the flour and cook for 1 minute. Whisk in the bouillon and half-and-half and simmer, partially covered, for 15 minutes. Add the orzo and cook until tender, about 5 to 7 minutes.

3. Fold in the crabmeat and parsley and just heat through. Correct the seasoning and serve hot, with a large grinding of black pepper.

Farm Stand Shellfish and Corn Chowder

To prepare: 20 minutes

To cook: 25 minutes

Serves 5 to 6

....

1 tablespoon unsalted butter

2 tablespoons olive oil

1 tablespoon finely minced jalapeño pepper or 1 small dried
red chili pepper, broken

1 medium onion, peeled and
finely minced

2 tablespoons all-purpose flour

6 cups chicken bouillon

4 large ears of fresh corn, cooked
and kernels removed

1 small zucchini, trimmed and
finely diced

1 small red bell pepper, cored,
seeded, and finely diced

Salt and freshly ground black
pepper

Optional: ½ cup diced smoked
turkey

⅓ cup heavy cream

½ pound medium shrimp, peeled
and diced

Pinch of cayenne pepper

GARNISH

Finely minced fresh cilantro,
chives, and/or parsley

H e r e is a quick summer soup that is as versatile as a minestrone. Many of summer's star vegetables are good additions to this chowder: Finely diced green peppers, leeks, green beans, and fresh tomatoes are all delicious. You can use either fresh, canned, or frozen corn. Since I like some smokiness in this kind of soup, I usually add a dicing of smoked turkey, ham, or sausage toward the end.

....

1. Melt the butter with the oil in a large casserole over medium heat. Add the jalapeño or dried chili pepper and onion and cook until soft and lightly browned. If using the dried pepper, remove and discard. Add the flour and cook for 1 minute longer. Immediately add the bouillon and whisk until the mixture comes to a boil. Add the corn and simmer, partially covered, for 15 minutes.

2. Add the zucchini and bell pepper, season with salt and pepper, and simmer until the vegetables are tender. Add the optional turkey, the cream, and shrimp and simmer over very low heat for 1 minute; do not overcook, or the shrimp with toughen. Correct the seasoning, adding the cayenne. Serve hot or at room temperature, garnished with cilantro, chives, and/or parsley.

Remarks: You can make a double batch of this soup and freeze it for later use, but do not add the shrimp to the soup until just before serving.

Although the cream adds a nice finishing touch to this soup, it is not a must and can be omitted.

T i p

I always cook corn on its cob and then let it sit in the water for 10 to 15 minutes, which renders the kernels sweeter and easier to remove from the cob.

Cool Cucumber Soup with Lime, Shrimp, and Cilantro

To prepare: 15 minutes
plus 30 minutes to drain

Serves 6 to 8

5 medium cucumbers, peeled, cut in half lengthwise, and seeded

Coarse salt

½ cup fresh cilantro leaves

6 scallions, finely minced

3 to 4 tablespoons fresh lime juice

1 quart buttermilk

1 pint sour cream or crème fraîche (see page 31)

¾ pound medium shrimp, peeled, cooked, and diced

Freshly ground white pepper

GARNISH
½ cup finely diced cucumber

Fresh cilantro leaves

T i p

You can also use large seedless cucumbers for this recipe. Use three of them, rather than five. Depending on where you live, they will be called English, burpless, or gourmet.

Uncooked soups are quick and welcome starters to warm-weather meals, and preparing one with crispy farm stand cucumbers is always my first choice. Fresh dill, chives, and tarragon are the classic accents, so for an interesting change I use a large sprinkling of fresh cilantro and a touch of lime. If you are one who dislikes cilantro, by all means use dill or tarragon. Follow the soup with Pan-Seared Salmon with Melted Leeks and Dill (page 211) or Grilled Salmon with Cracked White Pepper and Dill Rub (page 177). If you have the time, the Peach Gratin with Creamy Pecan Crumble (page 279) would be a nice seasonal dessert.

1. Sprinkle the cucumbers with coarse salt and let drain in a colander for 30 minutes.

2. Pat the cucumbers dry and chop coarsely. Puree in a blender, in several batches, with the cilantro, scallions, lime juice, buttermilk, and sour cream or crème fraîche until smooth.

3. Transfer to a serving bowl. Add the shrimp, season with salt and white pepper, and refrigerate for 2 to 3 hours. Serve chilled, garnished with the diced cucumber and cilantro leaves.

Cabbage, Potato, and Turnip Soup with Roquefort Toasts

~~~~~~

To prepare: 20 minutes
To cook: 1 hour
Serves 6

....

2 tablespoons unsalted butter

1 tablespoon corn oil

2 large onions, peeled, quartered, and thinly sliced

7 to 8 cups beef bouillon

1 pound Savoy cabbage, cored and sliced

3 medium all-purpose potatoes, peeled and cubed

4 medium turnips, peeled and cubed

2 large carrots, peeled and cubed

Salt and freshly ground black pepper

GARNISH

3 tablespoons finely minced fresh parsley

6 thin slices toasted French bread

4 ounces Roquefort or other mild blue cheese

E a r t h y , homey soups play a major role in my cool-weather repertoire. While they are good and tasty when first made, they get better and better if allowed to develop flavor for a day or two. So prepare a large batch and with minor variations such as the addition of a fresh herb or another type of cheese, you can easily make two or three meals out of this soup. Serve it as a one-dish meal with some crusty bread and sweet butter.

....

1. Melt the butter with the oil in a large casserole over medium-low heat. Add the onions and cook until soft and lightly browned. Add the bouillon and vegetables, season with salt and pepper, and simmer, partially covered, for 45 minutes.

2. Correct the seasoning. Serve hot in individual shallow soup bowls, sprinkled with the parsley and topped with toasted French bread spread with a thick layer of Roquefort.

T i p

....

Be sure to taste Roquefort before buying, since it can be very salty. If so, opt for another good and preferably mild blue cheese, such as Pipo crème, sweet Gorgonzola, or English Stilton.

Soup of Root Vegetables and Clams

To prepare: 15 minutes

To cook: 40 minutes

Serves 4 to 5

....

3 tablespoons olive oil

1 large leek, trimmed of all but 2 inches of greens, diced, and rinsed

2 medium carrots, peeled and finely diced

2 medium turnips, peeled and finely diced

2½ tablespoons all-purpose flour

3 cups chicken bouillon

2 cups bottled clam juice

2 cups shredded escarole

Optional: ¼ cup heavy cream

1 cup diced canned clams, drained

Salt and freshly ground black pepper

GARNISH

2 tablespoons finely minced fresh parsley

In Catalan cooking, the food I grew up with, root vegetables are often teamed with roast seafood. Here is a variation of a traditional soup that is extremely popular all along the coast north of Barcelona. The slightly briny, salty clam broth gives the soup its special punch. Serve with crusty bread either as a one-dish meal or as a starter followed by the Zucchini Frittata with Parmesan (page 95) or the Catalan Potato and Onion Tortilla (page 96).

....

1. Heat the oil in a 4-quart casserole over medium-low heat. Add the vegetables and cook, covered, for 20 minutes, or until soft. Stir in the flour and cook for 1 minute. Whisk in the bouillon and clam juice and simmer for 15 minutes longer.

2. Add the escarole and optional cream and simmer until the escarole is just wilted. Remove from the heat, add the clams, and season carefully with salt and pepper. Serve hot, sprinkled with the minced parsley.

T i p

Farm-raised mussels, which are inexpensive and available in many supermarkets, are a good substitute for the clams in this soup. Cook the mussels according to the directions on page 85. Dice them, and substitute their poaching liquid for the clam broth.

Yellow Pepper and Golden Zucchini Soup

To prepare: 15 minutes
To cook: 30 minutes
Serves 5 to 6

3 tablespoons extra-virgin olive oil

1 large onion, peeled and finely minced

5 large yellow bell peppers, cored, seeded, and cubed

2 tablespoons all-purpose flour

2 teaspoons ground cumin

½ teaspoon ground coriander

6 cups Chicken Stock (page 145) or chicken bouillon

2 cups diced golden zucchini or yellow squash

⅓ cup heavy cream or yogurt

Salt and freshly ground white pepper

GARNISH
Finely minced fresh cilantro, chives, or parsley

Tip

Golden zucchini is a relatively "new kid on the block." I prefer to use it because it is less watery, more flavorful, and has a better texture than yellow squash.

Just when I think that I have tried every possible variation of vegetable soup, I discover a "new" one. Of course, using red rather than yellow peppers and zucchini instead of yellow squash or golden zucchini is perfectly OK, but what makes this soup somewhat special is the extra sweetness that is achieved by using these golden vegetables, which complement each other so well. The soup is at its best when made a day ahead but it is quite tasty as soon as it is finished, which takes no more than thirty minutes.

1. Heat the oil in a large casserole over medium-low heat. Add the onion and cook until soft but not brown. Add the peppers and cook until soft. Add the flour, cumin, and coriander and stir well. Add the stock or bouillon and simmer, partially covered, for 15 minutes.

2. Puree the soup in a food processor in batches and return to the casserole. Add the golden zucchini or squash and simmer until just tender. Add the cream or yogurt and season with salt and white pepper. Garnish with cilantro, parsley, or chives and serve hot or at room temperature.

Starter Salads and Light Meals

We've come A LONG WAY FROM THE DAYS WHEN THE STANDARD SALAD WAS COMPOSED OF A WEDGE OF ICEBERG LETTUCE TOSSED WITH TASTELESS TOMATOES, ICY SLICED CUCUMBERS, AND BOXED CROUTONS, WITH OR WITHOUT BITS OF ERSATZ BACON. THIS UNAPPETIZING COMBINATION WAS SMOTHERED WITH YOUR CHOICE OF BOTTLED ITALIAN, FRENCH, RUSSIAN, OR THOUSAND ISLAND DRESSING—ONE TASTE OF WHICH COULD ALLOW ANY UPSTANDING CITIZEN OF FRANCE, ITALY, THE RUSSIAN REPUBLIC, OR THE THOUSAND ISLANDS TO SUE FOR FALSE ADVERTISING.

HAPPILY, THE WHOLE CONCEPT OF SALAD HAS BEEN THOROUGHLY RETHOUGHT, REINVENTED, REDEFINED, AND REFRESHED. AT ITS VERY SIM-

plest, a tossed salad is a bracing mix of crisp greens lightly coated with oil and vinegar in a silken, tangy harmony. But today's variations on a theme can turn a basic salad into anything from seasonal steamed vegetables in a tart vinaigrette to a warm curried chicken plate that's really more of a light meal.

Are Asparagus and Prosciutto Rolls in a Chive Vinaigrette (page 75) a salad or a light meal? How would you classify a combination of potatoes, roasted peppers, and salami (page 64)? Distinctions blur, but whether it's a salad or light meal, it's simple and satisfying as a first course or a light lunch.

The new variety and flexibility of salad making is a real boon to the Spur of the Moment cook who is looking for something healthful, but delicious, invigorating, and spontaneous that can be readily conjured up from a wealth of fresh ingredients and a range of seasonings. Bottled dressings have given way to simple vinaigrettes, which in turn have opened up a world of possibilities. Why not break some chunky blue cheese and walnuts onto a bed of arugula and Bibb, then substitute a fragrant walnut oil for olive oil in the vinaigrette? Why not spice up a plain vinaigrette with ginger and lime? Why not drizzle a mustardy balsamic vinaigrette over a bowl of warm new potatoes?

Delicious salads in all their infinite variety are enjoying well-deserved new popularity, and for that, I give a great deal of credit to the proliferation of salad bars across the country. The advent of the salad bar really helped redefine the salad—it no longer has to be green, raw, and crunchy and served cold at the beginning of the meal. It can be a far more imaginative, more substantial sampling, put together from dozens and dozens of possible choices. Unfortunately, the flip side of this is something I call "salad bar syndrome," a hodgepodge of tastes and textures that comes from heaping your plate with a little of everything. ("Do I want this or do I want that? I'll have them both!") Anything goes—but not together.

It's easy to avoid salad bar syndrome. Just remember that even though a salad can be a Spur of the Moment creation, it must be well conceived, well balanced, and well edited to succeed. Be creative: Experiment—add a little more, do a little more. Transform a salad by including an unexpected antipasto ingredient like warm roasted peppers. Slice chicken over the romaine and turn your salad into a light meal. But don't go overboard. Know when to stop. Make sure you respect each taste separately and in combination. Try not to be so clever that you risk losing the essence of a taste or a texture. Finally, remember my cardinal salad rule: If you have to stop eating to try to figure out *what* you're eating, you're in trouble!

Mediterranean Salad of Cucumbers, Radishes, and Feta

To prepare: 10 minutes
plus 1 hour to drain
cucumbers
Serves 4 to 6

....

2 pounds small cucumbers, preferably Kirby, peeled and thinly sliced

Coarse salt

1 cup plain yogurt

2 tablespoons red wine vinegar

3 tablespoons extra-virgin olive oil

1 large garlic clove, peeled and mashed

½ cup finely minced red onion

3 tablespoons finely minced fresh mint

Freshly ground black pepper

12 radishes (red and/or white), thinly sliced

1 cup diced feta cheese

T i p

....

I store feta in lightly salted water unless it is very salty to begin with. Change the water every 2 to 3 days.

H e r e is a salad that can be put together in a matter of minutes. What does take time is draining the cucumbers. This, however, is not a must, especially if you are willing to seed them or use the large gourmet or seedless variety. For a Viennese touch, add plenty of dill and minced green onions and some diced Gruyère or any other well-flavored Swiss-type cheese. I am especially fond of feta, with its lightly salty, briny flavor. You can now get pretty good feta in every supermarket but if you have a choice, I suggest that you try the French, Israeli, or Bulgarian varieties, which I find far less salty than the Greek import.

....

1. Place the cucumbers in a colander, sprinkle with coarse salt, and let drain for 1 hour.

2. Combine the yogurt, vinegar, oil, and garlic in a serving bowl and whisk until smooth. Add the onion and mint and season with a large grinding of pepper. Pat the cucumbers dry on paper towels and add to the vinaigrette together with the radishes and feta. Toss gently and correct the seasoning. Serve slightly chilled.

Remarks: The salad is best served 2 to 4 hours after tossing. The yogurt dressing can be made well in advance and kept refrigerated. It is equally delicious as a topping for garden greens, particularly young spinach leaves.

Endive and Young Spinach Salad with Roasted Cumin Vinaigrette

To prepare: 20 minutes
Serves 4

1 teaspoon cumin seeds, toasted and crushed

1 large shallot, peeled and finely minced

2 tablespoons balsamic vinegar

1½ teaspoons fresh lemon juice

6 tablespoons extra-virgin olive oil

Salt and freshly ground black pepper

½ pound young spinach leaves, stemmed, well washed, and dried

2 large Belgian endives, cored and cut crosswise into ½-inch slices

T i p

To toast cumin seeds, place them in a small dry nonstick skillet over medium heat and shake the skillet back and forth until the seeds are fragrant and golden brown. This can be done in quantity and the seeds stored in a covered jar for 2 to 3 weeks.

C o m e spring, much of the curly winter spinach gives way to New Zealand spinach, a variety grown in California that has a leaf similar to that of sorrel. This mild-flavored, rather delicate spinach is wonderful raw in salads, especially when combined with a julienne of Belgian endives. If possible, use toasted cumin seeds in the dressing rather than ground cumin—it makes a world of difference.

Combine the cumin, shallot, vinegar, and lemon juice in a large serving bowl. Slowly whisk in the oil until the mixture has emulsified. Season with salt and pepper, add the spinach and endives, and toss gently. Correct the seasoning and serve at once.

Remarks: This vinaigrette can easily be doubled or tripled and kept in a tightly covered jar in the refrigerator. Make sure to bring it back to room temperature before serving, and whisk until well blended.

Salad of Potatoes, Roasted Peppers, and Salami

To prepare: 20 minutes
To marinate: 30 minutes
To cook: 10 minutes
Serves 6

....

2 tablespoons balsamic vinegar

1 tablespoon sherry vinegar

2 large garlic cloves, peeled and mashed

Coarse salt and freshly ground black pepper

6 tablespoons extra-virgin olive oil

1 small red onion, peeled and thinly sliced

2 large bell peppers (1 red and 1 green), roasted, peeled (see page 182), and thinly sliced

8 to 10 medium red potatoes, unpeeled, cubed

1 tablespoon tiny capers, drained

1 small dill gherkin, finely diced

3 tablespoons finely minced fresh parsley

½ cup fine julienne of hard salami or smoked turkey

T i p

....

Dress the cooked potatoes in the vinaigrette while they are still warm and leave at room temperature for 30 minutes before serving.

Although its culinary heritage is nowhere near as famous as French bistro food, there are some wonderful home-style dishes in Austria and a real bistro cuisine that is gutsy and flavorful. Here is a typical potato salad that you can sample all over the country, where it is usually served as a side dish to an assortment of cold cuts and a cold glass of beer. The salad is good when it is freshly made and still warm, but leftovers are even better once the potatoes have a chance to absorb the vinaigrette. Serve with one or two other starter salads or a roast chicken left to cool to room temperature for a warm-weather supper.

....

1. Combine the vinegars and garlic in a large serving bowl and season with salt and pepper. Slowly whisk in the oil until well blended. Add the onion and peppers and let marinate at room temperature for 30 minutes.

2. Meanwhile, drop the potatoes into boiling salted water and simmer for 8 to 10 minutes, or until tender.

3. Drain the potatoes and, while still warm, add to the pepper mixture together with the capers, gherkin, parsley, and salami or smoked turkey. Toss gently, correct the seasoning, and serve at room temperature.

Curried Roast Chicken Salad

To prepare: 15 minutes
Serves 4 to 5

....

1 cup mayonnaise

1 teaspoon Madras curry powder

2 teaspoons finely minced jalapeño pepper

¼ cup finely diced red bell
  pepper

¼ cup finely diced yellow bell
  pepper

¼ cup finely minced red onion

2 tablespoons finely minced fresh
  parsley or cilantro

1 dill gherkin, finely diced

1 chicken (about 3 pounds),
  roasted (see page 229), meat
  removed and diced, or 4 cups
  diced leftover roast chicken or
  turkey

Salt and freshly ground black
  pepper

A delicious roast chicken (or roast turkey) makes for great leftovers. I love preparing a chicken "melt" with it or turning it into a flavor-packed salad. With some nicely dressed greens and a spoonful of a spicy chutney, you have the makings of an excellent easy lunch or supper.

....

1. Combine the mayonnaise, curry, jalapeño, bell peppers, onion, parsley or cilantro, and gherkin in a serving bowl, and whisk until well blended.

2. Add the roast chicken or turkey, season with salt and pepper, and fold gently but thoroughly. Serve lightly chilled.

T i p

....

Other spices are wonderful in this salad, especially cumin or the tandoori spice mix you can get in specialty shops.

Bell Pepper, Zucchini, and Smoked Salmon Salad

To prepare: 20 minutes
plus 30 minutes to 1
hour to marinate

Serves 4

3 large bell peppers (1 each red, yellow, and orange), cored, seeded, quartered, and cut into thin matchsticks

2 small zucchini, cut into 2-inch-long thin matchsticks (avoid the seedy center)

6 ounces smoked salmon, cut into thin matchsticks

⅓ cup Creamy Dill and Scallion Vinaigrette (page 89)

2 small bunches arugula, stemmed, rinsed, and dried

1 tablespoon balsamic vinegar

3 to 4 tablespoons extra-virgin olive oil

Coarse salt and freshly ground black pepper

GARNISH
Diced avocado

Finely minced fresh chives

M i x e d pepper salads tossed in either a cider vinegar and sugar dressing or a creamy vinaigrette like this one are extremely popular in Austrian bistros. By the time most chefs of this Alpine country woke up to nouvelle cuisine, the trend was over and it was back to basics. But some cooks decided to update the most classic fare, and with the addition of smoked salmon this traditional starter has indeed become far more interesting — and very tasty. For a less expensive variation, one that you can make with supermarket basics, use a julienne of smoked turkey breast instead.

1. Combine the peppers, zucchini, and salmon in a large bowl. Add the vinaigrette and toss gently. Marinate at room temperature for 30 minutes to 1 hour to develop flavor.

2. Combine the arugula with the balsamic vinegar, olive oil, and a touch of coarse salt and pepper in another large bowl. Toss lightly, and divide among 4 plates. Top each portion with some of the pepper and salmon mixture, and garnish with avocado and chives. Serve slightly chilled.

T i p

Be sure not to serve the salad too cold; it should just be lightly chilled. You can also add a julienne of Belgian endive to the arugula or toss the arugula with some spinach or Bibb lettuce leaves.

Calamari Salad with Avocado in a Lime-Ginger Vinaigrette

~~~

To prepare: 15 minutes
To marinate: 2 to 4
hours
To cook: 1 minute
Serves 4 to 5

....

1 pound fresh calamari, cleaned
and cut into ½-inch rings

Juice of 1 large lime

6 tablespoons extra-virgin olive oil

2 tablespoons soy sauce

1 large garlic clove, peeled and
mashed

2 teaspoons finely minced fresh
ginger, or more to taste

2 teaspoons finely minced jalapeño pepper

Freshly ground black pepper

1 cup thinly sliced red onions

1 large avocado, peeled, pitted,
and cubed

GARNISH
Tiny fresh cilantro leaves

T i p

....

To clean calamari, cut off the ten-
tacles. Rub or peel off the purplish
outer membrane under running
water. Pull out and discard the
white viscera and feather-shaped
quill. Dry on paper towels before
sautéing.

C a l a m a r i are sold two ways, cleaned and un-cleaned. Uncleaned calamari are less expensive but easy to prepare (see Tip). Calamari takes little more than thirty seconds to cook. Here the cooked calamari are dressed in a simple but zesty lime-ginger vinaigrette and tossed with ripe avocados at the very last minute. The salad is at its best when allowed to develop flavor for twenty minutes.

....

1.   Drop the calamari into boiling salted water and simmer until just opaque, about 30 seconds to 1 minute; do not overcook. Remove from the heat and immediately add ice cubes to stop further cooking. Drain well and set aside.

2.   Combine the lime juice and oil in a serving bowl and whisk until well blended. Whisk in the soy sauce, garlic, ginger, and jalapeño pepper. Add a large grinding of pepper and a touch more ginger if desired.

3.   Add the calamari together with the onions, toss gently, and marinate for at least 2 to 4 hours before serving. Just before serving, add the avocado. Garnish with cilantro and serve slightly chilled, accompanied by crusty bread.

Remarks: You can vary this salad by combining the calamari with ½ pound small bay scallops, lightly poached, for an interesting added texture.

Beet, Potato, and Endive Salad in Garlic-Dill Mayonnaise

To prepare: 15 minutes
To marinate: 1 hour
Serves 4 to 5

....

½ cup mayonnaise

⅓ cup sour cream

Juice of 1 large lemon

3 tablespoons finely minced
fresh dill

3 tablespoons finely minced
scallions

1 large garlic clove, peeled and
mashed

Salt and freshly ground black
pepper

1 pound cooked beets, cubed

1 pound small red potatoes, unpeeled, quartered, and
cooked

2 medium Belgian endives, cored
and cut crosswise into ½-inch
slices

T i p

....

When cooking beets, keep them from bleeding by leaving their roots and a full inch of their tops attached. Also, do not pierce them too often while testing for doneness.

T h e lovely custom of presenting two or three simple antipasto salads on the same plate is not unique to the Mediterranean. It is equally popular in Scandinavia and Central Europe, but I rarely see it here. It is a perfect way to eat simply and nutritiously, especially during the warm season when the last thing you want is to spend hours in the kitchen. This flavor-packed salad is good on its own but even better when teamed with two other light salads, such as the Calamari Salad with Avocado in a Lime-Ginger Vinaigrette (page 67) and some cherry tomatoes cut in half and tossed in a basil-garlic vinaigrette. The salad makes delicious leftovers, although the potatoes will be discolored by the beet juices.

....

1. Puree the mayonnaise, sour cream, lemon juice, dill, scallions, and garlic in a food processor until smooth. Season with salt and pepper and transfer to a large serving bowl. Add the beets, potatoes, and endives and let marinate at room temperature for 1 hour.

2. Just before serving, correct the seasoning. Serve at room temperature lightly chilled.

Swiss Country Salad

To prepare: 20 minutes
Serves 4

....

1 large shallot, peeled and finely minced

1 medium garlic clove, peeled and mashed

2 tablespoons balsamic vinegar

6 tablespoons extra-virgin olive oil

Salt and freshly ground black pepper

4 cups arugula leaves, washed and dried

3 large Belgian endives, cored and cut lengthwise into ½-inch julienne

1 cup julienne of Gruyère cheese

½ cup fine julienne of smoked ham

H e r e is a simple trattoria salad, one that you will find on the menu of many bistros throughout the French-speaking region of Switzerland. It makes a wonderful starter but with the addition of a julienne of smoked ham, it becomes a good, quick supper main course.

Combine the shallot, garlic, and vinegar in a large salad bowl. Add the oil in a slow steady stream, whisking constantly until the mixture has emulsified. Season with salt and pepper. Add the arugula, endives, Gruyère, and ham and toss gently but thoroughly. Correct the seasoning, and serve at room temperature.

T i p

This salad lends itself to many variations. I often use Jarlsberg, Comté, or Monterey Jack instead of the Gruyère. Smoked turkey or tongue makes a great substitute for the ham, and finely sliced radishes are a crisp and colorful addition as well.

Mixed Green Salad with Roasted Shiitakes and Parmesan Shavings

To prepare: 20 minutes
To cook: 15 minutes
Serves 6

....

2 tablespoons finely minced
   shallots

1½ tablespoons sherry vinegar

Juice of ½ lemon

¼ teaspoon dry mustard or 2 teaspoons Dijon mustard

Coarse salt and freshly ground
   black pepper

½ cup plus 1 tablespoon extra-
   virgin olive oil

8 cups mixed greens, such as
   frisée, Bibb lettuce, radicchio,
   and Belgian endives

18 medium shiitake mushrooms,
   stemmed

½ cup shavings of excellent-
   quality Parmesan cheese

T i p

....

*Shiitakes tend to absorb a great
deal of oil when sautéed. That is
why I prefer to roast them, which
also gives them a nongreasy,
lovely texture.*

A l l over Northern Italy you find a simple starter of mixed greens topped with a few long, thin "shavings" of excellent Parmigiano-Reggiano. For years I tried to make these shavings with a variety of peelers but at best the results were uneven. Now there are several Parmesan slicers and new vegetable peelers on the market that make it easy to slice the cheese into the superfine shavings.

For a seasonal variation, substitute two ripe Bartlett pears for the shiitakes. Quarter or cut the pears into eighths and roast with a touch of butter and sugar for ten minutes.

....

1. Preheat the oven to 400°F.

2. Combine the shallots, vinegar, lemon juice, and mustard in a salad bowl and season with salt and pepper. Whisk in the ½ cup oil until well blended. Add the greens but do not toss. Cover and chill.

3. Brush the mushrooms with the remaining tablespoon oil, place on a baking sheet, and roast for 10 minutes, or until tender and nicely browned.

4. To serve, toss the greens. Place on individual serving plates. Top with the warm mushrooms and shavings of Parmesan. Serve at once.

Remarks: Parmesan that gets hard and dry cannot be sliced, so keep the cheese in a plastic Ziploc bag, and bring it to room temperature before slicing.

Provençal Potato and Garlic Galette

To prepare: 5 minutes
To cook: 20 minutes
Serves 4

....

3 tablespoons olive oil

1 large garlic clove, peeled and finely minced

1 tablespoon finely minced fresh thyme or parsley

2 large Idaho potatoes, peeled and grated

Coarse salt and freshly ground black pepper

T h i s simple and gutsy potato pancake, similar to the Swiss potato rosti, makes a lovely accompaniment to any chicken preparation. Let the pan juices moisten the pancake to make it even more delicious. For a weekday supper, I often serve a wedge of pancake over an individual portion of a well-seasoned salad, often with the addition of two or three rashers of bacon.

....

1. Heat 2 tablespoons of the oil in a 9-inch non-stick skillet over medium-high heat. Add the garlic and thyme or parsley, and cook for 1 minute. Add the potatoes, toss well, and then press down lightly with a spatula. Cook for 10 minutes or until the bottom of the galette is nicely browned. Season with coarse salt and pepper.

2. Invert the galette onto a plate. Add the remaining 1 tablespoon oil to the skillet, carefully slip the galette back into the pan, bottom side up, and sauté for 5 to 10 minutes longer, or until nicely browned. Transfer to a large plate, season with salt and pepper, cut into wedges, and serve hot.

Remarks: Any leftovers can be easily reheated in the microwave. You can also make the galette in advance and place the skillet in a 200°F oven to keep warm. The galette will not be as crisp when reheated, but the taste will be as good as ever.

Souffléed Potato Cakes with Smoked Salmon and Sour Cream

To prepare: 20 minutes
To cook: 20 minutes
Serves 6

....

SAUCE

1 cup crème fraîche (see page 31) or sour cream

½ cup mayonnaise

Juice of ½ lemon

3 ounces smoked salmon

Salt and freshly ground white pepper

FRITTERS

2 medium baking potatoes (about 1 pound), peeled and cubed

2 extra-large eggs, separated

2 tablespoons finely grated onion

2 tablespoons all-purpose flour

Salt and freshly ground black pepper

Pinch of freshly grated nutmeg

3 to 5 tablespoons peanut oil or Clarified Butter (page 103)

GARNISH

Sprigs of fresh dill

T h i s is one of my grandmother's "classics." As a true Viennese, she usually made these cakes with left-over mashed potatoes. I used to love eating them nice and hot, right out of the skillet. Try these fluffy fritters as a side dish to a simple fish or chicken preparation or by themselves with a quick sauce of smoked fish mixed with sour cream and some lemon to give it a real kick. A topping of sour cream mixed with Dijon mustard and a teaspoon or two of strong horseradish also nicely complements the potato cakes.

....

1. Make the smoked salmon sauce: Puree all the sauce ingredients in a food processor until very smooth. Correct the seasoning and set aside.

2. Make the fritters: Cook the potatoes in boiling salted water until very tender. Drain well and pass through a food mill or potato ricer into a large bowl. Add the egg yolks, onion, and flour and mix well. Set aside.

3. Beat the egg whites until they hold firm peaks. Fold gently but thoroughly into the potato mixture and season generously with salt and pepper and a large pinch of nutmeg.

4. Cook the fritters in 2 to 3 batches: For each batch, heat 1½ tablespoons peanut oil or clarified butter in a nonstick skillet over medium heat. Add the batter by the tablespoon to the hot pan, without crowding, and cook for 1 to 2 minutes per side, or until nicely browned. Keep the cooked fritters warm in a 200°F oven while you fry the remaining batches.

5. Transfer the fritters to individual plates and spoon some of the smoked salmon sauce around each portion. Garnish with dill and serve at once.

T i p

The quality of the potatoes available at different times of the year will affect the texture of this batter. Sometimes you may need to add an extra tablespoon of flour, and additional seasoning to compensate. The best way to find out is by making your first fritter. If it holds up and tastes good, your batter is just right.

Crème Fraîche and Chive Fritters

To prepare: 5 minutes
To cook: 10 minutes
Serves 4 to 6

....

1 cup crème fraîche
(see page 31)

2 extra-large eggs

½ cup plus 2 tablespoons all-
purpose flour

½ teaspoon baking soda

¼ teaspoon baking powder

3 tablespoons finely minced fresh
chives

Salt and freshly ground black
pepper

2 to 3 tablespoons unsalted
butter

6 ounces smoked salmon, finely
minced and formed into
½-inch balls

T i p

....

*Homemade crème fraîche is far
better and more economical than
the store-bought varieties. It is not
a Spur of the Moment preparation, but it will keep for 2 to 3
weeks, so you can make these fritters spontaneously. If you choose
to buy crème fraîche, look for one
that has a low butterfat content.*

T h e s e savory little pancakes make a terrific quick appetizer or lunch on the weekend. For the smoked fish garnish, I usually buy smoked salmon trimmings, which are inexpensive and perfectly suitable to be minced or ground up in the food processor. You can serve the fritters with a variety of other toppings as well, depending upon what is easiest for you. Browned melted butter, sliced smoked mozzarella, or thin slices of goat cheese and a mincing of herbs all work well. Any leftover fritters can be reheated successfully and make a delightful side dish to grilled or pan-seared salmon, sea scallops, or swordfish.

....

1.   Combine the crème fraîche, eggs, flour, baking soda and powder, and chives in a large bowl. Season generously with salt and pepper and whisk until well blended.

2.   Cook the fritters in 3 to 4 batches: For each batch, heat 2 teaspoons butter in a large nonstick skillet over medium heat. Drop 2 tablespoons batter per fritter into the hot pan and cook for 1 to 2 minutes per side or until lightly browned. Serve warm, topped with the smoked salmon "tartare."

Asparagus and Prosciutto Rolls
in a Chive Vinaigrette

To prepare: 20 minutes
To cook: 5 to 7 minutes
Serves 6

....

½ cup olive oil

2 tablespoons sherry vinegar or
   red wine vinegar

1 tablespoon Dijon mustard

1 medium garlic clove, peeled
   and mashed

2 tablespoons finely minced fresh
   chives

Salt and freshly ground black
   pepper

36 fresh asparagus stalks of uniform size, trimmed and
   peeled

6 thin slices imported prosciutto,
   cut in half crosswise

GARNISH
Leaves of fresh Italian parsley

Tip

....

The best-tasting asparagus spears are not the pencil-thin ones but rather the fat stalks. Once they are cooked, I cut the stalks in half lengthwise, which makes them perfect for both serving and rolling up in either prosciutto or thinly sliced smoked ham.

I much prefer serving asparagus on its own and not as a side dish. You can find good-quality prosciutto in most supermarkets, making this an easy and tasty way to serve this superb vegetable. If you cannot find chives, finely minced green onions or minced shallots can be substituted. In Italy this dish is often served topped with an egg fried in olive oil, a nice way to make a meal out of the asparagus rolls.

....

1. Combine the oil, vinegar, mustard, and garlic in a small jar, cover, and shake until the dressing is well blended and smooth. Add the chives and season with salt and pepper.

2. Cook the asparagus in boiling salted water for 5 to 7 minutes, or until just tender. Run under cold water to stop the cooking and drain well on paper towels. Roll 3 stalks of asparagus up in each slice of prosciutto, place on a serving platter, and spoon the vinaigrette over them. Serve at room temperature, garnished with Italian parsley.

Artichokes with Curried Ginger-Lemon Vinaigrette

To prepare: 20 minutes

To cook: 25 minutes

Serves 4

....

4 large globe artichokes, trimmed (see Tip)

1 lemon, cut in half, plus juice of ½ lemon

1 teaspoon lightly beaten egg yolk

1 teaspoon Madras curry powder

One 1-inch piece fresh ginger, passed through a garlic press

1½ tablespoons sherry vinegar

2 teaspoons Dijon mustard

1 large garlic clove, peeled and mashed

¾ cup olive oil

2 tablespoons finely minced scallions or fresh chives

Optional: 3 flat anchovy fillets, finely minced

Salt and freshly ground black pepper

As I was brought up on the tiny chokeless artichokes of Mediterranean Europe, it took me a while to get used to the giant American globe artichoke. They take a long time to cook and, once served, require a bit of patience to get to the nutty and delicious heart. You may, of course, use your microwave, which will shorten the cooking time. Now I can settle down to savoring the leaves, dipping them into this tangy ginger-lemon dressing within thirty minutes of shopping. Other dressings in this book are also good accompaniments, particularly the Chive Vinaigrette (page 75), and, of course, there is always melted browned butter with a touch of lemon, anchovies, and a sprinkling of hot pepper.

....

1. Drop the artichokes into boiling salted water along with lemon halves and cook for 25 minutes, or until tender. Test by piercing the bottoms with the tip of a sharp knife.

2. While the artichokes are cooking, prepare the vinaigrette: Combine the beaten yolk, curry powder, ginger, vinegar, lemon juice, mustard, and garlic in a small bowl and whisk until well blended. Slowly add the oil, whisking constantly until thick and smooth. Add the scallions or chives and optional anchovies and correct the seasoning. (If using anchovies, you will probably not need salt, just a large grinding of pepper.) Set aside.

3. When the artichokes are done, drain well. Let cool slightly, then carefully spread the leaves out from the center, and scoop out the fuzzy chokes with a grapefruit spoon. Fill each with a little vinaigrette, place on a serving platter, and serve at room temperature. Pass any remaining vinaigrette separately.

T i p s

To extract ginger juice, peel a very fresh piece of ginger about the size of a walnut and pass through a garlic press. (Some kitchenware shops now carry ginger presses, which look just like garlic presses except that they have larger holes.) This sauce is equally delicious served with grilled scallops, shrimp, or fish steaks.

Cutting off the tops of artichokes allows them to cook faster. Be sure to rub the cut parts with a lemon half to keep them from discoloring. Always cook artichokes in plenty of lightly salted water.

Beef Carpaccio in a Viennese Mustard and Caper Sauce

To prepare: 20 minutes
plus time for freezing
beef

Serves 6

....

1¼ pounds fillet of beef or London broil, in one piece, trimmed of all fat

2 thin slices Italian bread

2 hard-boiled extra-large eggs, peeled

2 teaspoons Dijon mustard

½ cup extra-virgin olive oil

¼ cup corn oil

2 teaspoons tiny capers, drained

2 tablespoons finely minced dill gherkin

Salt and freshly ground black pepper

GARNISH
2 tablespoons extra-virgin olive oil

Coarse salt

Paper-thin sliced beef accompanied by a fragrant basil sauce called *salsa verde* is a classic Italian appetizer that has found its way into many French and American restaurants. Now you can sample tuna, salmon, and even lamb carpaccio, but to me, beef carpaccio is still the most flavorful. With top-quality beef, a splash of extra-virgin olive oil, a large grinding of black pepper, and a sprinkling of capers, it is a great dish. My favorite is this zesty Viennese version of a tartare sauce that is less overpowering than the ubiquitous salsa verde. The good news is that you can use very thinly sliced London broil instead of expensive beef tenderloin. You must, however, freeze the meat slightly first so as to be able to slice it very thinly. Placed on a warm plate, the sliced meat will defrost in a matter of seconds.

....

1. Wrap the beef in foil and freeze until completely frozen. Remove from the freezer and let sit for 15 to 20 minutes, or until easily pierced with the tip of a knife.

2. While the beef is sitting at room temperature, prepare the sauce: Puree the bread and eggs together with the mustard in a blender (not a food processor) until smooth. With the machine running, add the olive oil by droplets until emulsified. Add the corn oil, capers, and gherkin and blend until smooth. Season with salt and pepper, and reserve.

3. Slice the beef as thinly as possible. Cover each of 6 individual serving plates with a thin layer of beef, drizzle each serving with 1 teaspoon olive oil, and sprinkle with coarse salt. Spoon a little sauce by droplets over each portion and serve accompanied by crusty bread.

T i p

Rather than raw beef, I often opt for a piece of very rare quickly pan-seared or grilled beef. Cuts such as the rib-eye steak, flank steak, or London broil can be prepared this way and served thinly sliced with a variety of quick, zesty sauces, either warm or at room temperature.

Avocado, Tomato, and Bacon Bruschetta

To prepare: 10 minutes
Serves 4

4 slices peasant bread, cut ½ inch thick

5 tablespoons extra-virgin olive oil

1 large garlic clove, peeled and mashed in a garlic press

2 ripe avocados, peeled, pitted, and cubed

Juice of ½ lime, or more to taste

2 to 3 tablespoons finely diced red onion

Optional: 2 teaspoons finely minced jalapeño pepper

Coarse salt and freshly ground black pepper

6 to 8 slices bacon

GARNISH

6 to 8 ripe cherry tomatoes, quartered

Tiny fresh cilantro leaves

Freshly cracked black pepper

Tip

Whenever possible, I use Haas avocados, which have optimum flavor and the best texture. When perfectly ripe, the skin of the Haas should be almost black and the flesh should never be soft but rather give slightly to pressure.

H e r e is another simple Italian dish that has crossed the Atlantic successfully. The success of the bruschetta relies entirely on four ingredients: good bread, ripe tomatoes, fresh basil, and, of course, delicious extra-virgin olive oil. Since tomatoes are not always in season, I have found that many other toppings such as leftover roast chicken or turkey do nicely and produce a delicious open-faced sandwich that makes for a very satisfying light lunch or starter to a simple meal.

1. Preheat the broiler. Brush the bread with 2 tablespoons of the oil and the garlic, and run under the broiler until lightly browned. Set aside.

2. Combine the avocados, lime juice, red onion, and optional jalapeño pepper in a bowl. Season with coarse salt and pepper and add the remaining 3 tablespoons olive oil. Set aside.

3. Sauté the bacon in a nonstick skillet until almost crisp. Drain on paper towels and break into bite-size pieces.

4. Divide the avocado mixture among the bread slices, and top with the bacon. Garnish with cherry tomatoes and cilantro leaves, and serve with a sprinkling of cracked black pepper.

Catalan Open-Faced Tomato Sandwich

To prepare: 10 minutes
To cook: 2 to 3 minutes
Serves 6

....

1 small loaf French or Tuscan
  bread, cut in half lengthwise

2 large garlic cloves, peeled and
  cut in half

3 to 4 large ripe tomatoes, cut in
  half crosswise

3 tablespoons extra-virgin olive oil

Coarse salt and freshly ground
  black pepper

TOPPING
Thinly sliced red onions

6 small black oil-cured olives,
  pitted and cut in half

Tip

....

Optional toppings for this sandwich can include any of the following: Sardines or anchovies • Thinly sliced prosciutto, hard salami, chorizo, or andouille sausage • Leftover roast chicken (see page 228) • Leftover Catalan Potato and Onion Tortilla (page 96) • Thinly sliced goat cheese

T h i s open-faced sandwich is as common in Catalan cooking as the hot dog is in the United States. And all you need to satisfy a craving for "pa com tomat," as it is called in Barcelona, is dense, crusty bread, fruity olive oil, very ripe tomatoes, and coarse salt. If you like, the sandwich can be topped with anything from a quick omelette, sardines, or thinly sliced prosciutto to a simple basil leaf. In any case, it takes only minutes to prepare and is both filling and delicious.

....

1.   Preheat the broiler.

2.   Rub the cut sides of the bread with the cut sides of the garlic cloves. Cut each half of bread crosswise into 3 pieces. Arrange the bread on a baking sheet, place under the broiler about 6 inches from the source of heat, and broil until lightly browned. You may also grill the bread over hot charcoal.

3.   Rub the toasted bread with the cut sides of the tomatoes, soaking the bread with the tomato pulp. Discard the tomato shells. Drizzle the bread with the olive oil, and sprinkle lightly with coarse salt and pepper. Garnish each piece of bread with a few rings of red onion and 2 olive halves. Serve at once.

Smoked Cod, Potato, and Parsley Fritters

To prepare: 15 minutes
To cook: 30 minutes
Serves 6

....

4½ cups water

2 fish bouillon cubes

1 medium baking potato (about ½ pound), peeled and cut into eighths

1 pound smoked cod (finnan haddie) or fresh cod fillet, cut in half

1 large garlic clove, peeled and mashed

1 extra-large egg

1 extra-large egg yolk

3 to 4 tablespoons all-purpose flour

¼ cup finely minced fresh parsley

Coarse salt and freshly ground black pepper

3 tablespoons unsalted butter

2 tablespoons peanut oil

GARNISH
Leaves of fresh cilantro or Italian parsley

ACCOMPANIMENTS
Mustard, Caper, and Jalapeño Pepper Mayonnaise (page 187)

Lemon wedges

Melted unsalted butter

For years, fish cakes remained strictly in the domain of peasant cooking. Usually made with leftover bits of fish and stretched with either potatoes or bread crumbs, they provided the cook with an inexpensive flavorful main course. Now the spotlight is on this homey preparation, and it can be sampled in different variations in restaurants on both sides of the Atlantic. Here I use smoked cod, which goes by the name of finnan haddie (smoked haddock) and lends a smoky and assertive taste to the fritters. For the perfect side dish, go with Union Square Café's Slaw of Two Cabbages with Mustard and Champagne Vinaigrette (page 267) and possibly some lemon-accented braised zucchini or roasted mixed vegetables.

....

1. Combine the water and bouillon cubes in a casserole, add the potato, and simmer until very tender. Remove the potato with a slotted spoon and pass through a food mill. Set aside.

2. Add the smoked or fresh cod to the bouillon and simmer for 5 minutes, or until opaque. Transfer with a slotted spoon to a large bowl and mash with the back of a fork. Add the potato together with the garlic, egg, yolk, flour, and parsley and blend well. Season with salt and pepper and set aside.

3. Cook the fritters in 2 batches: For each batch, melt 1½ tablespoons butter together with 1 tablespoon oil in a nonstick skillet over medium heat. Add 2 tablespoonfuls of the cod mixture to the skillet for each fritter, flatten slightly, and cook for 3 minutes on each side, or until nicely browned.

4.   Transfer the fritters to individual plates, sprinkle with coarse salt, and garnish with cilantro or parsley leaves. Serve hot with the caper mayonnaise, lemon wedges, and a little melted butter.

T i p

I find that the taste of smoke is important in this dish, but if you cannot find finnan haddie, you can add two or three drops of mesquite or hickory Liquid Smoke to the potato and cod mixture for a nicely balanced smoky flavor.

Spicy Shrimp and Ginger Fritters

To prepare: 15 minutes
To cook: 5 minutes
Serves 6

....

1 pound medium shrimp, peeled
and cubed

¼ cup finely minced shallots

¼ cup finely minced scallions

Juice of 1 large lemon

1 tablespoon finely minced jalapeño pepper

2 tablespoons finely minced fresh
ginger

Coarse salt and freshly ground
white pepper

Peanut oil for frying

T i p

....

*When frying, use plenty of oil.
Food is less greasy when fried in
lots of oil rather than in a small
amount. Choose a flavorful oil.
My two favorites are peanut oil
and corn oil, both of which lend
good taste and a crispiness to fried
foods.*

E v e n the most restrained eater cannot hold back when it comes to these spicy little shrimp cakes. I am almost embarrassed to admit how often I make them, whether shaped into small finger-food sizes for an appetizer or larger for a main course, with a side dish of cabbage slaw or a spicy dipping sauce such as Ginger-Tamari Dipping Sauce (page 187). Be sure to make a few extra fritters to pop into the microwave the next day and enjoy for lunch or dinner with some salad greens dressed in a cumin vinaigrette.

....

1. Combine the shrimp, shallots, scallions, lemon juice, jalapeño pepper, and ginger in a food processor and puree until smooth. Season generously with salt and pepper.

2. Heat ½ inch of peanut oil in a nonstick skillet over medium-high heat. With wet hands, shape the shrimp mixture into 1½ inch-round disks, and fry in batches for about 1 minute per side, or until nicely browned. Season with a little coarse salt and serve immediately.

"Mussels on the Half-Shell" in Shallot, Crème Fraîche, and Herb Essence

To prepare: 10 minutes
To cook: 20 minutes
Serves 4

2 large shallots, peeled and finely minced

6 whole black peppercorns

2 tablespoons finely minced fresh thyme leaves or 1½ teaspoons dried

½ cup dry white wine

3 pounds small mussels, well scrubbed

½ cup crème fraîche (see page 31)

1 Beurre Manié (page 193)

2 tablespoons finely minced fresh tarragon

Fresh lemon juice to taste

Optional: 3 tablespoons unsalted butter

Tip

Many fish preparations benefit greatly from the addition of crème fraîche, which, unlike sour cream, does not curdle in cooking and gives the sauce a smooth, satiny texture and a delicious, slightly tart flavor.

L i k e scallops, shrimp, and clams, mussels should feature prominently in the cook's spontaneous repertoire. Almost any mussel dish I can think of takes only about ten minutes of preparation, and now that this superb shellfish is farm-raised in Maine, there is a good chance that you can get it truly fresh at your local seafood market or supermarket. You can also simplify this dish by keeping the mussels in their shells and tossing them with spaghettini that has been cooked al dente.

1. Combine the shallots, peppercorns, thyme, and wine in a large casserole. Add the mussels and simmer, covered, until the mussels open; discard any that do not. Remove with a slotted spoon, break off and discard the empty half shells, and place the mussels in a shallow serving dish.

2. Add the crème fraîche to the casserole and bring to a simmer. Whisk in bits of beurre manié until the sauce lightly coats a spoon. Add the tarragon, lemon juice, and optional butter, correct the seasoning, and pour over the mussels. Serve with plenty of crusty French bread for mopping up the sauce.

Roasted Portobello Mushrooms in Garlic, Caper, and Anchovy Cream

To prepare: 15 minutes

To cook: 15 to 20 minutes

Serves 6

....

4 tablespoons unsalted butter

4 to 6 flat anchovy fillets, drained and finely minced

1 large garlic clove, peeled and mashed

⅓ cup heavy cream

1½ tablespoons tiny capers, drained

Coarse salt and freshly ground black pepper

6 large portobello mushrooms

6 tablespoons extra-virgin olive oil

6 slices all-purpose white bread, cut with a round cookie cutter into the same size as the mushrooms

GARNISH

Tiny fresh Italian parsley or basil leaves

Portobello mushrooms have literally exploded onto the culinary scene. It seems as if only yesterday the choice in fresh mushrooms was limited to the all-purpose white variety. Portobellos, which are not a wild mushroom but rather cultivated much like shiitakes and the all-purpose mushrooms, have a meaty texture that allows for a variety of interesting preparations and sauces. Serve these mushrooms as a starter, as a side dish to a sauté of shrimp, pan-seared scallops, or Shallot and Herb–Infused Lamb Chops (page 199), or as a dramatic topping to a well-seasoned green salad.

....

1. Preheat the oven to 400°F.

2. Melt the butter in a small saucepan over low heat. Add the anchovies and garlic and cook for 3 minutes, or until the anchovies have melted. Whisk in the heavy cream, add the capers, and season with pepper. Taste for seasoning; you may not need to add salt. Keep warm.

3. Place the mushrooms on a baking sheet, brush with 2 tablespoons of the oil, and season with pepper. Roast for 10 minutes, or until tender.

4. While the mushrooms are roasting, sauté the bread rounds in 2 batches: For each batch, heat 2 tablespoons oil in a large nonstick skillet over medium heat. Add half the bread and sauté until nicely browned on both sides.

5. Season the mushrooms with coarse salt. Place a toast round on each of 6 individual appetizer plates, top with a mushroom, and coat with the sauce. Garnish with parsley or basil and serve immediately.

Remarks: You can broil the bread in the oven. You can also substitute olive oil for the butter in the sauce, adding lemon juice or balsamic vinegar for additional taste if desired.

T i p

The best way to prepare portobello and shiitake mushrooms is to roast them rather than sauté them. This way, the mushrooms do not absorb a great deal of oil. Also, roasting intensifies the mushroom taste and allows the texture to remain slightly firm rather than becoming soft and spongy.

Eggplant "Lasagna"

To prepare: 15 minutes
plus 1 hour to soak
To cook: 45 minutes
Serves 6

3 medium eggplants, unpeeled,
cut crosswise into ½-inch
slices

Coarse salt

½ to ¾ cup olive oil

4 thin slices smoked ham

2 large roasted red bell peppers
(see page 182) or jarred red
peppers, peeled and thinly
sliced

2 tablespoons finely minced fresh
oregano

½ cup freshly grated Parmesan
cheese

Freshly ground black pepper

1½ cups Tomato Fondue
(page 109)

T i p

If you do not have time to soak the eggplant in salted water, dust the slices lightly in flour and sauté in more oil than you would normally use. Then let the sautéed eggplant drain on a double layer of paper towels. Within minutes, it will release the oil it absorbed during cooking.

W h a t is so wonderful about eggplant is its incredible versatility. Sautéed, grilled, or baked and added to myriad other preparations, it is always delicious. This "lasagna" can be served as an appetizer, a side dish to grilled lamb or chicken, or as a main course following a salad or a soup and accompanied by a cool couscous salad. Salting and weighting down eggplant is the traditional way of removing the bitter eggplant juices. I find that soaking the slices in salted ice water does the job in much less time and is easier.

1.   Place the eggplant slices in a large bowl with ice water to cover. Add 2 teaspoons coarse salt and soak for 30 minutes. Drain well and pat dry with paper towels.

2.   Preheat the oven to 350°F.

3.   Heat ¼ cup of the oil in a large cast-iron skillet over medium-high heat. Add a few of the eggplant slices and sauté until nicely browned on both sides. Drain on paper towels. Sauté the remaining eggplant in same manner, adding more oil when necessary.

4.   Layer half the eggplant slices in a medium-size rectangular baking dish. Top with the smoked ham, peppers, oregano, and ¼ cup of the Parmesan. Season with salt and pepper. Spoon ¾ cup of the tomato fondue over the mixture. Top with the remaining eggplant and sauce and sprinkle with the remaining ¼ cup Parmesan. Bake, uncovered, for 35 minutes. Serve warm or at room temperature.

Creamy Dill and Scallion Vinaigrette

To prepare: 15 minutes
Makes about 1 cup

....

1 teaspoon lightly beaten
    egg yolk

2 teaspoons Dijon mustard

⅛ teaspoon dry mustard

1½ tablespoons balsamic vinegar

1½ teaspoons sherry vinegar

½ cup peanut oil

⅓ cup olive oil

1 large garlic clove, peeled and
    crushed

2 flat anchovy fillets, drained and
    finely minced

2 tablespoons finely minced
    fresh dill

2 tablespoons finely minced
    scallions

2 tablespoons sour cream

Salt and freshly ground black
    pepper

H e r e is a vinaigrette that I use constantly, both as a dressing and as a dip. It is a delicious accompaniment to many vegetables and salads and is well worth making in quantity. If you plan to make a large batch of this dressing to have on hand, do not add the garlic and anchovies until the last minute. Other herbs that work equally well are chives, fresh basil, and particularly sorrel (which should be blanched and pureéd prior to being added to the dressing).

....

1. Combine the egg yolk, mustards, and vinegars in a stainless steel bowl. Add both oils by droplets, whisking constantly, until the vinaigrette is creamy with a texture similar to a light mayonnaise.

2. Add the garlic, anchovies, dill, scallions, and sour cream and whisk until well blended. Season with a large grinding of pepper; do not add salt at this point. Set the vinaigrette aside for 1 hour, then taste, adding a pinch of salt if necessary. Covered and refrigerated, this vinaigrette keeps for up to a week.

T i p

Most commercially available fresh herbs, especially dill, basil, parsley, and cilantro, are grown in hothouses and do not have an assertive taste. You can therefore usually double or even triple the amount of herbs called for in this vinaigrette.

Lemon, Shallot, and Sherry Vinegar Dressing

To prepare: 5 minutes

Serves 6

....

2 tablespoons sherry vinegar

1 tablespoon fresh lemon juice

2 tablespoons finely minced shallots

Coarse salt and freshly ground black pepper

½ cup extra-virgin olive oil

This vinaigrette can be made two to three days ahead of time and kept refrigerated. Bring it back to room temperature about fifteen minutes before serving, and whisk once again until creamy.

....

Combine the vinegar, lemon juice, and shallots in a medium bowl. Season with coarse salt and pepper and whisk until well blended. Slowly add the oil, whisking constantly until smooth and creamy.

Balsamic Vinegar and Shallot Dressing

To prepare: 5 minutes

Serves 6

....

2 tablespoons balsamic vinegar

2 tablespoons finely minced shallots

Coarse salt and freshly ground black pepper

6 tablespoons extra-virgin olive oil

Combine the vinegar and shallots in a medium bowl. Season with coarse salt and pepper and whisk until well blended. Slowly add the oil, whisking constantly until smooth and creamy.

Walnut Oil and Sherry Vinegar Dressing

To prepare: 5 minutes
Serves 6

....

1 tablespoon sherry vinegar

2 tablespoons finely minced
shallots

Coarse salt and freshly ground
black pepper

6 tablespoons walnut oil

Combine the vinegar and shallots in a medium bowl. Season with coarse salt and pepper and whisk until well blended. Slowly add the oil, whisking constantly until smooth and creamy.

Eggs? Yes, *Eggs!*

It's small AND FRAGILE, SIMPLE AND DELICATE, UNDEMANDING AND INNOCENT. YET MILLIONS OF OTHERWISE SANE AMERICANS HAVE RECENTLY TURNED AGAINST IT WITH A VITRIOLIC PASSION. THE POOR EGG! I THINK IT'S TIME SOMEONE JUMPED TO ITS DEFENSE. AND WHO BETTER THAN A FOOD LOVER WHO GREW UP IN EUROPE, WHERE THE EGG IS CONSIDERED TO BE THE BACKBONE OF COOKING, THE FOUNDATION OF JUST ABOUT EVERY SAUCE AND DESSERT IN THE CLASSIC REPERTOIRE, THE CLOSEST THING TO A PERFECT FOOD THAT EXISTS?

YES, THE EGG IS HIGH IN CHOLESTEROL. BUT IT'S ALSO HIGH IN VITAMINS, MINERALS, PROTEIN, AND, LAST BUT NOT LEAST—TASTE! IT'S ALSO THE MOST versatile Spur of the Moment food I can think of. It goes with everything, from fresh sage to Gorgonzola cheese to smoked salmon. It does everything, from creating a voluptuous custard to dressing a Caesar salad. It's a breakfast food, a lunch food, a dinner food, a nursery food, a main dish, a side dish, an appetizer, a dessert. It's quick to cook. It's inexpensive. It's nourishing. It's satisfying. It can be anything from comfort food (just the very name "coddled egg" makes me feel better) to an elegant dinner party star. It's the only staple in the refrigerator that can instantly energize what's fresh at the farm stand, what's ripe and runny at the cheese counter, what's just snipped from the herb garden.

Oddly enough, as eggs have become less desirable here in America, they have been gaining a new popularity and cachet in Europe. Inventive young Spanish chefs are turning out sublime omelettes filled with Mediterranean prawns and napped with a light plum tomato sauce. On just about any day of the week you'll find at least six to eight omelettes on a restaurant menu in Paris, Lisbon, or Milan. In Barcelona, where eggs have always been the most popular appetizer, you can still practically set your watch by the moment when hungry Spaniards start scrambling eggs every evening.

There's no doubt in my mind that eggs will survive the violent attacks being waged against them here in America. But just in case they do need a little public relations boost, Spur of the Moment recipes like hearty Catalan Potato and Onion Tortilla (page 96) or a Savory Prune and Bacon Clafoutis (page 104) should help restore their excellent reputation.

Zucchini Frittata with Parmesan

To prepare: 15 minutes

To cook: 35 minutes

Serves 6

....

8 extra-large eggs

¼ cup plus 2 tablespoons freshly grated Parmesan cheese

Salt and freshly ground black pepper

4 tablespoons olive oil

1 large red onion, peeled, quartered, and thinly sliced

4 small zucchini (2 green and 2 golden), trimmed and thinly sliced

T i p

....

Vegetable frittatas tend to taste sweet because of the natural sugar in most vegetables. So be sure to season the eggs assertively, and use a large grinding of pepper. If the frittata still tastes sweet, serve it with a side dish of black oil-cured olives, Parmesan shavings, sliced salami, or feta cheese. A spicy high-quality commercial salsa is also a good accompaniment.

Open-faced frittatas like these are the mainstay of Catalan—and indeed all Spanish—home cooking. Not a day goes by that some kind of omelette is not served in most households. Quick to make, good-natured, and inexpensive, this is a good supper dish. Start with a soup and serve the frittata with a topping of goat cheese, a few oil-cured olives, or a salad and some crusty bread.

....

1. Preheat the oven to 375°F.

2. Combine the eggs and the ¼ cup Parmesan in a large bowl and whisk until well blended. Season with salt and pepper and set aside.

3. Heat 2 tablespoons of the oil in a 10-inch non-stick skillet over medium-low heat. Add the onion and cook until soft and lightly browned. Add the zucchini, season with salt and pepper, and cook, covered, for 6 to 8 minutes, or until tender. Drain well in a colander. Add the zucchini and onion to the egg mixture, season generously with salt and pepper, and fold in gently but thoroughly.

4. Add the remaining 2 tablespoons oil to the skillet. When hot, add the egg and squash mixture and cook for 1 minute, or until the bottom is lightly browned. Sprinkle with the remaining 2 tablespoons Parmesan and bake for 15 to 20 minutes, or until the eggs are set and the top is lightly browned. Serve warm or at room temperature, cut into wedges.

Catalan Potato and Onion Tortilla

To prepare: 15 minutes
To cook: 29 to 30
minutes
Serves 4

....

½ cup extra-virgin olive oil

2 medium baking potatoes or 3
all-purpose potatoes (about
1¼ pounds), peeled, quar-
tered, and cut into ¼-inch
slices

1 large onion, peeled, quartered,
and thinly sliced

Optional: ¼ cup diced chorizo

Salt and freshly ground black
pepper

4 to 5 extra-large eggs

Pinch of cayenne pepper

T h e r e must be as many versions of the traditional Catalan potato tortilla as there are cooks in
Spain. My friend Babette, whose cooking is both gutsy
and delicious, gave me this recipe and it is the best one
I know. The secret, draining the potatoes of their cooking oil, truly makes the difference. The omelette not
only is tasty with potatoes that retain their bite, but is
not at all greasy. Serve the omelette either right out of
the skillet, cut into wedges, or at room temperature. A
plateful of sliced tomatoes or of roasted peppers sprinkled with virgin olive oil is a nice simple side dish.

....

1.   Heat 6 tablespoons of the oil in a 10-inch cast-
iron skillet over low heat. Add the potatoes, onion,
and optional chorizo, season with salt and pepper,
and cook, covered, for 12 to 15 minutes, stirring often, until the potatoes are tender. Transfer the mixture to a strainer placed over a bowl and set aside
for 10 to 15 minutes. Reserve the potato mixture and
the drained oil separately.

2.   Beat the eggs in a large bowl. Season with salt
and black pepper and a pinch of cayenne and whisk
until well blended. Add the potato mixture and mix
well.

3.   Heat the reserved oil in a 9½-inch nonstick
skillet over medium-low heat. Pour the omelette
mixture into the skillet and cook for 5 to 7 minutes,
or until the bottom is lightly browned and the eggs
begin to set.

4. Invert the omelette onto a flat plate. Add the remaining 2 tablespoons oil to the skillet and, when hot, slide the omelette back into the skillet. Cook for 3 to 5 minutes longer, or until completely set. Transfer to a serving platter and let sit for 3 to 5 minutes. Cut into wedges and serve warm or at room temperature.

T i p

The type of skillet used in making a Catalan tortilla is extremely important. While my first choice for cooking the potato and onion mixture is a cast-iron skillet, I never finish making the omelette in it. Instead, I use a heavy 9½-inch nonstick skillet. If your skillet is 10 inches in diameter, increase the amount of the eggs to 6 and use an additional potato.

Caramelized Sweet Onion and Sour Cream Tart

~~~~~~

To prepare: 15 minutes

To cook: 50 minutes to 1 hour

Serves 6

....

¾ cup sour cream

1 cup heavy cream

3 extra-large eggs

½ cup grated Gruyère cheese

Salt and freshly ground black pepper

6 tablespoons olive oil

3 cups thinly sliced red onions

One 9-inch unbaked ready-made tart shell in a removable-bottom pan (see page 283)

3 tablespoons freshly grated Parmesan cheese

T i p

....

Although red onions are available year-round, the best ones, imported from Italy, are oval and quite small, and are available only in the fall. In the winter and spring months, I make this tart with large yellow Spanish onions, adding 1 to 2 tablespoons of fresh thyme to the mixture. For a variation, use a Cheddar or a Monterey Jack instead of the Gruyère.

A g o o d savory tart is so delicious and satisfying and really is easy to make. To me it is the perfect weekend food. Simply accompanied by a well-seasoned salad and some sliced salami, it makes for a complete meal. I have recently been experimenting with store-bought dough, with amazing results. Here is a tart that works beautifully with just such a dough. (Be sure to buy the variety that needs rolling out lightly by hand, not the one that is already placed into a pie tin and frozen.)

....

1. Preheat the oven to 400°F.

2. Combine the sour cream, heavy cream, eggs, and Gruyère in a large bowl, season with salt and pepper, and mix well. Set aside.

3. Heat the oil in a large skillet over high heat. Add the onions and cook for 5 minutes, stirring often. Reduce the heat and cook for another 10 minutes, or until soft and browned. Drain well, add to the sour cream mixture, and season generously with salt and pepper.

4. Pour into the tart shell, sprinkle with the Parmesan, and bake for 35 to 45 minutes, or until the top is nicely browned and the custard is set. Serve warm or at room temperature, cut into wedges.

Braised Leek, Smoked Ham, and Gorgonzola Flan

To prepare: 20 minutes
To cook: 45 to 50
minutes
Serves 6

....

3 tablespoons unsalted butter

12 small leeks (about ¾ inch in diameter), trimmed of all but 2 inches of greens

Salt and freshly ground white pepper

12 thin slices smoked ham, preferably Black Forest

3 extra-large eggs

3 extra-large egg yolks

2 cups heavy cream

4 ounces Gorgonzola cheese, crumbled

5 tablespoons freshly grated Parmesan cheese

T i p

....

If you use large leeks, cut them in half lengthwise before rolling up in the ham.

S t e a m e d , braised, baked, or grilled, leeks are delicious year-round. For this dish, I roll small leeks in thin slices of smoked ham and bake them in a savory custard. Serve as a main course, preceded by a soup or a salad and accompanied by sautéed or roasted mushrooms and crusty bread.

....

1. Preheat the oven to 375°F. Generously butter a heavy baking dish, using 1 tablespoon of the butter.

2. Cut the green part of the leeks in half lengthwise, and wash thoroughly under warm water. If time permits, soak the leeks in warm water to cover for about 20 minutes; drain well.

3. Place the leeks in a large skillet with water to cover, season with salt and pepper, and add the remaining 2 tablespoons butter. Simmer, covered, for 10 to 12 minutes, or until tender. Drain well and dry thoroughly on paper towels.

4. Wrap each leek in 1 slice of ham, roll up tightly, and place in a single layer, seam side down in the baking dish, leaving some space between each leek.

5. Combine the eggs, yolks, cream, Gorgonzola, and 2 tablespoons of the Parmesan in a food processor and puree until smooth. Season with salt and pepper, pour over the leeks, and sprinkle with the remaining 3 tablespoons Parmesan. Bake for 30 to 40 minutes, or until the custard is set and the top is lightly browned. Serve hot.

Chèvre Omelette with Fresh Tarragon

To prepare: 5 minutes

To cook: 5 minutes

Serves 2

....

6 extra-large eggs

6 tablespoons crumbled goat
cheese (about 4 ounces)

1½ tablespoons finely minced
fresh tarragon

Salt and freshly ground black
pepper

Dash of Tabasco sauce

2 tablespoons unsalted butter

1 tablespoon olive oil

T i p

....

When using goat cheese in cooking, I prefer slightly aged cheese. Aged goat cheese has a sharper, tangier taste that will stand up nicely when added to eggs, pasta dishes, risottos, and polenta.

E g g s and cheese are always in perfect harmony, but I particularly love an omelette in which herb-studded goat cheese is melted into the lightly scrambled egg mixture. Other herbs such as thyme, basil, or cilantro can be substituted for the tarragon here but freshness is a must. For an accompaniment I would opt for Pepper, Tomato, and Onion Compote (page 258). For an easier and always welcome accompaniment, good sourdough bread and sweet butter are the perfect solution.

....

1. Combine the eggs, cheese, and tarragon in a large bowl, season with salt and pepper and Tabasco, and set aside.

2. For each omelette, melt 1 tablespoon butter together with ½ tablespoon oil in an 8-inch nonstick skillet over medium heat. When hot, add half the egg mixture and cook for about 1 minute, or until the eggs begin to set. Stir with a fork to form a thick mass. Tilt the skillet away from you and, with a spatula, fold the part of the omelette that is farthest from you toward the center. Prod the part closest to you, pushing the omelette toward the far end of the skillet, then jerk the skillet roughly so that the omelette folds back onto itself.

3. Turn each omelette onto a plate and serve at once.

Scrambled Eggs with Smoked Salmon, Crème Fraîche, and Herbs

~~~

To prepare: 5 minutes
To cook: 5 minutes
Serves 4

....

8 extra-large eggs

2 tablespoons crème fraîche (see page 31)

Pinch of salt

Freshly ground black pepper

Dash of Tabasco sauce

3 tablespoons unsalted butter

1 to 1½ cups diced smoked salmon

2 tablespoons finely minced fresh dill

2 tablespoons finely minced fresh chives

GARNISH
Triangles of bread spread with a little butter or olive oil, broiled

Tip

....

A 1½-quart tin- or stainless steel–lined copper saucepan is my favorite for making scrambled eggs. A very heavy saucepan will do equally well, but be sure to take the eggs off the heat while they are still quite runny as they will continue to cook in the heat retained in the pan.

If I had to think of a single favorite Spur of the Moment dish, this would be the one! The French method of scrambling eggs in a heavy saucepan rather than a skillet produces a very different dish in both taste and texture. The eggs take a little longer to cook but the result is absolutely scrumptious. Be sure to add the smoked salmon to the eggs at the very last minute so it does not get tough. Place the buttered or oiled bread slices under the broiler while you whisk the eggs. Steamed spinach is another good choice as a bed for the eggs if you have the time. Season the spinach with some minced green onions and a touch of fresh dill.

....

1. Combine the eggs and crème fraîche in a large bowl, season with salt, pepper, and Tabasco, and whisk until well blended.

2. Melt the butter in a very heavy 2½-quart saucepan, preferably copper, over medium heat. Add the egg mixture and whisk constantly for 3 to 4 minutes, or until cooked to your preferred degree of doneness. Quickly remove from the heat, fold in the salmon and herbs, and correct the seasoning. Spoon onto individual serving dishes and serve at once with the bread triangles.

Cream Cheese and Herb Johnnycakes

To prepare: 10 minutes
plus 1 hour to rest
To cook: 10 minutes
Serves 6

8 ounces cream cheese

1 cup light cream or half-and-half

4 extra-large eggs, separated

1 cup cake flour

Salt and freshly ground black pepper

3 tablespoons finely minced fresh chives, parsley, or dill, or a mixture

3 tablespoons unsalted butter, melted

3 to 4 tablespoons Clarified Butter (page 103)

Tip

Clarifying butter is a simple technique that removes the milky residue and impurities that make butter burn quickly. Clarified butter is used for sautéing delicate foods, such as fish fillets, fritters, or anything that is breaded. You can use it in any recipe that calls for regular butter for sautéing.

Fritters, pancakes, and johnnycakes are the rage but the truth is that they have always been around. Now, however, they are teamed with both savory and sweet accompaniments. The great advantage of all fritters is that they are quick and easy to make since they generally require only basic ingredients that every cook has on hand. In this delicate fritter you can use fresh dill, parsley, or chives or omit the herbs entirely and instead add grated lemon or lime zest to the batter. My favorite accompaniment is smoked salmon or other smoked fish.

1. Combine the cream cheese with the light cream or half-and-half in a food processor and process until smooth. Add the yolks and flour, season with salt and pepper, and blend well. Transfer to a large bowl and whisk in the herbs and melted butter.

2. Beat the egg whites with a pinch of salt and fold gently but thoroughly into the cream cheese mixture; do not overmix. Let the batter rest for 1 hour at room temperature.

3. Cook the johnnycakes in 3 or 4 batches: For each batch, heat 1 tablespoon clarified butter in a nonstick skillet over medium heat. Add the batter by the tablespoon to the skillet without crowding and cook until the johnnycakes are nicely browned on both sides, about 1 minute per side. Serve warm with a little crème fraîche (see page 31) or brown butter.

Clarified Butter

Melt any desired amount of unsalted butter (but at least 8 tablespoons) in a heavy saucepan over low heat. As soon as the butter has melted and is very foamy, remove from the heat and carefully skim off the foam. Strain the clear yellow liquid through a fine sieve and discard the milky residue on the bottom of the pan. Refrigerate the strained, clear yellow liquid, the clarified butter, in a tightly sealed jar. It will keep for at least 2 weeks or can be frozen for several months.

Savory Prune and Bacon Clafoutis

To prepare: 10 minutes
To cook: 1 hour
Serves 6 to 8

....

1 pound large pitted prunes

4 extra-large eggs

¼ cup all-purpose flour

¾ cup milk plus ¾ cup heavy
cream or 1½ cups half-
and-half

Salt and freshly ground white
pepper

Large grating of nutmeg

2 tablespoons unsalted butter

5 ounces slab bacon, blanched
and finely diced, about 1 cup

T i p

....

*If slab bacon is difficult to find, I
often substitute thick-sliced bacon,
which does not need to be
blanched. Sauté the sliced bacon
without blanching until barely
crisp, and be sure to drain well on
a double layer of paper towels before using.*

T h e clafoutis is a traditional French country dessert usually made with cherries and a rather heavy custard. I came upon this preparation in a pastry shop in
the Southwest of France many years ago and have enjoyed making it ever since, especially during the fall
and winter months. It is a perfect accompaniment to a
roast turkey or a traditional baked ham.

....

1. Preheat the oven to 350°F.

2. Place the prunes in a small saucepan with water
to cover and simmer for 10 minutes. Drain and set
aside.

3. Combine the eggs, flour, and milk and cream or
half-and-half in a large bowl and whisk until well
blended. Season with salt and white pepper and nutmeg and set aside.

4. Melt the butter in a large skillet over low heat,
add the bacon, and sauté until almost crisp. Add the
prunes and stew for 3 to 4 minutes. Transfer the
prune mixture to a medium rectangular baking dish
in a single layer, and pour the egg mixture on top.
Bake for 35 to 40 minutes, or until a knife inserted
in the custard comes out clean. Let cool slightly before serving.

More Pasta

O n e o f MY FAVORITE COLLOQUIAL AMERICAN EXPRESSIONS IS "TOO MUCH AIN'T ENOUGH," AND ONE OF THE WAYS I THINK IT'S BEST USED IS TO DESCRIBE THE CURRENT AMERICAN PASSION FOR PASTA. NO MATTER HOW MUCH WE COOK, NO MATTER HOW MUCH WE EAT, NO MATTER HOW OFTEN WE EAT IT, NO MATTER HOW MANY NEW WAYS WE FIND TO MAKE IT, WE CAN'T WAIT TO HAVE MORE.

PASTA IS MORE THAN A FOOD—IT'S A PHENOMENON. EVERYONE FROM BABIES IN HIGH CHAIRS TO SERIOUS FOODIES CAN APPRECIATE IT. IT CAN GO ALL THE WAY FROM TRUCK-STOP SPAGHETTI AND MEATBALLS TO CAPPELLINI IN A DELICATE FRESH TOMATO SAUCE TO A SUPER-STAR PENNE WITH A RICH

caviar and zesty ginger-lemon vinaigrette. It can be beautifully cooked in a matter of minutes without sacrificing quality. It can taste "fancy" without fancy ingredients. It can feed hungry hordes for pennies. It can be made almost entirely from seasonal ingredients or just as successfully from ingredients in your pantry. It can even be reheated in the microwave with a fair amount of success. If Italians seem to be sunny and smiling more than the rest of us, it has to be that pasta is their national comfort food.

If "too much ain't enough" when

it comes to eating pasta, "less is more" is the right expression for cooking pasta—and another reason pasta is such a good choice for the Spur of the Moment cook. There is no need for endless "gourmet" ingredients such as sun-dried tomatoes and six other trendy additions to make what is essentially a simple soul food taste better. A basic tomato fondue, either spicy or lightly creamy, coupled harmoniously with two or three other ingredients is enough.

The Spur of the Moment cook needs only two things to make excellent pasta: the right basic ingredients to start with and a basic knowledge of when to stop. Chances are you don't have the time to make your own pasta, so look for top-quality dried varieties. If you crave fresh pasta, try different types until you find one that will cook without getting mushy and will maintain an al dente texture even when it's sauced. (Frankly, though, my own experience with store-bought fresh pastas all across the country has been consistently disappointing.)

To go with your pasta, you need to have on hand a good olive oil, a quality brand of canned tomatoes, fresh garlic, fresh parsley, possibly a hot chili pepper, and some nice moist Reggiano Parmesan. With these ingredients alone, you can create a variety of really outstanding pasta dishes. Given a little extra time for a stop at my local market, I can vastly expand my pasta repertoire by buying shrimp, clams, and mussels, bacon or fresh sausage, seasonal vegetables like winter leeks, sprightly spring peas, and colorful summer peppers, fresh herbs like rosemary and tarragon, a pungent goat cheese or blue cheese. When I start choosing ingredients, I try to think of what memorable combinations I've enjoyed in the past, here or in Europe. Or I ask myself, "If I were pasta, who would I like to be in the bowl with?" I know I'd only like to be sharing my bowl with a lively and harmonious group—a select few, not a crowd.

Make your pasta simple, make sure your ingredients are the best, don't try to be too creative or attempt something too complicated, make certain that the tastes aren't too jarring or too spicy. Then, most important of all, make sure you've made enough!

Penne with Broccoli, Cremini Mushrooms, and Tomato Fondue

To prepare: 20 minutes
To cook: 30 minutes
Serves 4

¾ pound broccoli, trimmed

3 tablespoons extra-virgin olive oil

2½ ounces slab bacon, blanched and diced, about ½ cup

6 cremini mushrooms, stemmed and cubed

2 large garlic cloves, peeled and finely minced

2 tablespoons finely minced shallots

3 tablespoons finely minced fresh parsley

1½ cups Tomato Fondue (see page 109)

1 tablespoon fresh thyme leaves

Salt and freshly ground black pepper

½ pound imported penne

½ cup freshly grated Parmesan cheese

H e r e is a rather robust dish that is somewhat more time-consuming if you decide to make your own tomato fondue, but in a pinch, I often doctor-up a good brand of supermarket fresh tomato sauce and add a touch of cream to mellow its flavor. Cremini mushrooms are becoming increasingly easy to find throughout the country but don't go out of your way if necessary to track them down. Instead use all-purpose mushrooms, and be sure to reduce the mushroom liquid to a syrupy consistency before adding to the pasta. For a variation, I like to grate smoked mozzarella into this dish, which gives it additional texture and flavor.

1. Cut the tops off the broccoli and separate into florets. Peel the stalks and slice them crosswise. Steam the florets and stalks separately in a vegetable steamer over simmering water until tender. Set aside.

2. Heat 2 tablespoons of the oil in a heavy skillet over medium heat. Add the bacon and cook until almost crisp. Set aside. Add the remaining 1 tablespoon oil to the pan and sauté the mushrooms until lightly browned. Add the garlic, shallots, and parsley and cook for 1 minute. Return the bacon to the pan together with the tomato fondue, thyme, and broccoli, season with salt and pepper, and just heat through. Remove from the heat and set aside.

3. Drop the penne into a large pot of boiling salted water and cook until just tender, or al dente. Drain well and return to the pot. Add the broccoli sauce and ¼ cup of the Parmesan and toss gently to just heat through. Correct the seasoning and serve hot, with the remaining Parmesan on the side.

T o m a t o   F o n d u e

Coarsely chop two 35-ounces cans Italian plum tomatoes. In a large heavy saucepan, heat ⅓ cup extra-virgin olive oil over medium heat. Add ½ cup finely minced shallots and 2 large garlic cloves, finely minced, and cook for 1 to 2 minutes or until soft but not browned. Add the tomatoes and 1 tablespoon fresh or 1 teaspoon dried thyme, and season with salt and freshly ground black pepper. Simmer, partially covered, for 40 to 45 minutes, or until all the liquid has evaporated. Store in the refrigerator until needed. The fondue will keep up to 2 weeks; it can also be frozen for 2 to 3 months.

Penne all'Alfredo with Wilted Greens

To prepare: 15 minutes
To cook: 20 minutes

Serves 4

....

2 tablespoons olive oil

2 large garlic cloves, peeled and
finely minced

1 head radicchio, torn into 2-inch
pieces

2 bunches arugula, stemmed and
thoroughly rinsed

4 tablespoons unsalted butter

¾ cup heavy cream

Salt and freshly ground white
pepper

1 Beurre Manié (page 193)

4 ounces mild goat cheese

½ pound imported penne

3 tablespoons finely minced fresh
chives

⅓ cup freshly grated Parmesan
cheese, plus additional for
serving

T i p

....

After adding pasta to boiling wa-
ter, stir gently with a wooden
spoon to prevent it from sticking
to the bottom of the pot and from
sticking together.

E v e n **a classic sauce such as an Alfredo can be
updated with simple seasonal touches. Cooked fresh
peas, asparagus tips, tiny Boston lettuce leaves, and
sautéed cremini mushrooms are just a few ingredients
that come to mind when I think of this superb sauce.
During the week, I usually serve the pasta as a main
course, preceded by either a salad, steamed globe artichokes (see page 76), or simply a plateful of cooked
young green beans dressed in extra-virgin olive oil and
a splash of balsamic vinegar.**

....

1. Heat the oil in a large skillet over medium heat.
Add the garlic and cook for 1 minute. Add the radicchio and arugula and sauté until just wilted. Transfer to a bowl and set aside.

2. Reduce the heat to low, add the butter to the
skillet, and whisk constantly until it starts to brown.
Immediately add the cream. Season with salt and
white pepper and reduce slightly. Whisk in bits of
beurre manié and simmer until the sauce lightly
coats a spoon. Whisk in the goat cheese and keep
warm.

3. Drop the penne into a large pot of boiling salted
water and cook until just tender, or al dente. Drain
immediately and return to the pot. Add the sauce,
the wilted greens, and the chives and toss gently.
Add the Parmesan and a large grinding of pepper,
and serve in shallow soup bowls with additional Parmesan on the side.

Ziti in a Roasted Onion, Fennel, and Tomato Compote

To prepare: 15 minutes
To cook: 45 minutes
Serves 4

1 large fennel bulb, trimmed and cut into eighths through the root end

1 large onion, peeled and cut into eighths through the root end

4 tablespoons extra-virgin olive oil

Coarse salt and freshly ground black pepper

2 large garlic cloves, peeled and finely minced

1 teaspoon fennel seeds

4 to 6 flat anchovy fillets, drained and finely minced

One 16-ounce can Italian plum tomatoes, drained and chopped, ¼ cup juice reserved

1 teaspoon fresh oregano leaves

2 teaspoons fresh thyme leaves

½ pound imported ziti

GARNISH
2 tablespoons finely minced fresh parsley

I f i r s t made this dish as a way of using leftover roasted vegetables. It has since become one of my favorite ways to prepare tubular pasta such as penne or ziti. If you are pressed for time, prepare this with about one cup of Tomato Fondue (page 109) or a doctored commercial tomato sauce. Serve as a main course, starting with **Endive and Young Spinach Salad with Roasted Cumin Vinaigrette (page 63).**

1. Preheat the oven to 425°F.

2. Place the fennel and onion on a nonstick baking sheet, drizzle with 2 tablespoons of the oil, and season with salt and pepper. Roast for 30 minutes, turning often, or until tender and browned.

3. While the vegetables are roasting, heat the remaining 2 tablespoons oil in a large skillet over medium heat. Add the garlic, fennel seeds, and anchovies and cook for 1 minute. Add the tomatoes and herbs, season with salt and pepper, and simmer for 5 minutes, or until slightly reduced.

4. When the fennel and onion are cooked, add them to the sauce. If the sauce seems too thick, add the reserved tomato juice. Keep warm.

5. Drop the ziti into a large pot of boiling salted water and cook until just tender, or al dente. Drain well, return to the pot, and add the fennel and onion fondue. Toss gently and serve hot, garnishing each portion with minced parsley.

Shrimp, Bacon, Spinach, and Mushroom Ragoût with Penne

To prepare: 20 minutes

To cook: 30 minutes

Serves 4 to 6

....

3 tablespoons unsalted butter

3 tablespoons extra-virgin olive oil

½ pound cremini mushrooms, stemmed and sliced

Salt and freshly ground black pepper

5 ounces slab bacon, blanched and cubed, about 1 cup, or 1 cup cubed prosciutto

1 pound medium shrimp, peeled

2 large garlic cloves, peeled and finely minced

¾ pound fresh spinach, rinsed and stemmed

½ cup heavy cream

¾ pound imported penne or ziti

A l t h o u g h I call for pasta in this dish, I very often make this quick shrimp stir-fry without pasta, accompanied just by crusty bread. Cremini mushrooms have a better texture than all-purpose mushrooms and will hold up nicely if this dish is to be reheated. Shiitake mushrooms, which are more readily available, are another good choice. If you use shiitakes, I suggest you roast them whole in a 400°F oven for ten to fifteen minutes and then slice them.

....

1.   Heat 1 tablespoon each of the butter and oil in a large heavy skillet over medium heat. Add the mushrooms and sauté just until nicely browned, about 2 minutes. Season with salt and pepper, transfer to a bowl, and set aside.

2.   Heat another tablespoon of butter and oil in the skillet. Add the bacon or prosciutto and sauté until almost crisp. Remove with a slotted spoon to a side dish.

3.   Add the remaining 1 tablespoon oil to the skillet and when hot, sauté the shrimp until just pink. Remove and set aside.

4.   Add the remaining 1 tablespoon butter to the skillet. Add the minced garlic and spinach and cook until the spinach is just wilted. Return the mushrooms, bacon, and shrimp to the skillet together with

the heavy cream and cook for 1 to 2 minutes. Season with salt and pepper and keep warm over the lowest possible heat.

5. Drop the penne or ziti into a large pot of boiling salted water and cook until just tender, or al dente. Drain well, add to the sauce, and toss gently. Correct the seasoning, adding a large grinding of pepper. Serve hot directly from the skillet.

T i p

Never go by package recommendation for time required to cook pasta. Keep tasting and using your palate. Fresh pasta usually takes no more than 1 to 3 minutes. Dried pasta may take as long as 7 to 10 minutes, depending on the shape.

Ziti with Smoked Bluefish and Summer Squash in Tarragon Cream

To prepare: 15 minutes
To cook: 20 minutes
Serves 4

1 cup heavy cream

½ chicken bouillon cube or 1 teaspoon chicken MBT

Salt and freshly ground black pepper

2 tablespoons finely minced fresh tarragon

3 tablespoons unsalted butter

½ pound imported ziti

2 small yellow squash, trimmed and cut into thick matchsticks (discard the seedy center)

2 small zucchini, trimmed and cut into thick matchsticks (discard the seedy center)

1 cup flaked smoked bluefish

GARNISH
Sprigs of fresh tarragon

Tip

When the pasta is just tender, add 2 cups cold water to the pot. This will prevent the pasta from overcooking. Then drain well and serve.

A touch of "smoke," be it bacon, sausage, or smoked fish, gives a simple dish of pasta in an herbed cream sauce a major boost. Smoked bluefish is particularly popular in the Northeast, especially around Cape Cod, where this fish is bountiful. But other smoked fish, such as tuna and mackerel, are excellent substitutes. Be sure to add the fish at the last minute to make sure it does not get tough or too salty.

1. Combine the cream and bouillon cube or MBT in a saucepan, season with salt and pepper, and simmer until slightly reduced. Whisk in the tarragon and butter and keep warm.

2. Drop the ziti into a large pot of boiling salted water and cook until just tender, or al dente.

3. While the pasta is cooking, steam the yellow squash and zucchini in a vegetable steamer over simmering water, covered, for 3 minutes, or until just tender.

4. Drain the pasta well and return to the pot. Add the tarragon sauce, squash, and zucchini and simmer gently to just heat through. Correct the seasoning, adding a large grinding of pepper, and serve hot, garnishing each portion with some of the smoked bluefish and sprigs of tarragon.

Cappellini with Pan-Seared Calamari, Tomatoes, and Lemon

To prepare: 20 minutes
To cook: 35 to 40 minutes
Serves 4

3 tablespoons extra-virgin olive oil

2 small dried red chili peppers, broken

1½ pounds cleaned calamari, cut into ¾-inch pieces

¼ cup finely minced shallots

3 large garlic cloves, peeled and finely minced

3 tablespoons finely minced fresh parsley

¼ cup dry white wine

3 large ripe tomatoes, peeled, seeded, and chopped

1 cup fish bouillon or chicken bouillon

Salt and freshly ground black pepper

½ pound imported cappellini

½ small lemon, cut into thin slices and finely diced

GARNISH
3 tablespoons finely minced fresh parsley

T i p

When draining pasta, save some of the cooking water for thinning out pasta sauces and adding taste.

N o w that you can find cleaned and ready-to-cook calamari practically year-round, they are well worth including in one's everyday cooking repertoire. They are the easiest of all fish to prepare. Just remember that calamari need no more than thirty seconds of sautéing or they will get tough—but if they are left to stew for thirty to forty minutes, they will become tender again. Stewed, they are perfect in a risotto, in any type of pasta or orzo, or mixed with cooked white beans. In the spring I add some peas and blanched asparagus tips to this dish for a touch of color.

1. Heat the oil in a large skillet over high heat. Add the chili peppers and heat until dark; remove and discard. Add the calamari and sauté for 30 seconds. Transfer to a side dish and set aside.

2. Add the shallots, garlic, and parsley to the skillet and cook for 1 minute. Add the wine and reduce to a glaze. Add the tomatoes, calamari, and bouillon, season with salt and pepper, and simmer, covered, for 20 to 30 minutes, or until the calamari are tender.

3. Drop the cappellini into a large pot of salted boiling water and cook until just tender, or al dente. Drain and return to the pot.

4. Add the calamari mixture and lemon to the pasta, mix well, and correct the seasoning. Serve hot, garnished with minced parsley.

Fricassee of Broccoli Rabe and Anchovies over Cavatelli

To prepare: 10 minutes
To cook: 20 minutes
Serves 5 to 6

....

1¼ pounds broccoli rabe, trimmed of all but 2 inches of stalks

⅓ cup extra-virgin olive oil

2 small dried red chili peppers, broken

3 large garlic cloves, peeled and finely minced

4 to 6 flat anchovy fillets, drained and minced

1 pound fresh or imported dried cavatelli

Salt and freshly ground black pepper

GARNISH

2 tablespoons pine nuts, sautéed in olive oil until golden (see page 269)

Freshly grated Parmesan cheese

T i p

....

Broccoli rabe is also called broccoli raab. With its slightly bitter flavor, it is an extremely versatile green, and it is now available from early winter through spring. Always remove two inches of the stalks and some of the larger leaves before using.

Cavatelli, a relatively new introduction to the world of pasta shapes, hold up beautifully to gutsy, robust sauces. Any dish calling for cavatelli also can be made with tubular pasta such as ziti, penne, or rigatoni. You may want to use some of the pasta cooking water in the sauce to give the dish the right texture without having to add too much olive oil.

....

1. Drop the broccoli rabe into boiling salted water, blanch for 30 seconds, and drain. Set aside.

2. Heat the oil in a small skillet over low heat. Add the chili peppers and cook until they darken; discard. Add the garlic and anchovies and stir until the anchovies are melted. Remove from the heat and set aside.

3. Drop the cavatelli into a large pot of boiling salted water and cook until just tender (the cavatelli are not done when they rise to the surface but, in fact, will need to cook longer). Drain well, return to the pot, and add the broccoli rabe and the anchovy sauce. Toss gently to just heat through. Correct the seasoning and serve hot, garnished with the pine nuts and a sprinkling of Parmesan.

Fettuccine in Chèvre Herb Cream

To prepare: 10 minutes
To cook: 10 minutes
Serves 4

....

3 tablespoons unsalted butter

¾ cup heavy cream

¼ cup crumbled mild goat cheese

2 tablespoons freshly grated Parmesan cheese

2 tablespoons finely minced fresh parsley

2 tablespoons finely minced fresh chives

1 tablespoon fresh thyme leaves

Salt and freshly ground black pepper

½ pound fresh fettuccine

2 medium ripe tomatoes, peeled, seeded, and diced

Optional: 2 to 3 tablespoons julienne of fresh basil

T i p

....

When buying young goat cheese, seek out some of our domestic brands. While they may be no less expensive than the imported varieties, they have a great deal of flavor and character. I particularly like Laura Chenel's, which is more widely available in the western states, and some of the ones produced in Vermont and Massachusetts.

I c o n s i d e r this a Cal-Italian pasta dish that is very much at home on both coasts. What's more, it is a year-round preparation that allows for endless Spur of the Moment seasonal variations. An especially good addition would be the fresh chanterelles that make their appearance in the fall. Sauté about half a pound with a mincing of shallots and add to the finished dish. In winter I like to add about sixteen double-poached garlic cloves (see page 41), and in the spring, a cupful of steamed asparagus tips or a handful of spinach leaves. For a variation in texture, you can also top each serving with diced ripe tomatoes dressed in some good olive oil and tossed with a julienne of basil.

....

1. Melt the butter in a skillet over medium heat and whisk constantly until light brown. Whisk in the cream and reduce slightly. Add the goat cheese, Parmesan, parsley, chives, and thyme, season with salt and pepper, and whisk until well blended. Keep warm.

2. Drop the fettuccine into a large pot of boiling salted water and cook until just tender, or al dente. Drain and return to the pot together with the goat cheese sauce, tomatoes, and optional basil, and toss gently to just heat through. Serve hot with crusty French bread.

Saffron-Infused Fettuccine with Braised Leeks

To prepare: 15 minutes
To cook: 20 to 25 minutes
Serves 4

....

4 tablespoons unsalted butter

2 medium leeks, greens removed, cut in half lengthwise, thinly sliced, and well rinsed

Salt and freshly ground black pepper

3 tablespoons water

¼ teaspoon saffron threads

½ cup chicken bouillon

⅓ cup heavy cream

½ pound fresh or imported dried fettuccine

G A R N I S H
Freshly grated Parmesan cheese

T i p

....

If you are fortunate enough to find powdered saffron, which is sold in tiny packages in some specialty stores, you can substitute it for the saffron threads. Use one whole packet in any preparation that calls for saffron. The advantage of powdered saffron is that it permeates the dish instantly, while saffron threads need 10 to 15 minutes of steeping before releasing all their flavor.

I l o v e leeks and try to use them whenever possible. Although they are at their best and least expensive in the fall, you can now get them year-round, making this an easy any-season dish. Leeks are amazingly good with pasta and here they are further enhanced by a gentle taste of saffron cream. Remember that simply "melted down" leeks, cooked in a touch of butter and bouillon, are a fabulous quick vegetable by themselves. A few pan-seared sea scallops would be a terrific addition to this dish.

....

1. Melt 2 tablespoons of the butter in a large skillet over low heat. Add the leeks, season with salt and pepper, and cook for 2 minutes. Add the water and simmer, covered, for 5 minutes, or until the leeks are tender and all the liquid has evaporated. Set aside.

2. Combine the saffron and bouillon in a saucepan and simmer until reduced by half. Add to the leeks together with the cream and keep warm.

3. Drop the fettuccine into a large pot of boiling salted water and cook until just tender, or al dente. Drain immediately and return to the pot.

4. Add the cream sauce together with the remaining 2 tablespoons butter and simmer for 1 to 2 minutes, being careful not to overcook the pasta. Correct the seasoning, adding a large grinding of pepper, and transfer to a serving bowl. Serve immediately, accompanied by some freshly grated Parmesan.

Fettuccine in Smoked Salmon and Chive Essence

To prepare: 10 minutes
To cook: 5 to 7 minutes
Serves 4 to 6

....

6 ounces smoked salmon

1 tablespoon finely grated onion

1¼ cups crème fraîche (see page 31)

Juice of ½ lemon, or more to taste

Coarse salt and freshly ground black pepper

¾ pound fresh fettuccine

3 to 4 tablespoons unsalted butter

3 tablespoons finely minced fresh chives

Optional: 1 cup steamed, diced asparagus

Tip

....

Whenever I plan to make this dish, I buy smoked salmon "trimmings," which are an inexpensive alternative, available in many specialty stores that sell a lot of the smoked fish. A good-quality packaged smoked salmon can also be used; be sure to look for packages with a sell-by date. A favorite is from Kendall-Brook in Maine.

If I had to pick a single favorite spring pasta dish, it would be this one. It takes minutes to prepare since the sauce is uncooked and simply heated by the warm pasta. As a garnish you can use your imagination—or whatever seems to appeal to you in the market. Since asparagus has a particular affinity for smoked salmon, I tend to opt for this delicious spring vegetable, but cooked fresh peas, a mincing of fresh dill, or a julienne of quickly braised leeks are other delicious alternatives.

....

1. Combine the salmon, onion, crème fraîche, and lemon juice in a food processor and process until smooth. Season with salt and pepper and set aside.

2. Drop the pasta into a large pot of boiling salted water and cook until just tender, or al dente. Drain well, transfer to a serving bowl, and toss with the butter. Add the salmon sauce, chives, and optional asparagus. Toss gently, correct the seasoning, and serve at once.

Fusilli with Fennel Sausage, Peas, and Creamy Tomatoes

To prepare: 15 minutes
To cook: 40 minutes
Serves 4 to 5

....

4 tablespoons extra-virgin olive oil

4 ounces slab bacon, blanched and diced, about ¾ cup

½ pound sweet Italian fennel sausage

1 medium onion, peeled and finely minced

2 large garlic cloves, peeled and finely minced

1 medium red bell pepper, cored, seeded, and diced

One 32-ounce can Italian plum tomatoes, drained and chopped

½ teaspoon dried oregano

½ teaspoon dried marjoram

½ teaspoon dried thyme

Salt and freshly ground black pepper

¼ cup heavy cream

1 cup fresh peas, cooked, or frozen peas, thawed

½ pound imported fusilli

GARNISH
¼ cup freshly grated Parmesan cheese

M o s t sweet Italian sausages are made with fennel seeds. Though some are very good, others can be too fatty, which is why I spend a lot of time searching for good fresh sausage in my local markets — and recommend you do the same. If you find one you like that is made without fennel, add a teaspoon of fennel seeds to this sauce. As for fresh peas, I've become spoiled since shelled peas are sold at produce markets all over New York City. If they are not available to you, use frozen peas and add them to the pasta right out of their box.

....

1.   Heat 2 tablespoons of the oil in a large skillet over medium heat. Add the bacon and cook until lightly browned. Remove with a slotted spoon and reserve. Add the sausage and cook until nicely browned on all sides. Cut crosswise into ¼-inch slices and set aside.

2.   Discard the fat from the skillet and add the remaining 2 tablespoons oil. Sauté the onion together with the garlic and red pepper until soft and lightly browned. Add the tomatoes and herbs, season with salt and pepper, and simmer, partially covered, for 20 minutes, or until thick.

3.   Puree the sauce in a food processor. Return to the skillet and add the cream, peas, bacon, and sausage. Keep warm.

4.   Drop the fusilli into a large pot of boiling salted water and cook until just tender, or al dente. Drain, return to the pot, add the sausage sauce, and simmer just to heat through. Correct the seasoning, transfer to a serving dish, and serve hot, sprinkled with the Parmesan cheese.

T i p

Fusilli is my favorite choice of dried pasta to use with sauces that are slightly runny, since the sauce gets trapped in the pasta instead of sinking to the bottom of the pasta bowl.

Fusilli with Broccoli, Peppers, and Smoked Mozzarella in Tomato-Basil Fondue

To prepare: 15 minutes
To cook: 50 minutes
Serves 4 to 5

....

5 tablespoons extra-virgin olive oil

1 large shallot, peeled and finely minced

4 large garlic cloves, peeled and thinly sliced

10 ripe plum tomatoes, peeled, seeded, and quartered, or one 35-ounce can Italian plum tomatoes, drained and quartered, or Tomato Fondue (see Tip)

1 tablespoon fresh oregano leaves or 2 teaspoons dried

½ cup fresh basil leaves, cut into a fine julienne or chopped

Salt and freshly ground black pepper

1 bunch broccoli, trimmed

½ cup chicken bouillon

2 large bell peppers (1 red and 1 yellow), cored, seeded, quartered, and thinly sliced

½ pound imported fusilli

1 cup finely diced smoked mozzarella

GARNISH
Freshly grated Parmesan cheese

I always have some Tomato Fondue (page 109) on hand, either in the refrigerator or in the freezer, which makes it much easier to come up with a pasta dish such as this almost on the Spur of the Moment. Smoked mozzarella is also best kept in the freezer. Let it thaw just enough to allow you to grate it into the finished pasta dish.

....

1.   Heat 3 tablespoons of the olive oil in a heavy 2-quart saucepan over medium heat. Add the shallot and half the garlic and cook for 1 minute. Add the tomatoes, oregano, and basil, season with salt and pepper, and simmer, covered, for 25 minutes, or until all the liquid has evaporated. Transfer to a food processor and process until coarsely chopped. Set aside.

2.   With a sharp knife, remove the broccoli florets and reserve. Peel the stalks and cut crosswise into ½-inch slices.

3.   Heat the remaining 2 tablespoons oil in a heavy skillet over medium heat. Add the remaining garlic together with the broccoli, bouillon, and peppers and simmer, covered, for 5 to 7 minutes, or until the vegetables are tender. Set aside.

4.   Drop the fusilli into a large pot of boiling salted water and cook until just tender, or al dente. Drain well and return to the pot. Add the tomato mixture, broccoli and peppers, and smoked mozzarella and toss gently. Correct the seasoning and serve immediately with a grating of fresh Parmesan.

T i p

Many recipes in this book call for a tomato fondue. The difference between a tomato fondue and a tomato sauce is that a fondue is rather "dry" and more intense, somewhat like an essence rather than a sauce. You can make a good tomato fondue with an excellent quality brand of canned tomatoes and either refrigerate it or freeze it (see page 109).

A tomato fondue can be used to enhance many dishes besides pasta preparations. It makes an excellent filling for an omelette, a seasoning for the pan juices of a roast, a sauce for sautéed eggplant, or even a topping to slices of French bread sautéed in olive oil.

Linguine with Spicy Shrimp al'Ajillo

To prepare: 15 minutes
To cook: 15 minutes
Serves 4

....

6 tablespoons extra-virgin olive oil

2 small dried red chili peppers, broken

1 pound medium shrimp, peeled

4 large garlic cloves, peeled and sliced

Coarse salt and freshly ground black pepper

½ pound imported linguine

¼ cup finely minced fresh Italian parsley

Tip

....

When shrimp are the main component of a dish, their utmost freshness is of great importance. Since most shrimp come into the market frozen, be sure to ask the "fish man" when the batch was defrosted. In fact, it is better to buy shrimp that are still lightly frozen than those that are sitting in a puddle of water or under a mountain of ice in the showcase.

Do not devein shrimp; it is simply not necessary. Deveining shrimp only makes them lose their juices during their cooking, rendering them tough.

Shrimp in garlic oil, *gambas al'ajillo*, is probably Spain's most popular little tapa dish. Usually served right out of a tiny clay casserole, it is eaten piping hot with crusty bread dipped into the spicy, garlicky oil. Here I combine the concept of this quick and delicious dish with linguine. If you see fresh calamari in the market, add some to the dish: cut three or four calamari into cubes, sauté them in hot oil for 30 seconds, and add to the finished pasta.

....

1. Heat 4 tablespoons of the oil in a large heavy skillet over medium heat. Add the chili peppers and cook until they darken; discard. Add the shrimp and cook until they just turn pink. Add the garlic and cook for 30 seconds longer. Season with coarse salt and pepper and set aside.

2. Drop the pasta into a large pot of boiling salted water and cook until just tender, or al dente. Drain well and return to the pot. Add the remaining 2 tablespoons olive oil, the shrimp mixture, and the parsley. Toss gently and correct the seasoning. Serve immediately.

Steamed Littlenecks with Linguine "Casera"

To prepare: 20 minutes
To cook: 20 minutes
Serves 6

1 medium onion, peeled and
finely minced

½ cup dry white wine

2 dozen littleneck clams,
scrubbed well

3 tablespoons extra-virgin olive oil

2 teaspoons finely minced fresh
ginger

2 teaspoons finely minced garlic

2 teaspoons finely minced jalapeño pepper

¼ cup finely minced scallions

½ cup finely diced red bell
pepper

½ cup finely diced yellow bell
pepper

1 cup finely diced zucchini skin
(with about ¼-inch pulp)

3 tablespoons mirin

6 ripe plum tomatoes, peeled,
seeded, and chopped

½ cup heavy cream

Salt and freshly ground black
pepper

1 pound imported linguine

GARNISH
¼ cup fresh cilantro leaves

Certain familiar preparations need no improvement, and a plateful of perfectly cooked linguine tossed with meaty, plump fresh clams and a touch of hot pepper, parsley, and garlic is just such a dish. But during a recent summer in Nantucket, I was in the mood for experimentation, and the result was this "East meets West" adaptation. We now like this version so much that it has become a new family classic. The word *casera* is a play on the Spanish word for "home-style," which perfectly describes this dish.

1. Combine the onion, wine, and clams in a large pot and steam, covered, until the clams open; discard any that do not. Remove from the shell, dice, and set aside. Strain and reserve ½ cup of the clam broth separately.

2. Heat the oil in large skillet over medium heat. Add the ginger, garlic, jalapeño pepper, scallions, bell peppers, and zucchini and cook for 2 minutes. Add the mirin and reduce to a glaze. Add the reserved clam broth and reduce by half. Add the tomatoes and cream, season with salt and pepper, and reduce slightly. Keep warm.

3. Drop the linguine into a large pot of boiling salted water and cook until just tender, or al dente. Drain well, return to the pot, and add the sauce. Toss gently but thoroughly, correct the seasoning, and serve hot garnished with the cilantro.

Mussels and Tomatoes alla Romagnola with Linguine

To prepare: 25 minutes
To cook: 30 minutes
Serves 4 to 6

⅓ cup finely minced shallots

½ cup dry white wine

1 tablespoon fresh thyme leaves

4 pounds small fresh mussels, well scrubbed (see Tip)

6 tablespoons extra-virgin olive oil

2 large garlic cloves, peeled and finely minced

1 tablespoon finely minced fresh ginger

¼ cup finely minced fresh parsley

4 large ripe tomatoes, peeled, seeded, and chopped

1 tablespoon finely minced fresh oregano

Optional: 1 Beurre Manié (page 193)

Freshly ground black pepper

1 tablespoon tiny capers, drained

¾ pound imported linguine

Salt

GARNISH
Tiny leaves of fresh basil

Mussels cooked in white wine, tomatoes, and herbs are a Mediterranean classic. Tossed with linguine, they become an earthy, homey pasta dish. I serve this as a one-dish meal, starting with a simple appetizer such as roasted peppers with mozzarella in an anchovy vinaigrette or a plate of roasted portabello or shiitake mushrooms sprinkled with extra-virgin olive oil and a few shavings of excellent Reggiano Parmesan.

1. Combine the shallots, wine, and thyme in a large heavy casserole and simmer for 1 minute. Add the mussels and steam, covered, until they open; discard any that do not. Remove with a slotted spoon and set aside. Reduce the cooking liquid to 1 cup, strain, and reserve.

2. Add the oil to the casserole and sauté the garlic, ginger, and parsley for 1 minute. Add the tomatoes and oregano, bring to a simmer, and cook for 5 minutes. Add the reserved mussel liquid and simmer for 5 minutes longer. If the sauce seems thin, whisk in bits of beurre manié and simmer until the sauce lightly coats a spoon. Season with a large grinding of pepper, add the capers, and keep warm.

3. Drop the linguine into a large pot of boiling salted water and cook until just tender, or al dente. Drain well, return to the pot, and add the mussels and sauce. Toss gently to heat through, and correct the seasoning. Transfer to a large serving bowl, garnish with basil, and serve at once with a crusty loaf of French bread and plenty of napkins.

T i p s

If you are as big a fan of mussels as I am, you may consider making this dish without the pasta and just serve a big bowl of the shellfish with a loaf of crusty bread.

If the mussels are very sandy, I soak them in a large bowl of cold water to which I add a tablespoon of all-purpose flour. The mussels absorb the flour and become larger and plumper. The flour also makes the mussels disgorge more of the sand that may be trapped in the shells.

Spaghettini in Sauce Basquaise (with Tuna, Tomatoes, and Black Olives)

To prepare: 20 minutes
To cook: 15 minutes

Serves 4

- ¼ cup extra-virgin olive oil

- 1 small dried red chili pepper, broken

- 2 tablespoons finely minced shallots

- 2 large garlic cloves, peeled and finely minced

- ¼ cup finely minced fresh parsley

- 4 large ripe tomatoes, peeled, seeded, and chopped, or one 35-ounce can Italian plum tomatoes, drained and chopped

- Coarse salt and freshly ground black pepper

- ½ cup small black oil-cured olives, preferably Gaeta

- 2 teaspoons finely grated lemon zest

- 1 tablespoon tiny capers, drained

- One 7½-ounce can chunk light tuna packed in olive oil, drained and flaked

- ½ pound imported spaghettini

Tip

I am a great fan of chunk light tuna packed in oil rather than the fancier white tuna. It is moister, more flaky, and more flavorful. Progresso and Pastene are my favorite brands.

This traditional pasta sauce remains a welcome standby at my house for Spur of the Moment cooking. It was the first dish my son made in college, and when I am out of town my husband can put it together as well in a matter of minutes since it calls for ingredients that we have on hand at all times.

Trendy restaurants are now using fresh tuna instead of canned, but the result is by no means better—in fact it is rather dry and less flavorful. Do use tuna packed in olive oil. If you cannot get black oil-cured olives, just leave the olives out. Serve this pasta dish as a main course following a soup such as the Yellow Pepper and Golden Zucchini Soup (page 57).

1. Heat the oil in large skillet over medium heat. Add the chili pepper and cook until it darkens; discard. Add the shallots, garlic, and parsley and cook for 1 minute. Add the tomatoes, season with coarse salt and pepper, and simmer for 5 minutes, stirring often. The mixture should remain quite juicy. Add the olives, lemon zest, capers, and tuna and set aside.

2. Drop the spaghettini into a large pot of boiling salted water and cook until just tender, or al dente. Drain well and add to the skillet. Toss gently over low heat, correct the seasoning, and just heat through. Serve directly from the skillet with crusty French bread.

Quick Potato Gnocchi

To prepare: 5 minutes
To cook: 20 minutes
Serves 5

....

1 pound all-purpose potatoes,
    peeled and cut into eighths

1½ extra-large egg yolks

¾ cup all-purpose flour

Salt and freshly ground black
    pepper

Optional: Pinch of freshly grated
    nutmeg

Tip

....

You must cook the gnocchi immediately after making the dough because the dough becomes much more soft and moist upon standing and very difficult to handle. On the other hand, once the gnocchi have been cooked, they will keep covered in the refrigerator for up to 1 week and they can also be frozen. To freeze, place the gnocchi on a baking sheet in the freezer until completely frozen. Transfer to plastic bags and store in the freezer for up to 1 month.

F o r years I have searched for a good recipe for these light little dumplings. Finally, thanks to Michael Romano of Union Square Café, here is a foolproof and delicious version. Not only are they easy and quick to make, you can cook them at your leisure and even freeze them and reheat in the microwave with excellent results. I like gnocchi best of all when simmered in a Parmesan cream, possibly with the addition of a few porcini mushrooms (see page 130), or in a rich Gorgonzola Cream sauce (page 131), but they are equally good tossed in a quick tomato sauce or even in a little brown butter enhanced with large shavings of Parmesan.

....

1. Drop the potatoes into boiling salted water and cook until very tender. Drain and pass through a food mill or potato ricer into a large bowl. While still warm, add the yolks and flour, season with salt and pepper and the optional nutmeg, and mix well. Transfer to a lightly floured surface and knead quickly into a smooth ball; the dough will be slightly moist. Roll quickly with floured hands into ½-inch-thick logs, and cut crosswise into 1-inch pieces. Set aside.

2. Set a pan of ice water near the stove top. Drop the gnocchi a few at a time into a large pot of boiling salted water and cook just until they rise to the surface. Remove immediately with a slotted spoon and plunge into the bowl of ice water. When completely cool, drain well on kitchen towels, cover, and refrigerate until needed.

Two Sauces for Potato Gnocchi

To prepare: 5 minutes
To cook: 30 minutes
Serves 4

....

½ ounce dried porcini mushrooms, well rinsed

1 cup chicken bouillon

4 tablespoons unsalted butter

¾ cup heavy cream

Optional: 1 Beurre Manié
(page 193)

¼ cup freshly grated Parmesan
cheese, plus additional for
serving

Salt and freshly ground black
pepper

1 recipe Quick Potato Gnocchi
(page 129)

1. Combine the porcini and bouillon in a saucepan and simmer, covered, for 20 minutes, or until the mushrooms are tender. Drain well, finely dice, and reserve. Pass the bouillon through a double layer of cheesecloth and reserve.

2. Melt the butter in a heavy skillet over medium-low heat and whisk constantly until a light hazelnut brown. Immediately add the cream and reserved mushroom broth and simmer until reduced by one quarter. Whisk in bits of the optional beurre manié and simmer until the sauce lightly coats a spoon. Add the porcini and Parmesan and season with salt and pepper.

3. Add the gnocchi to the skillet and simmer gently until just heated through. Serve at once with a grating of Parmesan.

To prepare: 5 minutes
To cook: 10 minutes
Serves 4

5 tablespoons unsalted butter

1¼ cups heavy cream

1 Beurre Manié (page 193)

4 ounces Gorgonzola cheese, crumbled

3 tablespoons freshly grated Parmesan cheese, plus additional for serving

Salt and freshly ground white pepper

1 recipe Quick Potato Gnocchi (page 129)

1. Melt the butter in a heavy skillet over medium-low heat and whisk constantly until a light hazelnut brown. Immediately add the cream and simmer until reduced by one quarter. Whisk in bits of the beurre manié and simmer until the sauce lightly coats a spoon. Add the Gorgonzola and Parmesan, season with salt and white pepper, and simmer until the cheeses have melted.

2. Add the gnocchi to the skillet and simmer gently until just heated through. Serve at once with a grating of Parmesan.

Penne Salad with Caviar and Ginger-Lemon Vinaigrette

To prepare: 20 minutes
To cook: 10 to 12 minutes
Serves 4 to 5

½ pound imported penne

1 teaspoon lightly beaten egg yolk

Juice of 1 large lemon

1 tablespoon Dijon mustard

2 teaspoons finely minced fresh ginger

1 large garlic clove, peeled and crushed

½ cup extra-virgin olive oil

¾ cup mayonnaise

Salt and freshly ground black pepper

Pinch of cayenne pepper

2 small bell peppers (1 red and 1 yellow), cored, seeded, and cut into a fine julienne

3 medium scallions, finely minced

2 ounces red salmon caviar

6 ounces smoked salmon, cut into a fine julienne

GARNISH
Tiny leaves of fresh cilantro

Optional: ½ cup finely diced roasted red pepper (see page 182)

Diced avocado

O K , so pasta salads are passé. Does it mean that you can't still enjoy one that is good? Here is a delicious, somewhat "East meets West" version that everyone in my house loves. Be sure to season the salad assertively — and plan for leftovers, which get better and better tasting as they stay around.

1. Drop the penne into a large pot of boiling salted water and cook until just tender, or al dente.

2. While the pasta is cooking, combine the egg yolk, lemon juice, mustard, ginger, and garlic in a large bowl. Slowly whisk in the oil until emulsified. Fold in the mayonnaise and season with salt and black pepper and cayenne.

3. Drain the pasta well. Add to the vinaigrette together with the peppers, scallions, caviar, and salmon and toss gently but thoroughly. Correct the seasoning. Garnish with cilantro, the optional red pepper, and the avocado and serve at room temperature or lightly chilled.

T i p

When it comes to pasta salads, there is only one word of advice: Be patient. More than a potato salad or any other salad, pasta salads need time to absorb the flavor of a vinaigrette. If you are in a rush, then double the amount of vinaigrette and season the salad assertively with lots of freshly ground pepper.

Great Grains

Just before CHRISTMAS 1989, I GOT A CALL FROM THE FOOD EDITOR OF THE *LOS ANGELES TIMES* ASKING ME WHAT I THOUGHT THE BIG FOOD TREND OF THE 1990S WOULD BE. MY GUT REACTION WAS TO ANSWER "BAGELS," SINCE I WAS SURE THEY WERE ABOUT TO TAKE OFF. BUT I SENSED FROM THE EDITOR'S TONE OF VOICE THAT SHE WAS SOMEWHAT DISAPPOINTED IN SOMETHING SO UNCHIC AND UNSEXY, SO I TRIED AGAIN. "GRAINS WILL BE VERY BIG," I VENTURED. "RICE, POLENTA, COUSCOUS, AND BULGUR WILL ALL FINALLY GET THE ATTENTION THEY DESERVE."

TO A LARGE EXTENT, BOTH OF MY PREDICTIONS CAME TRUE, AND I JUST WISH I WAS AS GOOD AT PREDICTING HORSE RACES AND HOT STOCKS AS I

am food trends. But since I am passionate about grains I am especially delighted that more cooks are discovering their infinite variety and potential.

Polenta was the first of my picks to really catch on, and if it at first seemed a shade too exotic to many American cooks, it redeemed itself by being an Italian staple. Clearly, any food the Italians can't get enough of must be terrific!

And terrific it is: substantial enough to be wonderfully satisfying, versatile enough to go with just about anything from spicy jalapeño peppers to creamy mascarpone cheese, and easy to cook now that quick polenta varieties are readily available in the supermarket. Polenta is so good you usually won't have leftovers, but if you do, you can fry it, sauté it in butter, grill it, or simply reheat it, and it will be delicious all over again!

If ease of preparation has helped polenta become more accessible to Spur of the Moment cooking, much the same thing has happened to rice. Having grown up in Barcelona, I know nothing can top the taste of saffron-tinged paella rice that's cooked for hours. But there are a number of terrific skillet rice dishes in Catalan cooking that are far less time-consuming than traditional paella and quite good. My skillet paella (see page 142) or skillet shrimp pilaf (see page 137) are just two examples of Spur of the Moment possibilities.

Even risottos, which have always demanded a great deal of time and attention from the cook, are possible to create with a shortcut method that doesn't shortcut the rich, intense taste. I think my simplified version (see page 144) is perfect for the Spur of the Moment cook. I'm no longer rigid about how I make risotto or how I serve it: I often make it the main course, preceded by a soup or a salad or a quick skillet sauté of shellfish. When I choose a grilled or pan-seared fish as my main course, I balance it with a hearty risotto as an appetizer.

The only thing better than simple preparation and a short cooking time is no cooking time, and that is the joy of making couscous and bulgur, two grains that require no cooking whatsoever. Just soak them in broth, stock, or bouillon—they'll plump up to a fluffy consistency in very little time. Good quick couscous, especially one of the superior French varieties, is ready in about ten minutes. Add a little butter and some melted scallions and you've got a lovely and effortless dish. Dice some tomatoes and slice some cucumbers into a bowl of bulgur, sprinkle with fresh cilantro, lemon juice, and olive oil, and you're ready to serve a tangy grain salad that's a refreshing change of pace.

Whether you choose a pilaf or a paella, a risotto or a couscous dish, grains give you myriad fresh, imaginative ways to expand your cooking repertoire.

Piquant Parsley and Lemon Pilaf

To prepare: 5 minutes
To cook: 25 minutes
Serves 4

....

2 tablespoons unsalted butter

1 small onion, peeled and finely minced

1 cup Arborio rice or long-grain rice

2 cups chicken bouillon

Salt and freshly ground black pepper

3 tablespoons finely minced fresh Italian parsley

1 teaspoon finely grated lemon zest

Optional: 2 tablespoons unsalted butter for enrichment

T i p

....

Curly parsley and Italian flat parsley are interchangeable in many recipes, but there is quite a difference in flavor between the two. While curly parsley is more decorative, the Italian flat type is far more intensely flavored and more suitable for stocks and those dishes in which you are looking for distinct parsley flavor.

T h e key to a successful pilaf lies in the quality of the rice you use. My first choice is always Arborio rice. But long-grain rice is an inexpensive basic that is good to have on hand, and when enhanced by fresh lemon or lime juice and a generous amount of minced Italian parsley, it becomes a quick and tasty side dish that works well with stews and ragoûts. Any leftover pilaf can be turned into a tasty rice salad by adding Balsamic Vinegar and Shallot Dressing (page 90). Serve the pilaf with lamb chops, shish-kebabs, or a juicy lamb burger.

....

1. Melt the butter in a 2-quart saucepan over low heat. Add the onion and cook until soft but browned. Add the rice and mix well. Add the bouillon, season with salt and pepper, and simmer, covered, for 20 minutes, or until the rice is tender.

2. Add the parsley, lemon zest, and optional butter and fold in gently. Correct the seasoning and serve hot.

Remarks: The rice can be kept warm, covered, in a low oven. It can also be reheated in the microwave. Be sure to cover the rice with microwave-safe plastic wrap so that it does not dry out.

Shrimp, Tomato, and Red Onion Pilaf à la Catalane

~~~~~~~~~~

To prepare: 10 minutes
To cook: 40 minutes
Serves 4 to 5

....

5 tablespoons extra-virgin
    olive oil

1 small dried red chili pepper,
    broken, or ½ teaspoon red
    pepper flakes

15 large shrimp, peeled

2 large red onions, peeled, quar-
    tered, and thinly sliced

2 large garlic cloves, peeled and
    crushed

1 teaspoon dried oregano

1 teaspoon dried thyme

2 large ripe tomatoes, cubed

1¼ cups Italian rice, preferably
    Arborio

2¾ cups chicken bouillon

Salt and freshly ground black
    pepper

G A R N I S H
Quartered lemons

Strips of pimiento

T i p

....

*Pilafs calling for Arborio rice can
also be made with imported Spanish paella rice, which is less expensive than the Arborio.*

T h i s dish, a cross between a risotto and a paella, is popular in Catalan cooking but has never gained the fame of paella. It is a perfect Spur of the Moment one-dish meal. All you should need to buy are the fresh ingredients that constitute the dominant taste, in this case, shrimp and tomatoes; the rest are pantry basics that you probably have on hand. Instead of shrimp, you can use more than one kind of seafood or a combination of sweet and spicy sausage. The pilaf is wonderful the next day served at room temperature, tossed with Lemon, Shallot, and Sherry Vinegar Dressing (page 90). It can also be reheated in the microwave.

....

1. Heat 2 tablespoons of the oil in a cast-iron skillet over high heat. Add the chili pepper or red pepper flakes and shrimp and cook until the shrimp are bright pink. Let cool slightly, then cube and set aside.

2. Add the remaining oil to the skillet. Reduce the heat to low. Add the onions, garlic, and herbs and cook for 10 minutes, or until the onions are soft and nicely browned. Add the tomatoes and rice and mix well. Add the bouillon, season with salt and pepper, and simmer, covered, for 25 minutes, or until the rice is tender and all the liquid has been absorbed.

3. Add the shrimp and fold in gently. Correct the seasoning and serve the pilaf directly from the skillet, garnished with lemons and pimiento strips.

Tomatillo, Cilantro, and Green Chili Pilaf

To prepare: 5 minutes
Serves 6 to 8

8 tomatillos, husks removed, well scrubbed and blanched (see Tip)

3 large garlic cloves, peeled and finely minced

1 serrano chili, finely minced

1 cup fresh cilantro leaves

½ cup fresh parsley leaves

Optional: 5 leaves fresh spinach, stemmed

Juice of 1 lime, or more to taste

Salt and freshly ground black pepper

4 cups hot cooked rice

Tip

Tomatillos look like small, husk-covered green tomatoes. They have a tart, citrus flavor. When purchasing tomatillos, look for firm, bright green ones. Remove the husks and rinse them under warm water. It is always best to blanch them in boiling water for 1 minute before using.

I am always fascinated by new ingredients and, especially, "new" varieties of fruits and vegetables. That's what happened when tomatillos first appeared in the market. Now I find myself using them quite often, especially in dishes such as this simple pilaf. Their subtle acidity complements the other ingredients in this easy side dish, which is best served with grilled fish or chicken.

1.   Puree the tomatillos together with the garlic, serrano, cilantro, parsley, and optional spinach in a food processor until almost smooth. Add the lime juice and season with salt and pepper.

2.   Pour the mixture into the hot rice and mix thoroughly. Correct the seasoning and serve immediately.

Caramelized Onion Pilaf

To prepare: 10 minutes

To cook: 50 minutes

Serves 6

....

2 tablespoons unsalted butter

1 tablespoon olive oil

2 large onions, peeled, quartered, and thinly sliced

Salt and freshly ground black pepper

Pinch of granulated sugar

1½ cups Italian rice, preferably Arborio

3 cups chicken bouillon or Chicken Stock (page 145)

Optional: ¼ cup heavy cream

¼ cup freshly grated Parmesan cheese

GARNISH

2 tablespoons finely minced fresh parsley

T i p

....

For a variation, you can add ¼ cup crumbled mild blue cheese and about 12 double-poached garlic cloves (see page 41) to the finished pilaf.

T h e secret to caramelizing onions quickly is to use plenty of oil and a pinch of sugar. Once the onions are well browned, place them in a colander over a bowl and drain them of excess oil. Combined with rice in a tasty pilaf, they make a terrific flavor-packed side dish to a roast chicken. The pilaf can be prepared ahead of time and reheated in either a low oven or the microwave.

....

1. In a heavy 3-quart casserole, melt the butter together with the oil over medium heat. Add the onions and season with salt and pepper and a pinch of sugar. Cook for 5 minutes, stirring constantly, until the onions begin to brown.

2. Reduce the heat and cook, partially covered, until the onions are very soft and nicely browned, about 25 minutes.

3. Add the rice to the casserole and stir to blend well. Add the bouillon or stock and bring to a boil. Reduce the heat, season with salt and pepper, and simmer, covered, for 20 to 25 minutes, or until the rice is tender.

4. Add the optional cream and the Parmesan and stir gently. Transfer to a serving bowl, sprinkle with the parsley, and serve hot.

Skillet-Braised Shrimp, Zucchini, and Pepper Paella

To prepare: 20 minutes
To cook: 1 hour
Serves 4 to 6

....

4 tablespoons extra-virgin olive oil

½ pound medium shrimp, peeled

2 teaspoons finely minced jala-
    peño pepper

1 large Spanish onion, peeled,
    quartered, and thinly sliced

2 large bell peppers (1 red and
    1 green), cored, seeded, and
    thinly sliced

2 large garlic cloves, peeled and
    finely minced

1½ teaspoons imported paprika

1 tablespoon fresh thyme leaves

1 small zucchini, trimmed and
    diced

1 small yellow squash, trimmed
    and diced

4 large ripe tomatoes, peeled,
    seeded, and chopped

Salt and freshly ground black
    pepper

1¼ cups Italian rice, preferably
    Arborio

2 cups chicken bouillon

G A R N I S H
Finely minced fresh parsley

Lemon wedges

P a e l l a , like risotto, comes in many variations and degrees of difficulty. In spite of the number of ingredients in this recipe, however, the preparation is really very easy and not at all time-consuming. Still, you may prefer to reserve this dish for weekend cooking, mainly because the leftovers are so delicious and reheat well in the microwave for an easy Sunday night supper. The great advantage of a paella is that you can be as creative as you wish. If you are near the shore or have access to great seafood, by all means use several kinds. There are few musts in a homey paella such as this. Just be sure to pay attention to the rice and do not overcook it. Serve this as a main course right from the skillet, starting with a simple salad and followed by a light fruit dessert.

....

1. Heat 2 tablespoons of the oil in a large deep cast-iron skillet over medium-high heat. Add the shrimp and sauté quickly until lightly browned. Remove with a slotted spoon and set aside.

2. Add the remaining 2 tablespoons oil to the skillet and reduce the heat. Add the jalapeño pepper, onion, and bell peppers and cook, stirring often, for 10 minutes, or until the vegetables are barely tender. Add the garlic, paprika, thyme, zucchini, yellow squash, and tomatoes, season with salt and pepper, and bring to a simmer. Cook, covered, for 10 minutes longer.

140   *Great Grains*

3. Add the rice and bouillon and mix well. Simmer, covered, over low heat for 20 minutes. Add the shrimp and simmer for 5 minutes longer, or until the rice is tender and all the liquid has been absorbed. Correct the seasoning, garnish with minced parsley and lemon wedges, and serve hot, directly from the skillet.

T i p

The success of all paellas, be it the classic kind or this "poor man's" version, depends upon the quality of the sofrito. The sofrito is the onion and tomato base to which the rice and seasonings are added. In a good sofrito, the onions must be cooked until well browned and caramelized and then cooked further with the tomatoes. The mixture must be well reduced and intensely flavored. It is this base that will ultimately give the rice its true paella flavor.

Spicy Basque Smoked Chicken Paella

To prepare: 10 minutes

To cook: 55 minutes

Serves 4 to 6

3½ cups Chicken Stock (page 145) or chicken bouillon

1 teaspoon saffron threads

2 tablespoons olive oil

2 small dried red chili peppers, broken

2 medium onions, peeled, quartered, and thinly sliced

3 large garlic cloves, peeled and finely minced

1½ cups peeled, seeded, and chopped Italian plum tomatoes or one 16-ounce can, drained and chopped

2 large bell peppers (1 red and 1 green), cored, seeded, and thinly sliced

Large sprig of fresh thyme

Large sprig of fresh oregano

Salt and freshly ground pepper

1¼ cups Arborio rice

¾ pound smoked chicken, cut into ½-inch cubes

½ cup cooked fresh peas or thawed frozen peas

GARNISH

Lemon wedges and thinly sliced pimientos

2 to 3 tablespoons minced parsley

My mother used to call this dish "leftover paella," but there was really little in the way of leftovers used, only some grilled chicken or diced roast lamb. Here is a version of her homey dish using smoked chicken, which adds character to an otherwise simple preparation. Remember that there are few leftovers more tasty than paella. Reheated in the microwave, this Spanish peasant dish tastes even better two or three days later.

1. Combine the stock or bouillon and saffron in a small saucepan and simmer until reduced to 3 cups. Set aside.

2. Preheat the oven to 350°F.

3. Heat the oil over medium heat in a deep ovenproof skillet. Add the chili peppers, onion, and garlic and cook, stirring often, for 10 minutes, or until soft and lightly browned. Add the tomatoes, bell peppers, thyme, and oregano, season with salt and pepper, and cook until the liquid has evaporated.

4. Add the rice and saffron broth, mix well, and bring to a boil. Cover tightly, placed in the oven, and bake for 20 minutes. Fold in the smoked chicken and peas and bake for 5 to 10 minutes longer, or until the rice is tender. Correct the seasoning and garnish with lemon wedges, parsley, and pimientos. Serve directly from the skillet with a crusty loaf of bread.

T i p

When buying Arborio rice, you will find that you have more than one choice these days. The best quality, called "super-fino," comes in large sacks, but those that are sold in 2-pound bags are equally good. Be sure to transfer the rice to an airtight container for storage. If you're not planning to use it right away, I suggest refrigerating it, since Arborio rice seems to draw tiny bugs that would not make a flavorful addition to any risotto.

Risotto with Smoked Trout, Tomatoes, and Herb Cream

To prepare: 15 minutes

To cook: 30 minutes

Serves 4 to 5

⅓ cup mascarpone

2 tablespoons finely minced fresh chives

2 tablespoons finely minced fresh dill

3 tablespoons unsalted butter

2 medium leeks, trimmed of all but 2 inches of greens, thinly sliced, and well rinsed

2 large ripe tomatoes, peeled, seeded, and chopped

1¼ cups Italian rice, preferably Arborio

3½ to 4 cups Chicken Stock (page 145) or chicken bouillon

Salt and freshly ground black pepper

1 cup skinned and flaked smoked trout or bluefish

GARNISH
Sprigs of fresh dill

T o me, a good risotto is as satisfying as any pasta dish. What's more, risottos are custom-made for the Spur of the Moment cook. With a few basics on hand, a little ingenuity, and an ingredient or two that has caught your fancy at the market, you can be on your way to preparing a dish that very few restaurants do well.

Here is a quick method that produces a terrific risotto without having to resort to the microwave. Using leeks rather than the usual onions produces a more delicate taste, which is further enhanced by a garnish of smoked trout. Other smoked fish will do as well, especially scallops, salmon, tuna, and mackerel. Do not use seafood that is either too salty or too smoky or one that will fall apart.

1. Whisk together the mascarpone, chives, and dill. Set aside.

2. Melt the butter over low heat in a heavy 3-quart casserole. Add the leeks and cook, covered, for 5 minutes. Add the tomatoes and cook, uncovered, until all the juices have evaporated. Add the rice and 2 cups of the stock or bouillon, reduce the heat to very low, and simmer, covered, for 10 minutes.

3. Raise the heat to medium, uncover the saucepan, and add the remaining stock or bouillon ¼ cup at a time, stirring constantly for the next 10 minutes, until each addition has been absorbed; you may not need all the remaining stock. The rice should be tender on the outside but still chewy on the inside. Season with salt and pepper.

4. Fold in the mascarpone mixture and smoked fish and correct the seasoning, adding a large grinding of pepper. Serve at once in shallow soup bowls, garnished with sprigs of fresh dill.

C h i c k e n   S t o c k

Combine one 3-pound chicken, quartered; 14 chicken wings; 2 carrots, cut in half; 2 celery stalks, cut in half; 10 sprigs fresh parsley; 2 leeks, cut in half and rinsed; 8 black peppercorns; and a large pinch of salt in an 8-quart pot. Add water to cover by 2 inches. Slowly bring to a boil, skimming the surface often. Reduce the heat and simmer, partially covered, for 1 hour and 30 minutes. Strain and cool, uncovered. Then refrigerate, uncovered, overnight. The next day, remove the solidified fat from the surface. Transfer the stock to a large pot and bring to a boil. Pour into 1-quart containers and cool, uncovered. Cover and refrigerate for up to 1 week (bringing back to a boil every 2 days) or freeze for up to 1 month.

Al Porto's Risotto with Basil, Rosemary, and Mascarpone

To prepare: 10 minutes

To cook: 25 minutes

Serves 4

3 tablespoons unsalted butter

1 medium onion, peeled and finely diced

1½ cups Italian rice, preferably Arborio

4 cups hot Chicken Stock (page 145) or chicken bouillon

Salt and freshly ground black pepper

2 large ripe tomatoes, peeled and diced

⅓ cup mascarpone

¼ cup julienne of fresh basil

2 tablespoons finely minced fresh rosemary

2 to 3 tablespoons freshly grated Parmesan cheese

GARNISH

Sprigs of fresh basil

Freshly grated Parmesan cheese

I n 1975, when risottos first appeared on the food scene, I decided that I needed some in-depth mastery of how to make this great rice. I chose to work in a restaurant in Milan called Al Porto, which specialized in risottos of all kinds but whose most famous rice dish was black risotto made with the ink of squid. The other day, while looking through my old notebooks, I came upon this risotto from Al Porto that I had never done before. I am not quite sure why—possibly because at the time mascarpone was hard to come by. Now all of the ingredients for this dish are readily available. Like pasta, there are still many new ways of enjoying one of Italy's most creative dishes.

1. Melt the butter in a heavy 3-quart saucepan over low heat. Add the onion and cook until soft. Add the rice and cook for 1 minute, stirring constantly.

2. Add 2 cups of the stock or bouillon and simmer over the lowest possible heat, covered, for 10 minutes. Raise the heat to medium, uncover the saucepan, and add the remaining stock or bouillon ¼ cup at a time, stirring constantly for the next 10 minutes, until each addition has been absorbed; you may not need all the remaining stock. The rice should be tender on the outside but still chewy on the inside. Season with salt and pepper.

3. Fold in the tomatoes, mascarpone, herbs, and Parmesan and correct the seasoning. Serve immediately in shallow soup bowls, garnished with basil and accompanied by grated Parmesan.

T i p

....

If you cannot get mascarpone, you can still make this risotto by adding 2 tablespoons of heavy cream or crème fraîche (see page 31) to the rice. If getting good Parmesan, preferably Reggiano, is a problem, it is better not to use it at all, since this is a rather delicate risotto that could easily be overpowered by a strong or salty cheese.

Zucchini and Basil Risotto with Parmigiano

To prepare: 10 minutes
To cook: 30 minutes
Serves 4

....

1 cup tightly packed fresh basil
    leaves

1 large garlic clove, peeled and
    mashed

2 to 3 tablespoons olive oil

3 tablespoons unsalted butter

1 medium onion, peeled and
    finely diced

1½ cups Italian rice, preferably
    Arborio

1 cup finely diced zucchini

4 cups hot Chicken Stock (page
    145) or chicken bouillon

Salt and freshly ground black
    pepper

¼ cup heavy cream

¼ cup freshly grated Parmesan
    cheese

GARNISH

2 ripe tomatoes, diced and driz-
    zled with a little sherry vine-
    gar and extra-virgin olive oil

Freshly grated Parmesan cheese

C o m e summer, with its overabundance of zuc-chini, yellow squash, and golden zucchini, a risotto is one of the best ways to use these delicate yet delicious vegetables. When the dish is further enhanced with plenty of fragrant sweet basil, you feel as if the summer kitchen is truly complete. Serve this risotto as either a starter or a light warm-weather main course. I like to top each serving with a dicing of ripe tomatoes, gently marinated for a few minutes in extra-virgin olive oil and a touch of sherry vinegar.

....

1. Combine the basil and garlic in a food processor and finely mince. Add enough oil to make a smooth paste. Set aside.

2. Melt the butter in a heavy 3-quart saucepan over low heat. Add the onion and cook until soft. Add the rice and zucchini and cook for 1 minute, stirring constantly.

3. Add 2 cups of the stock or bouillon and simmer, covered, over the lowest possible heat for 10 minutes. Raise the heat to medium, uncover the saucepan, and add the remaining stock or bouillon ¼ cup at a time, stirring constantly for the next 10 minutes, until each addition has been absorbed; you may not need all the remaining stock. The rice should be tender on the outside but still chewy on the inside. Season with salt and pepper.

4. Add the basil paste, cream, and Parmesan and just heat through. Correct the seasoning, sprinkle with the diced tomatoes, and serve at once, with a bowl of Parmesan on the side.

T i p

The more delicate the risotto, the more important the quality of the stock. A full-bodied homemade Chicken Stock (page 145) will make all the difference in a rice dish in which the vegetables are delicate or lack an assertive flavor. For the Spur of the Moment cook, doctoring up chicken bouillon with some root vegetables and a few chicken wings is a quick and extremely flavorful alternative.

Tangy Lemon Orzo with Red Peppers and Scallions

To prepare: 10 minutes

To cook: 15 minutes

Serves 4 to 5

....

6 tablespoons extra-virgin olive oil

¾ cup finely minced scallions

1 red bell pepper, cored, seeded, and finely diced

2 tablespoons water or chicken bouillon

Salt and freshly ground black pepper

1 cup orzo, preferably imported

2 tablespoons finely minced fresh parsley

Juice of ½ lemon, or more to taste

T i p

....

You can be quite creative with this dish, using both red and yellow peppers and adding any variety of fresh herbs, such as cilantro, chives, basil, or thyme, as a garnish.

I t i s hard to believe that orzo, a longtime supermarket staple, has suddenly become so popular. Now it ranks up there with polenta and Arborio rice on the menus of many three-star restaurants. It was because of Alfred Portale of Gotham Bar and Grill, who makes the best orzo salad that I have ever tasted, that I started to cook this rice-shaped pasta, with some terrific results.

....

1. Heat 2 tablespoons of the oil in a medium skillet over medium heat. Add the scallions and red pepper and cook for just 1 minute. Add the water or bouillon, season with salt and pepper, and simmer, covered, for 3 to 4 minutes, or until the vegetables are tender.

2. While the pepper mixture is braising, cook the orzo in boiling salted water for 5 minutes, or until just tender; do not overcook. Drain.

3. Add the orzo to the pepper mixture together with the parsley, toss well, and transfer to a serving bowl.

4. Combine the lemon juice and remaining 4 tablespoons oil in a small bowl and whisk until well blended. Season with salt and pepper, add to the orzo, and mix well. Serve warm or at room temperature.

Creamy Polenta with Jalapeño Peppers, Corn, and Two Cheeses

To prepare: 10 minutes
To cook: 25 minutes
Serves 6

....

3¼ cup skim milk (or half whole milk and half water)

Salt

¾ cup fine semolina or yellow cornmeal

3 tablespoons unsalted butter

1 to 2 teaspoons finely minced jalapeño pepper (see Tip)

One 11-ounce can corn niblets, drained

Freshly ground black pepper

2 ounces extra-sharp white Vermont Cheddar, finely grated

2 ounces Monterey Jack cheese, finely grated

T i p

....

To control the hotness that a jalapeño will impart, cut the peppers in half lengthwise and remove the seeds and white membranes. Taste a seed—if it is quite spicy, use only a few. Be sure to taste a tiny bit of the pepper itself. If it is very spicy, start by using only a teaspoon of minced pepper, then add more to taste if you like.

N o w that pasta and even risotto have moved into the mainstream of American cooking, polenta is the new Italian favorite. I still prefer the old-fashioned variety, although it does take time to cook and requires plenty of attention. Quick-cooking polenta is a good choice for the busy cook and can be substituted in many recipes, including this one. In this version, diced jalapeño and a sprinkling of corn kernels give zest to the basic preparation, and the cheese further enriches it, making it a perfect accompaniment to simple grilled or pan-seared fish and veal chops or roast chicken.

....

1. Combine the skim milk (or whole milk and water) and ¾ teaspoon salt in a heavy 3½-quart saucepan and bring to a boil. Sprinkle in the semolina or cornmeal very slowly, whisking constantly. Reduce the heat to very low and simmer, covered, for 20 minutes, stirring often (a film will form on the bottom of the pan; do not be alarmed).

2. While the polenta is cooking, melt the butter over low heat in a small skillet. Add the jalapeño pepper and cook for 30 seconds. Add the corn, season with salt and pepper, and just heat through. Set aside.

3. When the polenta is done, add the corn mixture and the cheeses and stir until just melted. Correct the seasoning and serve at once.

Wild Mushroom Polenta with Thyme and Aged Goat Cheese

To prepare: 10 minutes

To cook: 35 minutes

Serves 6

....

½ ounce dried porcini mushrooms

4 to 4½ cups chicken bouillon

4 tablespoons unsalted butter

1 medium shallot, peeled and
finely minced

½ pound shiitake mushrooms,
stemmed and thinly sliced

Salt and freshly ground black
pepper

1 cup fine semolina or yellow
cornmeal

2 tablespoons finely minced fresh
thyme

½ cup crumbled aged goat
cheese

A g e d goat cheese is harder and a little saltier than the fresh young type. If you can't find it in your local market, simply freeze a soft goat cheese until firm and grate it into the cooked polenta. Since this is a flavor-packed side dish, I usually team it with something as simple as a hamburger or a juicy veal chop. I must admit that I like polenta so much that I often serve it as a light main course with just some cooked asparagus, green beans, or a medley of oven-roasted peppers.

....

1.   Combine the porcini and 1 cup of the bouillon in a small saucepan and simmer, covered, for 10 minutes, or until the mushrooms are tender. Drain, reserving the broth. Mince the porcini and set aside. Combine the mushroom broth with enough of the remaining bouillon to measure 3½ cups. Set aside.

2.   Melt 2 tablespoons of the butter in a 10-inch skillet over medium heat. Add the shallot and shiitake mushrooms and sauté until nicely browned. Season with salt and pepper and set aside.

3.   Bring the reserved chicken-mushroom broth to a boil in a 3-quart casserole. Slowly add the cornmeal, stirring constantly until the mixture thickens. Reduce the heat to very low and simmer, covered, for 20 minutes, stirring often (a film will form on the bottom of the pan; do not be alarmed).

4. Fold the porcini, shiitakes, thyme, and goat cheese into the polenta. Add the remaining 2 tablespoons butter, season with salt and pepper, and just heat through. Transfer to a serving dish and serve hot.

T i p

Don't be afraid to enrich polenta to your heart's content. Like mashed potatoes, polenta loves the company of butter, lots of good Parmesan, and, above all, mascarpone, the creamy, buttery, smooth Italian cheese. If you cannot get it, try other creamy Italian cheeses, such as Gorgonzola Dolce, or Taleggio, or diced Fontina.

Semolina Gnocchi with Anchovies, Garlic, and Rosemary

To prepare: 25 minutes
plus 1 hour to chill
To cook: 30 minutes
Serves 4

ANCHOVY BUTTER

1 large garlic clove, peeled and finely minced

1 tablespoon finely minced fresh rosemary

2 tablespoons finely minced fresh parsley

4 flat anchovy fillets, drained and finely minced

6 tablespoons unsalted butter, softened

Salt and freshly ground black pepper

GNOCCHI

1 quart skim milk

Salt

1 cup fine semolina or yellow cornmeal

2 tablespoons unsalted butter

½ cup plus 3 tablespoons freshly grated Parmesan cheese

Freshly ground black pepper

S e m o l i n a gnocchi are not intended for the quick cook since it takes time for the polenta to cool properly before it can be cut into squares or rounds. Still, it is a perfect choice on the weekend when I want to serve creamy polenta one day and have terrific leftovers, with a minimum of effort. As a variation, the gnocchi can be dipped into beaten egg and then in cornmeal and fried in oil. A superb dish that is well worth the calories.

1. Start by making the anchovy butter: Combine the garlic, rosemary, parsley, anchovies, and butter in a food processor and process until smooth. Season with salt and pepper and refrigerate.

2. Make the gnocchi: Combine the skim milk and 1 teaspoon salt in a heavy 3½-quart saucepan and bring to a boil. Sprinkle in the semolina or cornmeal very slowly, whisking constantly. Reduce the heat to very low and simmer, covered, for 15 minutes, stirring often. Remove the pan from the heat, add the butter and the ½ cup Parmesan, season with salt and pepper, and mix well.

3. Rinse a rectangular baking pan or cookie sheet with cold water. Spoon the polenta into the pan and smooth evenly with a wet spatula into a ½-inch-thick layer. Chill for 1 hour.

4. Preheat the oven to 350°F.

5. With a 1-inch round cookie cutter, cut the polenta into disks. Place them, slightly overlapping, in a well-buttered heavy baking dish. Dot with the anchovy butter, sprinkle with the remaining 3 tablespoons Parmesan, and bake for 30 minutes. Serve at once, directly from the baking dish.

T i p

If you want to cut down on the fat and the calories in this dish, you can omit the anchovy butter and instead add a large mincing of herbs right into the gnocchi mixture. Once the mixture is cold, the gnocchi can be cut and sautéed in just a touch of olive oil or grilled.

Soft Polenta with Braised Leeks and Mascarpone

To prepare: 5 minutes
To cook: 30 minutes
Serves 4 to 6

2 large leeks, trimmed of all but 2 inches of greens

5 tablespoons unsalted butter

3¼ cups skim milk (or half whole milk and half water)

Salt

¾ cup fine semolina or yellow cornmeal

½ cup mascarpone

Freshly ground black pepper

Tip

Members of the onion family make excellent flavorings for creamy polenta: red and yellow onions, scallions, and leeks. Be sure to cook the onions first in some butter and bouillon until very soft and then add to the polenta just before it is done.

Polenta has become the new favorite Italian side dish. Traditional polenta calls for only three ingredients: milk, cornmeal, and a touch of butter plus seasoning, but the dish allows for many delicious seasonal Spur of the Moment adaptations.

1. Quarter the leeks lengthwise and then cut crosswise into ½-inch pieces. Place in a colander and run under warm water to remove all traces of sand.

2. Melt 2 tablespoons of the butter in a medium skillet. Add the leeks and 2 tablespoons water and simmer, partially covered, until tender. Set aside.

3. In a heavy 3½-quart saucepan, combine the skim milk (or whole milk and water) and ¾ teaspoon salt and bring to a slow boil. Sprinkle in the semolina or cornmeal very slowly, whisking constantly. Reduce the heat to very low and simmer, covered, for 20 minutes, stirring often (a film will form on the bottom of the pan; do not be alarmed).

4. Remove the pan from the heat. Add the leeks, the remaining 3 tablespoons butter, and the mascarpone and fold in gently. Correct the seasoning, adding a large grinding of black pepper. Serve at once.

Curry-and-Cumin-Scented Couscous with Toasted Walnuts

To prepare: 10 minutes

To cook: 10 minutes

Serves 4 to 5

....

2 tablespoons unsalted butter

2 tablespoons walnut oil or olive oil

1 medium onion, peeled and finely minced

1 teaspoon Madras curry powder

½ teaspoon ground cumin

Pinch of cayenne pepper

½ cup toasted walnuts, broken

1 cup couscous, preferably imported

2 cups chicken bouillon

Salt and freshly ground black pepper

T i p

....

Leftover couscous makes a great salad or filling for tomatoes. Add a shallot, balsamic vinegar, and olive oil vinaigrette to it and season assertively. Let sit for at least 30 minutes or even overnight — the taste will only get better.

C o u s c o u s is a "great grain" that loves the company of spices, raisins, and myriad vegetables. Here, good curry powder adds a unique taste to a simple preparation that calls only for your pantry's basics. For those who like their food spicy, add a dicing of fresh cayenne or jalapeño pepper to the oil before adding the onion. Serve the grain with lamb or Spicy Grilled "Kebab-burgers" (page 169) and a Mediterranean cucumber salad, made with seedless cucumbers tossed in yogurt with a touch of garlic and mint.

....

1.   Melt the butter with the oil in a 2-quart saucepan over low heat. Add the onion and cook until soft. Add the curry powder, cumin, cayenne, and walnuts and cook for 1 minute. Add the couscous and the bouillon and season with salt and pepper. Bring to a boil, cover, and remove from the heat. Set aside for 5 minutes.

2.   Fluff the couscous with a fork and serve hot.

Saffron Couscous with Spinach and Red Peppers

To prepare: 15 minutes
To cook: 25 minutes
Serves 4

....

2½ cups chicken bouillon

1 teaspoon saffron threads

2 tablespoons unsalted butter

½ cup finely diced red bell pepper

1 large carrot, peeled, quartered lengthwise, and thinly sliced

2 medium scallions, trimmed and finely minced

1 cup couscous, preferably imported

¼ teaspoon turmeric

1 large garlic clove, peeled and finely minced

1 cup tightly packed fresh spinach leaves, washed, dried, and coarsely chopped

Salt and freshly ground black pepper

Q u i c k couscous takes well to assertive spices such as saffron. This is one of my most popular teaching recipes. The combination of golden couscous with flecks of bright green spinach and red pepper is both colorful and tasty. Serve with marinated pan-seared lamb chops, sautéed fresh tuna, or grilled fish steaks.

....

1. Combine the bouillon and saffron in a saucepan and simmer, covered, for 20 minutes, or until reduced to 2 cups. Set aside.

2. Melt the butter in a 2-quart casserole over low heat. Add the red pepper and carrot and cook, covered, until tender. Add the scallions and cook until just wilted. Add the couscous, saffron broth, and turmeric. Bring to a boil, cover, and remove from the heat. Set aside for 5 minutes.

3. Return the couscous to low heat, add the garlic and spinach, and stir until the spinach is wilted. Season with salt and pepper and serve at once.

T i p

True saffron is Spanish saffron and is generally bought in threads. Now you can also purchase powdered saffron in tiny packages, each one good for one dish. Powdered saffron cannot be stored for any length of time; be sure to keep it refrigerated, preferably in a dark container.

Carrot, Raisin, and Pine Nut Couscous

To prepare: 10 minutes
To cook; 10 minutes
Serves 4

2 tablespoons unsalted butter

2 teaspoons corn oil

1 small onion, peeled and finely minced

1 medium carrot, peeled and diced

1 cup couscous, preferably imported

2 cups chicken bouillon

Salt and freshly ground black pepper

⅓ cup dark raisins, plumped

2 to 3 tablespoons pine nuts, lightly toasted (see page 269)

Juice of ½ lemon, or more to taste

Tip

To plump raisins, place them in a saucepan with water to cover. Bring to a boil, and immediately remove the pan from the heat. Let cool and drain well.

This couscous works particularly well as a side dish to something spicy, such as Grilled Flank Steaks in a Chili-Ginger Marinade (page 174). I usually double the recipe and make a salad with the leftovers by adding the juice of one or two limes, several tablespoons of extra-virgin olive oil, and a large mincing of fresh cilantro. Serve the couscous at room temperature with Roast Chicken Legs with Chili and Cinnamon Rub (page 226).

1. Melt the butter with the oil in a medium saucepan over low heat. Add the onion and carrot and cook until tender. Add the couscous and bouillon, season with salt and pepper, and bring to a boil. Cover, remove from the heat, and set aside for 5 minutes.

2. Fold the raisins, pine nuts, and lemon juice into the couscous. Correct the seasoning, adding a large grinding of pepper and more lemon juice if necessary. Serve at once.

Couscous with Melted Scallions

To prepare: 10 minutes

To cook: 10 minutes

Serves 5

....

4 tablespoons unsalted butter

1 bunch scallions, trimmed and finely minced

1 cup couscous, preferably imported

2 cups chicken bouillon

Salt and freshly ground black pepper

Q u i c k couscous can be made with almost any vegetable, including every member of the onion family. The great delicate taste of what I call melted scallions is especially complementary to the grain, and since I consider scallions a "vegetable bin basic," this dish is something I can put together in a matter of minutes. Serve the couscous with pan-seared scallops or shad, Brochettes of Grilled Shrimp in Sesame Marinade (page 176), or Oven-Braised Salmon Fillets in Lemon Crème Fraîche (page 238).

....

1. Melt the butter in a medium saucepan over low heat. Add the scallions and cook, covered, for about 8 minutes, or until tender. Add the couscous and bouillon, season with salt and pepper, and bring to a boil. Cover, remove from the heat, and set aside for 5 minutes.

2. Correct the seasoning, adding a large grinding of pepper, and fluff the couscous with a fork. Serve at once.

T i p

....

To "melt" scallions, always be sure to add them to warm, not hot, butter and let them cook over very low heat in a touch of broth or water. Adding scallions to very hot fat will give them a bitter aftertaste.

From the Grill

When I FIRST CAME TO AMERICA, I FELL IN LOVE WITH SKYSCRAP-
ERS, MY HUSBAND-TO-BE, AND AMERICAN BARBECUES. I'M HAPPY TO SAY
THAT TWENTY YEARS LATER ALL THESE FEELINGS ARE STILL GOING STRONG.
NO WONDER I FELT SUCH A PASSION FOR BARBECUES. WHAT COULD BE
MORE FOREIGN AND CAPTIVATING TO A EUROPEAN PALATE THAN JUICY CHAR-
BROILED HAMBURGERS, PLUMP HOT DOGS, AND THREE-INCH-THICK T-BONE
STEAKS? NOT TO MENTION EXOTIC CONDIMENTS LIKE TOMATO KETCHUP AND
BRIGHT YELLOW MUSTARD, BOTTLED BARBECUE SAUCE, AND SUPERMARKET
POTATO SALAD AND COLESLAW. EVEN THE SPONGY PACKAGED HAMBURGER
AND HOT DOG ROLLS, WITH ALMOST NO TEXTURE AND VERY LITTLE FLAVOR,

tasted ambrosial when they were lightly toasted on the grill.

Grilling has always been the quintessential Spur of the Moment technique—it's quick, easy, fun, and incredibly delicious. There is no one who doesn't like the tangy, savory charcoal taste of food sizzling from the grill. Somehow even a badly cooked, boring hamburger is pure heaven when it's grilled. And just the scent of the neighbor's grill heating up can make your mouth start watering.

In the past few years, grilling has evolved from basic American picnic food to an imaginative, creative, even sophisticated cuisine that combines the best of American regional tastes with an eclectic assortment of international flavors. And while it remains quick, that's no longer its strongest *raison d'etre*. It now has all the qualities a Spur of the Moment meal should possess: It's spirited, seasonal, flavorful, satisfying, spontaneous. It's the difference between a good plain grilled lamb chop and a show-stopping Sweet-and-Spicy Grilled Butterflied Leg of Lamb with Jalapeño Pepper Marinade (page 170).

If the concept of grilling has been updated, so has the technique. Instead of waiting for coals to heat up (and never knowing if the fire is going to be too hot or too weak), we have powerful gas-jet grills, efficient top-of-the-stove grills, and even recipes for using woks as grills. Serious foodies swear by exotic woods like lilac and apple to subtly flavor foods. We're cooking more vegetables, fish, and side dishes on the grill, and seasoning them with more herbs, more spices, more marinades, more exotic condiments. Char-Grilled Pork Tenderloins in Crushed Coriander and Mustard Marinade (page 173) is a far cry from yet another barbecued chicken breast. Charcoal-roasted eggplant and a salad of sweet roasted peppers are alternatives to a plain baked potato in foil, and not much more demanding.

Spur of the Moment grilling does call for some thought, planning, and organization. Since grilling demands total attention (a steak can go from medium rare to shoe leather in seconds!) and can't wait once it's ready, have your side dishes made ahead of time and keep them warm or at room temperature. Or grill your side dishes while you're doing your main course. Tomatoes, zucchini, eggplant, squash, peppers, and onions are all vegetables that can be grilled directly over the flame with beautiful results. Sometimes I pack a variety of vegetables from my garden into foil packages and "braise" them on the grill alongside my main course.

There's so much about grilling that makes it a winner for today's cook. It's easy to shop for: simple ingredients, inexpensive cuts of meat, basic vegetables. It's easy to substitute one ingredient for another: You're out of lemons, use limes. No olive oil? Try peanut oil. It's easy to make extra and have great leftovers: Tonight's Grilled Chicken Breasts with Chinese Mustard and Honey Glaze (page 164) is tomorrow's sliced chicken sandwich on rosemary focaccia. And when you're outdoors at the end of the perfect summer day, watching a gorgeous sunset, sipping a glass of chilled white wine, laughing with your friends and family, and anticipating a delicious dinner, it's easy to understand why grilling will always be America's favorite way to cook.

Grilled Chicken Breasts with Chinese Mustard and Honey Glaze

To prepare: 5 minutes
To cook: 6 minutes
Serves 6 to 8

6 tablespoons pure honey

1 tablespoon plus 1 teaspoon imported paprika

2 teaspoons dry Chinese mustard

1 teaspoon cayenne pepper

4 whole boneless and skinless chicken breasts, cut in half

2 tablespoons olive oil

Coarse salt

T i p

For freshness, don't trust the sell-by date on the poultry package, unless you shop in a market that has major turnover. Ask the butcher to take the chicken out of its wrapping so that you can smell it, to assure that it is fresh.

F o r the Spur of the Moment cook's repertoire, chicken breasts are a must! They are done in a matter of minutes and go with just about every seasonal vegetable. These delicious, quickly seared chicken breasts are best when grilled on a charcoal or gas grill but can also be sautéed in a skillet and then run under the broiler. I especially like to serve them with steamed spinach flavored with a mashed garlic clove and a touch of butter.

1. Combine the honey, paprika, mustard, and cayenne in a bowl and mix well.

2. Prepare the grill.

3. Brush the chicken with the oil, sprinkle with coarse salt, and grill over white-hot coals for 5 to 6 minutes, turning once. Brush with the honey mixture and grill 1 minute longer, or until the chicken is nicely glazed. Serve hot with steamed spinach or Curried Leek and Raisin Chutney (page 257).

Grilled Chicken in Lemon-Cumin Marinade

To prepare: 10 minutes
To marinate: 30 minutes
To cook: 30 minutes
Serves 4 to 6

....

Juice of 1 large lemon

6 tablespoons extra-virgin olive oil

1½ teaspoons ground cumin

2 tablespoons finely minced fresh thyme or 1 tablespoon dried thyme

Large pinch of cayenne pepper

1 teaspoon coarsely ground black pepper

2 large garlic cloves, peeled and mashed

8 small chicken legs with thighs attached

Coarse salt

Tip

....

Since the coals will still be nice and hot after grilling the chicken, take advantage of them and roast some tomatoes (cut in half and placed on heavy-duty foil) or some colorful peppers, which you can set aside for another meal.

H e r e is a recipe particularly suited to the Weber kettle grill, which I use constantly from early spring through late fall. You can, however, achieve excellent results by using a gas grill or a broiler. As a variation, I often prepare quartered Cornish hens the same way, and I always make use of the coals for a side dish as well, such as Charcoal-Roasted Eggplant with Lemon-Scallion Mayonnaise (page 183), or grilled thickly sliced zucchini.

1. Combine all the ingredients except the salt and the chicken in a small bowl and whisk until well blended. Pour the marinade into a large Ziploc bag, add the chicken, and seal the bag. Marinate at room temperature for at least 30 minutes, or marinate in the refrigerator for 1 hour or longer.

2. Prepare the charcoal grill with briquettes on one side only. Open all the vents.

3. When the coals are almost all white, sprinkle the chicken with salt and place it, skin side down, directly above the coals. Grill for 5 minutes, or until browned on all sides. Move the chicken to the side of the grill away from the coals, brush heavily with the marinade, and sprinkle with additional coarse black pepper. Grill, covered, for 20 minutes, or until the juices run pale yellow, turning the chicken and basting once or twice with the marinade. Transfer to a serving platter and serve.

Grilled Cornish Hens in a Tangy Lime and Onion Marinade

To prepare: 15 minutes
To marinate: 6 hours, or
overnight
To cook: 1 hour and 10
minutes
Serves 4 to 6

....

3 Cornish hens, quartered and
  backbone removed

4 large garlic cloves, peeled and
  finely minced

Juice of 5 limes

1 tablespoon finely minced jalapeño pepper or 3 small dried
  red chili peppers, broken

2 to 3 tablespoons finely minced
  fresh thyme or 1½ teaspoons
  dried thyme

6 tablespoons extra-virgin olive oil

Coarse salt and freshly ground
  black pepper

5 medium onions, peeled and
  thinly sliced

1 bay leaf, preferably Turkish,
  crumbled

½ to ¾ cup chicken bouillon

1 teaspoon arrowroot mixed with
  a little bouillon

GARNISH
Sprigs of fresh thyme

S i n c e I love the taste of marinated foods, I make this marinade in quantity and keep it refrigerated until needed. Spices such as chili powder, curry, cumin, and garam masala (an Indian blend of spices) can also be added, as well as minced ginger and a mixture of herbs such as oregano and rosemary.

....

1.   Place the Cornish hen pieces in a large Ziploc bag. Combine the garlic, lime juice, jalapeño or chili peppers, thyme, and 2 tablespoons of the oil in a mixing bowl and whisk until well blended. Season with coarse salt and black pepper, and add the onions and bay leaf. Pour the marinade over the chicken, seal the bag, place in a shallow dish, and refrigerate for at least 6 hours, or overnight, turning the hens several times in the marinade.

2.   Remove the hens from the marinade. Strain the marinade and set the onions and the marinade aside separately.

3.   In a heavy 12-inch skillet, heat the remaining 4 tablespoons oil over medium-high heat. Add the onions and cook for 5 minutes, stirring constantly, until they begin to brown. Reduce the heat and continue to cook, partially covered, until the onions are very soft and nicely browned, about 30 to 35 minutes. Add the reserved marinade and reduce, uncovered, to a glaze. Remove from the heat and set the skillet aside.

4. Prepare the charcoal grill.

5. When the coals are white-hot, place the Cornish hen pieces on the grill directly above the coals and grill, turning once or twice, until nicely browned on all sides.

6. Transfer the hens to the 12-inch skillet and spoon the onion mixture over them. Add 2 to 3 tablespoons bouillon and bring to a simmer. Simmer, partially covered, for 15 to 20 minutes, or until the juices run pale yellow, adding a little bouillon to the skillet every 5 to 10 minutes.

7. Transfer the hens to a serving platter and, using a slotted spoon, top them with the onions. Add the remaining bouillon to the skillet, bring to a boil, and whisk in the arrowroot mixture bit by bit until the sauce lightly coats a spoon. Taste and correct the seasoning. Spoon the sauce over the hens. Garnish with sprigs of thyme and serve hot.

T i p

Small whole chicken legs, with thighs attached, can be substituted for the Cornish hens. Use 8 whole legs and cut them in half at the joint, which will give you 8 thighs and 8 drumsticks. They will take about 20 to 25 minutes of simmering in the onion mixture.

Yogurt-and-Ginger-Marinated Smoked Chicken Wings

To prepare: 20 minutes
To marinate: 6 hours, or
overnight
To cook: 30 minutes
Serves 4

1 medium onion, peeled and
quartered

4 large garlic cloves, peeled

One 1-inch piece fresh ginger,
peeled and coarsely chopped

1 small jalapeño pepper or 1 teaspoon red pepper flakes

2 cups plain yogurt

Optional: 1½ tablespoons tandoori seasoning

1 tablespoon ground cumin

20 chicken wingette pieces

Coarse salt and freshly ground
black pepper

1 cup hickory chips, soaked in
water for 30 minutes

1 recipe Spicy Warm Peanut
Sauce (page 186)

T i p

Instead of hickory chips, try the "designer" wood chips now avail-able, or simply use fresh green woods such as apple, lilac, or cherry, which impart a delicious, subtle smoky flavor.

"**W i n g e t t e s** '' are one of the new supermar-ket staples. I find myself cooking them often, especially during the warmer months when I can use the grill. These juicy little morsels make a quick and easy main course when served with the Endive and Young Spin-ach Salad with Roasted Cumin Vinaigrette (page 63).

1. Process the onion, garlic, ginger, and jalapeño pepper or pepper flakes in a food processor until finely minced. Add the yogurt, optional tandoori sea-soning, and cumin and process until smooth. Trans-fer to a large Ziploc bag, add the wingettes, and seal the bag. Refrigerate for at least 6 hours, or over-night, turning the bag often.

2. Prepare the charcoal grill with briquettes on one side only. Open all the vents.

3. When the coals are white-hot, remove the win-gettes from the marinade, sprinkle with coarse salt and pepper, and place on the grill directly above the coals. Grill for 3 to 5 minutes, or until browned on all sides. Move the wings to the side of the grill away from the coals. Drain the hickory chips and add to the coals. Cover the grill and "roast" for 20 to 25 minutes, or until the juices run pale yellow.

4. Transfer the wingettes to a platter and serve hot with a bowl of the peanut sauce on the side.

Spicy Grilled "Kebab-burgers"

To prepare: 20 minutes
To cook: 3 to 5 minutes
Serves 4

....

1 pound ground lamb

1 cup fresh bread crumbs

2 tablespoons grated onion

3 tablespoons finely minced fresh
   parsley

2 large garlic cloves, peeled and
   mashed

⅛ teaspoon cayenne pepper, or
   more to taste

¼ teaspoon ground cinnamon

1 teaspoon ground cumin

2 extra-large eggs

3 tablespoons pine nuts, sautéed
   in a little olive oil until golden
   (see page 269)

Salt and freshly ground black
   pepper

4 wooden skewers, soaked in
   water for 30 minutes

T i p

....

*To fry the kebab-burgers: Heat ¼
inch of peanut oil in a heavy skillet over medium-high heat. Roll
the balls lightly in flour, shaking
off the excess, and add to the hot
oil, without crowding. Sauté until
nicely browned on all sides but
still rare in the center, about 4 to
5 minutes. Drain on paper towels.*

H e r e is a classic **Middle Eastern** dish that is perfectly suited for the Spur of the Moment cook. You can
experiment with the spices, making the ground meat
mixture more or less spicy. If you cannot buy lamb
already ground, purchase lamb shoulder and finely
mince in a food processor. My favorite accompaniment
is a vegetable paella, but if you are pressed for time, a
side dish of garlic-flavored yogurt along with the Fricassee of Peppers in Spicy Crème Fraîche (page 259)
will make for a perfect weekday meal.

....

1.   Combine the lamb, bread crumbs, onion, parsley, garlic, spices, eggs, and pine nuts in a large bowl
and mix well. Season generously with salt and pepper. You might want to sauté a little of the mixture
to taste for seasoning and add more cayenne, cinnamon, cumin, salt, and/or pepper to taste.

2.   Shape the meat mixture into 1½-inch balls.
Thread the kebab-burgers onto the skewers and set
aside.

3.   Prepare the charcoal grill.

4.   When the coals are white-hot, place the kebabs
on the grill directly above the coals and grill for 3
to 5 minutes, turning several times, until nicely
browned but still rare in the center. Serve hot.

Sweet-and-Spicy Grilled Butterflied Leg of Lamb with Jalapeño Pepper Marinade

To prepare: 10 minutes
To marinate: 1 to 6
hours, or overnight
To cook: 25 to 30
minutes
Serves 4 to 6

....

2 cups diced onions

3 large garlic cloves, peeled and
minced

1 jalapeño pepper, sliced

1 tablespoon finely minced fresh
ginger

1 cup fresh cilantro leaves

Juice of 2 lemons

1 teaspoon coriander seeds,
toasted and crushed

⅓ cup olive oil

Coarse salt and coarsely cracked
black pepper

1 leg of lamb (about 6 to 6½
pounds), boned and butterflied

THE GLAZE
3 tablespoons pure honey

2 tablespoons soy sauce

1 egg yolk

2 cups mesquite chips, soaked in
water for 30 minutes

A g r i l l e d butterflied leg of lamb has replaced
the steak as our favorite warm-weather food. Here is a
version that is rather spicy and extremely flavorful.
The lamb takes minutes to prepare but needs to marinate for at least one hour at room temperature, or four
to six hours or overnight in the refrigerator, so save
this recipe for your weekend repertoire. Serve with
Charcoal Roasted Eggplant with Lemon-Scallion Mayonnaise (page 183) and a fricassee of summer vegetables.

Any leftover sliced lamb makes a fabulous open-
faced sandwich served on lightly grilled bread and
topped with cilantro and sliced avocados. A drizzle of
Roasted Cumin Vinaigrette (page 63) gives this supper
sandwich a flavorful finishing touch.

....

1.   Combine the onions, garlic, jalapeño pepper,
ginger, cilantro, lemon juice, coriander seeds, and oil
in a food processor and process until finely minced.
Season with coarse salt and cracked pepper. Pour
the marinade into a large Ziploc bag, add the lamb,
and seal the bag. Marinate at room temperature for
1 hour or, preferably, refrigerate for 4 to 6 hours,
or overnight.

2.   Prepare the charcoal grill.

3.   Combine the glaze ingredients and set aside.

4. When the coals are almost all white, sprinkle the drained mesquite chips over them. Remove the lamb from the marinade. Place directly above the coals and grill for 10 minutes. Turn and grill for another 15 minutes for medium-rare; the lamb will register an internal temperature of 135° to 140°F in the thickest part, on a meat thermometer. Brush with the glaze and grill for another 1 to 2 minutes. Cut crosswise on the bias into thin slices and serve at once.

T i p

Although butterflied leg of lamb is one of the great cuts of meat, it is difficult to grill evenly since it is usually much thicker in some parts than in others. If you want to be sure that all the lamb is evenly cooked, have the lamb cut into cubes for shish-kebabs and skewer it, which will cut way back on the grilling time and give you a more even result.

Pepper-and-Sage-Grilled Pork Tenderloins

To prepare: 5 minutes
To cook: 20 minutes
Serves 4

2 teaspoons black peppercorns

2 small dried red chili peppers, broken

1½ teaspoons coarse salt

3 large garlic cloves, peeled

3 tablespoons fresh sage leaves

2 pork tenderloins (about 1½ pounds total), trimmed of all fat

2 tablespoons olive oil

GARNISH
Fresh sage leaves

Tip

Pork tenderloins, commonly sold in packages of two, have usually been frozen and then defrosted by the supermarket before they go on sale. Use them by the expiration date on the label, and do not re-freeze.

On a busy day, my choice for a flavorful and easy main course is often tenderloin of pork. It is quick to prepare, widely available. Try it with Curried Leek and Raisin Chutney (page 257) or Tuscan Fricassee of Savoy Cabbage and Pancetta (page 251). Or take advantage of the hot fire and grill some eggplant (see Charcoal-Roasted Eggplant with Lemon-Scallion Mayonnaise, page 183, for the technique). Peel and chop the grilled eggplant and toss with fruity olive oil and plenty of mashed garlic.

1. Combine the peppercorns, chili peppers, and coarse salt in a small grinder and process to a medium grind. Add the garlic and sage and process to a paste. Rub the paste all over the tenderloins and set aside.

2. Prepare the charcoal grill with briquettes on one side only. Open all the vents.

3. When the coals are almost white, brush the tenderloins with the olive oil and place directly above the coals. Grill for 5 minutes, or until browned on all sides. Move the tenderloins to the side of the grill away from the coals, cover, and "roast" for 10 to 12 minutes, or until the juices run pale pink and the internal temperature registers between 145° and 150°F on a meat thermometer.

4. Transfer to a cutting board and let sit for 5 minutes. Then slice crosswise on the bias into ½-inch slices. Place on a serving platter and garnish with sage leaves. Serve hot or at room temperature.

Char-Grilled Pork Tenderloins in Crushed Coriander and Mustard Marinade

To prepare: 5 minutes
To marinate: 1 hour, or
overnight
To cook: 20 minutes
Serves 4

5 tablespoons soy sauce

3 tablespoons red wine vinegar

2 tablespoons Dijon mustard

2 large garlic cloves, peeled and mashed

1 tablespoon coriander seeds, toasted and crushed

1 teaspoon cracked black pepper

1 tablespoon Chinese sesame seed oil

2 pork tenderloins (about 1½ pounds total), trimmed of all fat

GARNISH
Sprigs of fresh cilantro

Tip

Pork, unlike beef, has a short shelf life, so always use it the day you purchase it, unless it is vacuum-packed.

If pork tenderloins are not available, Cornish hens are equally good bathed in this zesty marinade and grilled. Good side dishes are the Creamy Polenta with Jalapeño Peppers, Corn, and Two Cheeses (page 151), a red onion jam, or a quick stir-fry of colorful bell peppers.

1. Combine the soy sauce, vinegar, mustard, garlic, coriander seeds, black pepper, and sesame seed oil in a small bowl and whisk until well blended. Pour into a large zip-lock bag, add the pork, and seal the bag. Set aside at room temperature for 1 hour, or refrigerate overnight.

2. Prepare the charcoal grill with briquettes on one side only. Open all the vents.

3. When the coals are almost white, place the tenderloins directly above the coals and grill, turning occasionally, for 5 minutes, or until browned on all sides. Move the pork to the side of the grill away from the coals, cover, and "roast" for 10 to 12 minutes, or until the juices run pale pink and the internal temperature registers between 145° and 150°F on a meat thermometer.

4. Transfer to a cutting board and let sit for 5 minutes. Then slice crosswise on the bias into ½-inch slices. Place on a serving platter, garnish with cilantro, and serve hot.

Grilled Flank Steaks
in a Chili-Ginger Marinade

To prepare: 15 minutes
To marinate: 1 hour, or
overnight
To cook: 15 minutes
Serves 4 to 6

2 large garlic cloves, peeled and
finely minced

1 tablespoon finely minced fresh
ginger

1 medium onion, peeled and
thinly sliced

2 tablespoons finely minced fresh
cilantro

1 tablespoon ground cumin

1 tablespoon pure chili powder

2 teaspoons dried oregano

½ cup olive oil

Juice of 1 large lemon

2 tablespoons black soy sauce

1 to 2 canned smoked chipotle
peppers in adobo sauce,
finely minced

2 flank steaks (about 1½ to 2
pounds each), trimmed of
all fat

Coarse salt

GARNISH
Sprigs of fresh cilantro

I consider flank steak one of the best cuts of meat. If I see them on sale at the market, I will often buy more than one. I marinate flank steaks in a variety of marinades, and this spicy flavor-packed one is probably my favorite. Be sure not to overcook the meat. Serve with Curried Leek and Raisin Chutney (page 257), Wild Mushroom Polenta with Thyme and Aged Goat Cheese (page 152), or a medley of roasted vegetables. Leftover flank steak makes a terrific open-faced sandwich topped with a red onion jam and served with Savory Prune and Bacon Clafoutis (page 104).

1. Combine the garlic, ginger, onion, cilantro, cumin, chili powder, oregano, oil, lemon juice, soy sauce, and chipotle peppers in a mixing bowl. Pour into a large zip-lock bag. Add the steaks, seal the bag, and set aside at room temperature for 1 hour, or refrigerate overnight, turning the steaks in the marinade several times.

2. Prepare the charcoal grill.

3. Remove the steaks from the marinade and set aside, reserving the marinade separately.

4. When the coals are red-hot, sprinkle the steaks on both sides with coarse salt. Brush the grill with vegetable oil and place the steaks directly above the hot coals. Grill for 5 to 6 minutes, or until the steaks are nicely browned on one side and they begin to tighten up and slightly curl; brush often with the marinade. Turn over and grill for another 3 to 4 minutes for medium-rare (about 130° to 135°F internal temperature on a meat thermometer).

5.   Transfer the steaks to a cutting board and let sit for 5 minutes before slicing. Cut the meat across the grain, on the bias, into thin slices. Garnish with sprigs of cilantro and serve warm or at room temperature.

T i p

Flank steak is a cut of meat that is at its best when marinated, but if you do not have the time to marinate it, simply brush the marinade on during the grilling time. Be sure to use a highly seasoned marinade with plenty of spice and character to infuse the meat with flavor.

Brochettes of Grilled Shrimp
in Sesame Marinade

To prepare: 10 minutes
To marinate: 30 minutes
To cook: 4 minutes
Serves 6

....

2 tablespoons soy sauce

¼ cup rice vinegar

1 tablespoon minced fresh ginger

2 large garlic cloves, peeled and finely minced

1 tablespoon granulated sugar

1 teaspoon finely minced jalapeño pepper

⅓ cup olive oil

1 tablespoon Chinese sesame seed oil

3 to 6 drops Tabasco sauce

30 large shrimp, peeled

Coarse salt and freshly ground black pepper

6 wooden skewers, soaked in water for 30 minutes

GARNISH
Sprigs of fresh cilantro

T i p

....

Be sure to limit your marinating time for shrimp to 30 minutes, or the shellfish will "cook" in the marinade.

H e r e is a marinade that doubles as a delicious vinaigrette or dipping sauce. You can use it with pan-seared or grilled sea scallops instead of shrimp, or with grilled chicken breasts cut into one-and-a-half-inch pieces. For a more interesting and colorful presentation, alternate the shrimp with thick onion slices and large cubes of different colored peppers. Serve with a side dish of the marinade and a curried couscous (see page 157).

....

1.   Combine the soy sauce, vinegar, ginger, garlic, sugar, and jalapeño pepper in a medium mixing bowl. Whisk in the olive and sesame seed oils in a slow stream, then add the Tabasco. Add the shrimp and marinate for 30 minutes at room temperature.

2.   Prepare the charcoal grill.

3.   Remove the shrimp from the marinade and thread 5 on each skewer. Sprinkle with a little coarse salt and cracked pepper and grill over very hot coals for 1 to 2 minutes per side, or until pink and nicely browned. Transfer the brochettes to individual serving plates, garnish with cilantro, and serve hot.

Grilled Salmon with Cracked White Pepper and Dill Rub

To prepare: 5 minutes
plus 45 minutes to cure
salmon
To cook: 10 minutes
Serves 4

....

2 teaspoons coarse salt

2 teaspoons white peppercorns,
   coarsely ground

2 teaspoons granulated sugar

Juice of 1 large lemon

⅔ cup finely minced fresh dill

1½ pounds salmon fillet in one
   piece, preferably center-cut,
   with skin on

2 teaspoons olive oil

GARNISH
A few drops of lemon juice

Sprigs of fresh dill

ACCOMPANIMENT
1 recipe Tomato and Cucumber
   Vinaigrette (page 187)

H e r e is a dry marinade that follows the principles of the famous "gravlax" concept — but while gravlax requires twelve to twenty-four hours of marinating, this "cure" produces excellent results for salmon in about forty-five minutes. Since the salmon is cured only for a short time, it should then be grilled or pan-seared. I like this dish best when accompanied by sautéed cucumbers, butter-glazed beets, or skillet-braised Belgian endives.

....

1. Mix together the salt, pepper, sugar, lemon juice, and minced dill and rub all over the salmon. Set aside at room temperature for 45 minutes.

2. Prepare the charcoal grill.

3. Wipe the marinade off the salmon, brush with the oil, and sprinkle with a little coarse salt and white pepper. Grill over hot coals for 4 to 5 minutes per side, or until just opaque in the center; the internal temperature should register 120° to 125°F on a meat thermometer. Sprinkle with lemon juice, garnish with sprigs of dill, and serve warm with the vinaigrette on the side.

T i p

....

To me, most fish, particularly salmon and tuna, is at its best when undercooked. To test for doneness, insert the tip of a paring knife into the thickest part of the fish for 10 seconds. Then place the flat side of the blade gently against your cheek or wrist. If the blade is cold, the fish is undercooked. If just warm, the fish is done. If hot, the fish is overcooked.

Grilled Tuna Steaks with Basil-Scented Orzo

To prepare: 20 minutes
To marinate: 30 minutes
To cook: 15 minutes
Serves 4

....

Juice of 1 lemon

6 tablespoons extra-virgin olive oil

2 tuna steaks (about ¾ pound each), cut ¾ inch thick

1 large garlic clove, peeled and finely minced

¼ cup fresh basil leaves

⅓ cup mayonnaise

Coarse salt and freshly ground black pepper

1 cup orzo

2 teaspoons coarsely cracked black pepper

GARNISH
Tiny fresh basil leaves

Here is a recipe that came about in a rather strange way. Because of my new passion for orzo, I was trying to figure out a way I could serve these little pasta jewels as a one-dish meal. After trying to team the orzo with a variety of shellfish, I turned to a lovely piece of tuna I had just bought. It complemented the orzo so nicely that I have since kept this marriage of ingredients with occasional seasonal changes, substituting parsley, dill, and/or chives for the basil.

....

1. Whisk together the lemon juice and 4 tablespoons of the oil in a small bowl. Pour over the tuna and let marinate at room temperature for 30 minutes.

2. Prepare the charcoal grill.

3. While the tuna is marinating, prepare the orzo: Puree the garlic, basil, and remaining 2 tablespoons oil in a food processor until smooth. Add the mayonnaise and season with salt and pepper. Reserve.

4. Drop the orzo into boiling salted water and cook for 6 to 8 minutes, or until just tender. Drain well and toss with the basil mixture. Correct the seasoning and keep warm in a double boiler over lukewarm water.

5. When the coals are white-hot, remove the tuna from the marinade and sprinkle both sides with coarse salt and the cracked pepper. Place the tuna on the grill directly above the coals. Grill for 3 to 4 minutes per side, or until nicely browned on the outside but still translucent in the center.

6.   Cut the tuna steaks crosswise, against the grain, into ½-inch slices. Serve warm on individual plates, garnished with tiny basil leaves and the warm orzo on the side.

T i p

Always choose tuna that is uniform in color and with flesh that looks shiny and translucent. Avoid tuna with flesh that looks dull and/or has very dark areas.

Charred Red Peppers Filled with Couscous in a Cumin Vinaigrette

To prepare: 20 minutes
To marinate: 1 hour
To cook: 15 minutes
Serves 6

....

VINAIGRETTE
Juice of 1 lemon

1 tablespoon sherry vinegar

1 large garlic clove, mashed

½ teaspoon cumin seeds, toasted
    and crushed (see page 63),
    or ½ teaspoon ground cumin

6 to 8 tablespoons extra-virgin
    olive oil

Salt and freshly ground black
    pepper

COUSCOUS
2 tablespoons olive oil

½ cup finely minced scallions

½ cup finely diced red bell
    pepper

½ cup finely diced zucchini

1 cup imported quick couscous

2 cups chicken bouillon

Salt and freshly ground pepper

3 tablespoons finely minced fresh
    parsley

6 roasted red bell peppers (see
    page 182), peeled and left
    whole

Charcoal or gas-charred—as opposed to oven-broiled—peppers retain much of their crispness and lend themselves well to stuffings. For a lovely and quick appetizer, I like to toss couscous in a well-flavored vinaigrette, stuff it into the roasted peppers, and serve them on individual plates with two or three sprigs of arugula. Half a pepper is often enough for a starter or side dish to grilled meats, poultry, or fish.

....

1. Start by making the vinaigrette: In a small bowl, combine the lemon, vinegar, garlic, and cumin. Slowly add the oil, whisking constantly until smooth and creamy. Season with salt and pepper.

2. Make the couscous: Heat the oil in a 2½-quart saucepan over medium heat. Add the scallions, red pepper, and zucchini and cook, covered, for 5 minutes, or until tender. Add the couscous and bouillon and season with salt and pepper. Bring to a boil, cover tightly, and immediately remove from the heat. Set aside for 10 minutes.

3. Pour the vinaigrette over the couscous, add the parsley, and correct the seasoning. Toss gently with a fork and let marinate at room temperature for at least 1 hour.

4. To serve, carefully cut a circle around the stem of each roasted pepper with a sharp knife. Remove and discard the stems and carefully remove all the seeds from the inside of each pepper with a small spoon, keeping the peppers whole. Fill the peppers with the couscous, and serve at room temperature.

T i p

You can substitute a variety of vinaigrettes for the cumin vinaigrette. Also, any extra couscous can be served at room temperature as an accompaniment to grilled meats or fish.

Fire-Roasted Bell Peppers

To prepare: 10 minutes
To cook: 5 to 8 minutes

....

Red, green, yellow, and/or
orange bell peppers

Tip

....

If you roast peppers on an outdoor grill, put them directly on the hot coals and turn them often to char them evenly. I usually use the coals when they are just starting to heat up. Be sure to use an electric starter, rather than lighter fluid, if you are going to grill peppers this way.

R o a s t e d peppers will keep for several days in the refrigerator if covered with olive oil. You may also roast variety peppers (jalapeño, Anaheim, poblano) and fresh tomatoes in the same manner. Tomatoes do not need to be wrapped in damp towels after roasting, just set aside to peel and seed.

....

To char the peppers outdoors:

1. Prepare the charcoal grill.

2. When the coals are red-hot, place the peppers directly on top of the coals and grill until the skins are somewhat blackened and charred on all sides. Remove from the grill, wrap in damp paper towels, and set aside to cool completely.

3. Peel off the charred skin, core the peppers, and remove the seeds.

To char peppers indoors, on an electric or gas stove:

Pierce each pepper with a long fork through the stem end. For an electric stove, place the peppers directly on the coils of a burner at medium-high heat and char on all sides. For a gas stove, set the peppers over a medium-high flame and char on all sides. Wrap in damp paper towels, set aside to cool completely, and proceed as directed in step 3 above.

Charcoal-Roasted Eggplant with Lemon-Scallion Mayonnaise

To prepare: 10 minutes
To cook: 10 minutes
Serves 4

....

2 medium eggplants

Juice of ½ lemon, or more to taste

½ to ¾ cup mayonnaise, to taste

1 large garlic clove, peeled and mashed

¼ cup finely minced scallions

Salt and freshly ground black pepper

OPTIONAL GARNISH
Small black oil-cured olives

Small ripe cherry tomatoes, halved

Tip

....

When grilling whole eggplants, be careful not to pierce the skin. Use tongs to turn them since pricking would release the delicious juices, making the eggplant lose much of its smoky taste.

There are dishes one grows up with that simply become family treasures. Smokey charcoal-grilled eggplant, diced and bound with a few tablespoons of mayonnaise and minced scallions, is just such a dish. I serve it often as an appetizer on grilled peasant bread with a plate of cherry tomatoes or as a filling for small ripe tomatoes. Mostly it is a favorite accompaniment to almost anything grilled, be it chicken, beef, or lamb. It can be prepared outside, directly on hot charcoal, or indoors, over a gas flame. It takes more time to cook on the coils of an electric stove, but the result is still terrific. Purchase eggplants that are firm and light in weight for their size.

....

1. Prepare the charcoal grill.

2. When the coals are very hot, place the eggplants directly on the coals and grill until the skin is charred on all sides and the eggplants are quite tender. Be careful not to char beneath the skin.

3. Remove the eggplants carefully from the grill, transfer to a cutting surface, and cut in half lengthwise. Scoop out the pulp, cut it into cubes, and place in a shallow serving dish. Add the lemon juice, mayonnaise, garlic, and scallions, season with salt and pepper, and fold gently. Correct the seasoning, adding more lemon juice if necessary. Serve warm or at room temperature, garnished with the optional black olives and cherry tomatoes.

Apple Wood Smoked Turkey with Mustard-Herb Crust

To prepare: 5 minutes
To cook: 1 hour and 30 minutes
Serves 6 to 8

....

3 large garlic cloves, peeled and mashed

2 teaspoons dried thyme

2 teaspoons dried marjoram

1 tablespoon imported paprika

2 tablespoons Dijon mustard

1 fresh whole turkey (about 7 pounds)

Coarse salt and freshly ground black pepper

1 pound fresh green apple wood twigs

GARNISH
Sprigs of fresh watercress

I am a great believer in cooking small turkeys and would rather use two eight- to nine-pound turkeys than one sixteen pounder. The larger the turkey, the more chances for it to dry out during roasting. A small turkey should be roasted either in a 450°F oven or on the grill. In either case, it will take only about one and a half hours and will be nice and juicy.

....

1. In a small bowl, combine the garlic, thyme, marjoram, paprika, and mustard and mix well. Dry the turkey thoroughly with paper towels and rub the herb mixture over the entire surface of the bird. Season with coarse salt and pepper inside and out and truss.

2. Prepare a round kettle-type charcoal grill about 22½ inches in diameter (preferably Weber): Open all the vents. Place 30 briquettes on the lower grill and ignite the charcoal. When the coals are white-hot, carefully push them to one side. Set a rectangular disposable roasting pan, slightly larger than the turkey, alongside the coals. Position the cooking grill in the kettle with one handle directly over the mound of coals; this will allow you to add briquettes through the opening by the grill handle during smoking.

3.   Place the turkey on the cooking grill, breast side up, directly over the roasting pan. Add a few twigs of apple wood to the pile of coals, cover, and "roast" the turkey for about 12 minutes per pound, or until it registers an internal temperature of 180°F on a meat thermometer. The turkey will need no basting or turning, but every 20 minutes, add 6 more briquettes and a few twigs of apple wood to the pile of burning coals (through the opening at the grill handle).

4.   When the turkey is done, transfer to a carving board and remove the trussing string. Let sit for 15 minutes before carving.

5.   Carve the turkey and place on a large serving platter. Garnish with the watercress and serve with Sweet Yellow Corn Pudding (page 263) and Red Onion Jam with Red Wine and Cassis (page 249).

T i p

Good-quality paprika is usually imported from Hungary and comes in cans that are labeled either "hot" or "sweet." I prefer the sweet paprika since this allows you to flavor a dish to your taste and does not impose a hot spicy taste on every preparation. Be sure to refrigerate paprika once the can has been opened since the delicate aroma of this spice dissipates easily.

Sauces for Grilled Fish

All serve 4 to 6

TANGY LIME AND CHIPOTLE PEPPER DIPPING SAUCE

Combine ½ cup mayonnaise, ½ cup sour cream, 1 tablespoon grated onion, 2 finely minced garlic cloves, 1 to 2 finely minced canned chipotle peppers in adobo sauce, and the juice of ½ lime in a bowl and mix well. Season with salt and more lime juice if necessary. Serve with grilled shellfish.

CRÈME FRAÎCHE, SHALLOT, AND CHIVE SAUCE

Combine ¾ cup crème fraîche (see page 31), 2 tablespoons finely minced shallots, ¼ cup finely minced fresh chives, and 2 teaspoons red wine vinegar in a small bowl and whisk until well blended. Season with salt and freshly ground black pepper and serve at room temperature with pan-seared or grilled salmon.

CHILLED LEMON-DILL SAUCE

Combine ½ cup each crème fraîche (see page 31) and softened cream cheese, 1 tablespoon fresh lemon juice, and the finely grated zest of 1 lemon in a small bowl and whisk until well blended. Fold in 3 tablespoons finely minced fresh dill or chives and 2 tablespoons red salmon caviar (optional) and season with salt and freshly ground black pepper. Serve lightly chilled with braised or sautéed fish steaks or fillets.

SPICY WARM PEANUT SAUCE

Heat 1 tablespoon peanut oil over low heat in a small skillet. Add 2 teaspoons each finely minced garlic and ginger and 1 teaspoon tomato paste and cook for 1 minute. Add ⅔ cup chicken bouillon, 1½ teaspoons chili paste, and 2 tablespoons each hoisin sauce and smooth peanut butter and whisk until well blended. Simmer for 2 to 3 minutes and whisk in 2 teaspoons of Chinese sesame seed oil. Serve warm with grilled shellfish.

MUSTARD, CAPER, AND JALAPEÑO PEPPER MAYONNAISE

Combine 1 cup mayonnaise, 2 tablespoons sour cream, 2 teaspoons Dijon mustard, 1 tablespoon drained tiny capers, 2 tablespoons finely minced shallots, 1 finely minced hard-boiled egg, 1 teaspoon fresh lemon juice, 1½ tablespoons finely minced dill gherkins, and 1 teaspoon finely minced jalapeño pepper in a small bowl. Season with salt and freshly ground white pepper and mix well. Serve chilled with fish fritters or with grilled fish or shellfish.

TOMATO AND CUCUMBER VINAIGRETTE

Sprinkle ½ cup very finely diced peeled and seeded cucumber with a little coarse salt in a strainer and drain for 30 minutes. Then squeeze gently in a kitchen towel and set aside. Puree 3 large ripe peeled, seeded, and chopped tomatoes together with 1 tablespoon finely minced red onion, 2 tablespoons sherry vinegar, and ½ cup extra-virgin olive oil in a food processor until smooth. Pass through a sieve into a small bowl. Add the cucumber and ¼ cup finely minced fresh dill and season with salt and freshly ground black pepper. Serve with grilled or pan-seared salmon, scallops, or swordfish.

GINGER-TAMARI DIPPING SAUCE

Combine 3 tablespoons tamari or thin soy sauce, the juice of 2 limes, 6 tablespoons extra-virgin olive oil, 1 peeled and mashed large garlic clove, one ½-inch piece peeled fresh ginger, mashed through a garlic press, and 3 tablespoons finely minced scallions in a small bowl. Season with freshly ground white pepper and whisk until well blended. Serve with fish fritters or with a carpaccio of tuna.

Quick Sautés and Skillet Skills

Everything in LIFE SEEMS TO GO IN CYCLES, FROM HEM-
LINES TO ARCHITECTURE TO COOKING TECHNIQUES. SKILLET COOKING, FOR
EXAMPLE, HAS BEEN A BASIC AMERICAN COOKING TECHNIQUE FOR GENER-
ATIONS. AND WELL-SEASONED BLACK CAST-IRON SKILLETS (ALONG WITH THE
FAMILY FRIED CHICKEN RECIPE!) WOULD BE PASSED DOWN FROM MOTHER TO
DAUGHTER. BUT BY THE TIME I MOVED TO THIS COUNTRY FROM EUROPE, I
WAS SURPRISED TO SEE THAT HARDLY ANYONE WAS DOING TOP-OF-THE-
STOVE COOKING. OVEN-COOKING AND BROILING HAD BECOME THE TWO MOST
POPULAR WAYS TO COOK FOOD SIMPLY AND QUICKLY.

YEARS LATER, HEMLINES ARE UP, POST-MODERN ARCHITECTURE IS
out, and skillet cooking is back. Sau-
téing, pan-searing, and top-of-the-
stove braising are enjoying a
delicious renaissance. This is especially good news for the Spur
of the Moment cook, since, to my
mind, there is simply no faster or
more rewarding way to produce good food in a matter of minutes.

The introduction of classic
French and Mediterranean cooking
to the American kitchen, along with
the irresistible tastes of the New
American cuisine, clearly hastened
the cycle. Who hasn't relished the
smoky, savory taste of a blackened

redfish, mustardy pan-seared lamb chops, or a crackling pepper-coated tuna steak? Quickly seared, highly seasoned, immensely juicy, and intensely flavorful—it makes you wonder how skillet cooking fell out of favor!

And just about anything goes: scallops, scaloppine, swordfish, steak. Once you understand the basic procedure and pick the right skillet, you can do everything from caramelizing corn to stir-frying carrots or mushrooms. With chicken and meat, the technique is the same. The object is to make the food nice and brown on the outside while keeping it juicy and tender inside. First, the foods are browned quickly over high heat. Then they're usually braised, covered, over low heat, moistened with stock, bouillon, or wine. Once you've sautéed and braised, you deglaze the pan juices with anything from lemon juice to a touch of cream. Fresh herbs, capers, and a variety of separately sautéed

vegetables can top it all off.

Cooking fish is just as foolproof. A nonstick skillet helps retain all the natural juices. Be sure to buy fish with the skin on. Sautéed, covered, skin side down in a touch of butter and oil, most fish fillets don't even need to be turned over. Transfer them to a hot dinner plate, skin side up, and they'll be cooked to perfection.

Skillet cooking does demand a little more knowledge and experience than some other techniques. You need to sauté in the right pan, with the right amount of oil and butter, at the right temperature. You have to work quickly, to know when something is properly browned and thoroughly cooked. But once you gain confidence in your skills, there's no end to what you can do. You'll probably be like me, with two skillets going at once, stirring a vegetable sauté with my left hand and sautéing chicken legs with my right without skipping a beat!

Sauté of Chicken Breasts with Roasted Pepper and Chive Coulis

To prepare: 15 minutes
To cook: 10 minutes
Serves 4

2 whole boneless and skinless chicken breasts, cut in half

Coarse salt and freshly ground black pepper

All-purpose flour for dredging

2 to 3 tablespoons unsalted butter

1 to 2 teaspoons peanut oil

⅓ to ½ cup Chicken Stock (page 145) or chicken bouillon

¾ cup crème fraîche (see page 31) or heavy cream

1 Beurre Manié (page 193)

⅓ cup diced roasted red bell pepper (see page 182) or jarred roasted red pepper

1 teaspoon finely minced jalapeño pepper

2 tablespoons finely minced fresh chives

OPTIONAL GARNISH
Leaves of fresh cilantro or julienne of fresh basil leaves

R o a s t e d peppers, whether fresh or out of a jar, make for an instant finishing garnish. Here the sauce should be "short" and intense. You can vary the garnish using other seasonal herbs besides basil and cilantro. Serve with **Tangy Lemon Orzo with Red Peppers and Scallions (page 150)** or **Tomatillo, Cilantro, and Green Chili Pilaf (page 138).**

1. Season the chicken breasts with coarse salt and pepper and dredge very lightly in flour, shaking off the excess.

2. Melt 2 tablespoons butter together with 1 teaspoon oil over high heat in a heavy skillet. Add the chicken and brown on both sides. If the fat has burned, discard it and replace with 1 tablespoon butter and 1 teaspoon oil. Add the stock or bouillon and simmer, covered, for 4 to 6 minutes or until the chicken juices run pale yellow. Remove the chicken and set aside.

3. Add the crème fraîche or cream and reduce slightly. Whisk in bits of beurre manié and simmer until the sauce lightly coats a spoon. Add the red and jalapeño peppers and chives and season with salt and pepper. Return the chicken to the skillet and just heat through. Transfer to a platter and serve hot, garnished with optional cilantro or basil.

T i p

A beurre manié *is a flour and butter paste used to thicken
sauces at the end of cooking. You will need only 1 to 2
teaspoons of beurre manié for any recipe in this book since
it is preferable to reduce the sauce naturally before thickening it so as to intensify the flavor.*

B e u r r e M a n i é

*Process 8 tablespoons softened unsalted butter and 8 table-
spoons all-purpose flour in a food processor until smooth.
Divide the mixture into 8 equal parts and, with floured
hands, shape each into a ball. Place the beurre manié in a
tightly covered jar and refrigerate for up to 1 week. Beurre
manié can also be frozen for 2 to 3 months.*

Sauté of Chicken Legs with Red Peppers and Fennel Sausage

To prepare: 20 minutes
To cook: 40 minutes
Serves 4 to 6

....

2 tablespoons extra-virgin olive oil

½ pound sweet Italian fennel
sausage

8 small chicken legs with thighs
attached

Salt and freshly ground black
pepper

2 tablespoons finely minced
shallots

⅓ cup dry white wine

2 to 3 large garlic cloves, peeled
and thinly sliced

3 tablespoons finely minced fresh
parsley

One 32-ounce can Italian plum
tomatoes, drained and
chopped (see Tip)

3 red bell peppers, cored,
seeded, and thinly sliced

1 tablespoon fresh thyme leaves

½ cup chicken bouillon

Optional: 2 teaspoons arrowroot
mixed with a little bouillon

1 tablespoon tiny capers, drained

GARNISH
3 tablespoons finely minced fresh
parsley mixed with 1 finely
minced garlic clove

Although this homey and flavor-packed dish takes a little more time to prepare than most of the recipes in this book, it is so good-natured that I feel it is well worth it, particularly if you keep your side dish quite simple. And you can vary this dish according to the seasons. A combination of zucchini and peppers would be great in the summer, and be sure to use ripe plum tomatoes instead of canned tomatoes whenever available (see Tip).

....

1. Heat the oil in a heavy 12-inch skillet over medium-high heat. Add the sausage and sauté until nicely browned but still pink in the center. Transfer to a cutting board, cut crosswise into ¼-inch slices, and set aside.

2. Discard all but 3 tablespoons of the fat from the skillet. Add the chicken and sauté until nicely browned. Remove from the skillet, season with salt and pepper, and set aside.

3. Reduce the heat, add the shallots to the skillet, and cook for 1 minute. Add the wine and reduce to a glaze. Add the garlic, parsley, tomatoes, peppers, and thyme. Return the chicken to the skillet, add the bouillon, and simmer, partially covered, for 20 to 25 minutes, or until the juices run pale yellow. Ten minutes before the chicken is done, add the sausage to the skillet.

4. Transfer the chicken and sausage to a deep serving platter and keep warm. If the sauce seems thin, whisk in a little of the optional arrowroot mixture and simmer until it lightly coats a spoon. Add the capers. Spoon the sauce over the chicken, sprinkle with the parsley mixture, and serve hot, accompanied by crusty French bread.

T i p s

You can substitute 6 to 8 ripe plum tomatoes for the canned tomatoes. You do not need to peel or seed them, just coarsely chop.

Browning chicken can be a messy and lengthy task since commercial chickens are usually very watery. To prevent splattering, wrap the chicken pieces tightly in an absorbent kitchen towel — not paper towels — and keep them at room temperature for 20 to 40 minutes before sautéing. Always season chicken with salt after it has been browned, since seasoning before releases the juices, preventing it from browning properly.

Pan-Seared Chicken Breasts in Asparagus and Dill Sauce

To prepare: 20 minutes
To marinate: 3 to 4 hours, or overnight
To cook: 15 minutes

Serves 6

....

3 whole boneless and skinless chicken breasts, cut in half

Juice of 1 large lemon

2 tablespoons finely minced fresh thyme

4 tablespoons extra-virgin olive oil

Salt and freshly ground black pepper

½ pound asparagus, peeled and cut into 1-inch pieces

2½ cups Chicken Stock (page 145) or chicken bouillon

Optional: 1 teaspoon arrowroot mixed with a little stock

2 tablespoons finely minced fresh dill, parsley, or chives

Tip

If you like to serve chicken a few times a week, I suggest that you prepare the dark meat in gutsy tomato-based or brown sauces and save the chicken breasts for the more delicate white sauces or for pan-searing or grilling.

I usually serve asparagus as a starter, but I often cook a few extra stalks to use in this quick and flavorful sauce that goes well with both chicken breasts and salmon fillets. The pureed asparagus thickens the sauce, making it unnecessary to use any thickening agent.

....

1. Place the chicken breasts in a Ziploc bag. Add the lemon juice, thyme, 2 tablespoons of the oil, and black pepper, seal the bag, and marinate in the refrigerator for 3 to 4 hours, or overnight.

2. Combine the asparagus and 2 cups of the stock or bouillon in a saucepan and cook until the asparagus is very tender. Puree in a food processor until very smooth. Set this sauce aside.

3. Heat 1 tablespoon of the oil in a large nonstick skillet over high heat. Remove the chicken from the marinade and sauté until nicely browned on both sides. Season with salt and pepper, add a little stock or bouillon, and simmer, covered, for 3 to 4 minutes or until the chicken juices run pale yellow. Transfer the chicken to a serving platter, cover, and keep warm.

4. Add the asparagus sauce to the skillet and simmer until slightly reduced. If the sauce seems too thin, add a little of the optional arrowroot mixture and simmer until it lightly coats a spoon. Add the herbs and correct the seasoning. Spoon over the chicken and serve hot, accompanied by sautéed mixed peppers or warm couscous.

Scaloppine of Turkey with Chanterelles, Tarragon, and Tomato Concassée

To prepare: 15 minutes
To cook: 20 minutes
Serves 4

....

3 tablespoons unsalted butter

1 tablespoon olive oil

1 large shallot, peeled and finely minced

½ pound fresh chanterelles, trimmed and thinly sliced

Salt and freshly ground black pepper

1 pound turkey cutlets

All-purpose flour for dredging

1 large ripe tomato, unpeeled, diced

1 cup Chicken Stock (page 145) or chicken bouillon

2 tablespoons finely minced fresh tarragon

1 teaspoon finely grated lemon zest

1 tablespoon fresh lemon juice

Optional: 3 tablespoons heavy cream

D o not be alarmed by the number of ingredients called for in this recipe: Most of them are basics that you are bound to have on hand, so your shopping should be easy. This is a dish that benefits tremendously when made with fresh chanterelles, which are at their best in the fall. I usually make this dish on the Spur of the Moment when I see these mushrooms in the market. Fresh tarragon and ripe tomatoes also make a difference in taste, and when all of these good ingredients come together, you will find that it is well worth the effort. Serve with Piquant Parsley and Lemon Pilaf (page 136) or Mascarpone and Chive Mashed Potatoes (page 248).

....

1. Melt 1½ tablespoons of the butter together with ½ tablespoon of the oil in a large cast-iron skillet over medium heat. Add the shallot and mushrooms and cook for 2 to 3 minutes, or until tender. Season with salt and pepper and remove to a side dish.

2. Season the turkey with salt and pepper and dredge lightly in flour, shaking off the excess. Add the remaining 1½ tablespoons butter and ½ tablespoon oil to the skillet. When hot, add the scaloppine and sauté quickly until nicely browned on both sides. Add the tomato and a little stock or bouillon and simmer, covered, for 5 minutes.

(continued)

3. With a slotted spoon, transfer the turkey to a side dish. Add the mushroom mixture to the skillet together with the tarragon, lemon zest, lemon juice, and remaining stock or bouillon and simmer until most of the liquid has evaporated. Add the optional cream, season with salt and pepper, and spoon the sauce over the turkey. Serve hot.

T i p

Fresh chanterelles are one of our few truly wild mushrooms that are now available commercially. While they are abundant in the Northwest during the fall, they are often hard to find and very expensive elsewhere. So be sure to be spontaneous and use them only when you see them very fresh. Good chanterelles should be firm and moist, not dry or mushy and broken. Never soak the mushrooms; simply rinse them briefly and trim off just the stem ends. The rest of the mushroom, including the stem, can be chopped and used in many delicious preparations.

Shallot and Herb-Infused Lamb Chops

To prepare: 10 minutes
To cook: 15 minutes

Serves 4

....

4 tablespoons unsalted butter,
softened

2 tablespoons finely minced
shallots

2 tablespoons finely minced fresh
parsley

Optional: 1 tablespoon finely
minced fresh sage or tarragon

Coarse salt and freshly ground
black pepper

2 tablespoons Clarified Butter
(page 103)

4 to 8 loin lamb chops, about ¾
inch thick

GARNISH
Sprigs of fresh rosemary

Tip

....

An herb butter is always good to have on hand. I usually make mine in quantity, using ½ pound of salted butter, which I blend together in the food processor with 1 finely minced medium shallot, 2 large garlic cloves, and 2 tablespoons minced fresh parsley. The herb butter can be kept in the refrigerator for up to 2 weeks. Put a dollop on each chop for a super taste boost.

A juicy, crisp, well-seared lamb chop needs little in the way of a sauce, but there is nothing wrong with a little enrichment from a delicious herb butter, such as this one that melts nicely into the chop. You can vary the herb, keeping in mind that lamb has a particular affinity to character herbs such as rosemary, sage, tarragon, and oregano as well as, of course, garlic and shallots. Serve the chops with Mascarpone and Chive Mashed Potatoes (page 248) or Soft Polenta with Braised Leeks and Mascarpone (page 156).

1. Combine the softened butter, shallots, parsley, and optional sage or tarragon in a small bowl. Season with coarse salt and pepper.

2. Bring a small amount of water to a simmer in a 2-quart saucepan. Set a heavy heatproof 10-inch dinner plate on top of the pan and place half of the herb butter on it. Keep warm over low heat.

3. Heat the clarified butter in a heavy skillet over high heat until almost smoking. Add the chops and sauté for 2 to 3 minutes. Turn the chops and sauté for 3 to 4 minutes, or until nicely browned and medium-rare.

4. Transfer the chops to the plate with the herb butter, cover tightly with foil, and let absorb the butter for about 3 minutes. Serve at once, topped with the remaining herb butter and garnished with rosemary.

Lamb Chops with Mustard, Balsamic Vinegar, and Herb Marinade

To prepare: 5 minutes
To marinate: 30 minutes
To cook: 6 to 7 minutes
Serves 4

....

12 to 16 rib lamb chops, about ½ inch thick

2 tablespoons balsamic vinegar

2 large garlic cloves, peeled and crushed

2 teaspoons Dijon mustard

½ cup extra-virgin olive oil

1 tablespoon finely minced fresh rosemary

1 tablespoon finely minced fresh thyme

1 teaspoon dried oregano

Coarsely ground black pepper

Coarse salt

Tip

....

Avoid buying aged lamb. Many markets recommend it, but while aging is good for beef, it produces a strong, mutton-like flavor in lamb. Buy lamb that is pinkish with white, almost translucent, fat.

T h e r e are few more delicious foods than a juicy pan-seared rib lamb chop. I buy them no thicker than half an inch thick and trim them of all fat, leaving just the "eye" on the bone. These little chops cook in two minutes and are best picked up with your fingers and enjoyed with crusty peasant bread or some roasted potatoes and a well-seasoned salad.

....

1.   Place the chops in a shallow dish.

2.   Combine the vinegar, garlic, mustard, and 6 tablespoons of the oil in a bowl and whisk until well blended. Add the herbs, season with coarse pepper, and pour over the chops. Marinate at room temperature for 30 minutes.

3.   Heat the remaining 2 tablespoons oil in a large cast-iron skillet over medium-high heat. Remove the lamb chops from the marinade, add the chops, without crowding the skillet, and sauté until browned on both sides, about 6 to 7 minutes. Sprinkle with coarse salt and transfer to a platter. Serve hot or at room temperature.

Remarks: These marinated chops are also delicious seared quickly either on a gas or charcoal grill over white-hot coals.

Skillet Steak in Tarragon and Green Peppercorn Sauce

To prepare: 5 minutes
To cook: 30 minutes
Serves 3 to 4

3 tablespoons Clarified Butter (page 103)

1½ pounds shell or rib-eye steak, cut 2 to 2¼ inches thick

Coarse salt and freshly ground black pepper

2 tablespoons finely minced shallots

½ cup Scotch whiskey

1 cup beef bouillon

1 teaspoons green peppercorns packed in brine, drained

2 teaspoons arrowroot, dissolved in a little bouillon

2 tablespoons finely minced fresh tarragon

Optional: 12 double-poached garlic cloves (see page 41)

Tips

Look for green peppercorns packed in brine, not pickled in vinegar.

You can age beef steaks in your refrigerator by placing them on a plate, loosely covered with butcher paper, for 2 to 3 days.

Food trends come and go: Beef in green peppercorn sauce, the "in" dish of the Seventies, now seems somewhat outdated. But in contrast to many unlikely combinations, this marriage of flavors deserves its place among the classics and, personally, I still love teaming beef with a variety of peppercorns. The addition of fresh tarragon and double-poached garlic cloves gives a new dimension to this classic. Serve this steak with **Roasted Portobello Mushrooms (page 86).**

1. Heat the butter in a cast-iron skillet over high heat. Add the steak and sauté for 3 minutes. Turn and sauté for another 3 minutes, or until nicely browned. Season with salt and pepper, reduce the heat, and cook for 10 minutes. Turn the steak once more and cook for 8 to 10 minutes longer for medium-rare. Transfer to a cutting board and let rest.

2. Discard all the fat from the skillet. Add the shallots and cook for 1 minute. Add the Scotch and reduce to a glaze. Add the bouillon and green peppercorns and whisk in enough of the arrowroot mixture so the sauce lightly coats a spoon. Add the tarragon and optional double-poached garlic, and correct the seasoning.

3. Slice the steak crosswise on the bias into thin slices, place on a serving platter, and spoon the sauce over. Serve at once.

Skillet-Seared Flank Steak in Spicy Ginger Marinade

To prepare: 5 minutes
To marinate: 30 minutes
to 1 hour
To cook: 10 minutes
Serves 2 to 3

....

2 tablespoons balsamic vinegar

2 tablespoons soy sauce

1 tablespoon Dijon mustard

1 tablespoon finely minced jalapeño pepper

1 tablespoon finely minced fresh
ginger

2 large garlic cloves, peeled and
finely minced

1 teaspoon coarsely ground black
pepper, or more to taste

¼ cup plus 2 tablespoons
olive oil

1½ to 2 pounds flank steak

Salt

T i p

....

Since flank steak has little fat, it is best to serve it medium-rare for maximum juiciness. Always cut the steak into thin slices on the bias, against the grain.

F o r the Spur of the Moment cook who likes beef, flank steak is a great choice. For years I thought of this cut as one that is best reserved for the grill and Chinese preparations, but recently I have been pan-searing it with excellent results. A heavy cast-iron skillet is essential since it allows you to cook the meat over high heat, searing the outside while keeping it rare on the inside, a must for this chewy but flavorful cut. Serve the steak with Tuscan Fricassee of Savoy Cabbage and Pancetta (page 251) and Wild Mushrooms Roasted with Rosemary and Thyme (page 262).

....

1.   Combine the vinegar, soy sauce, mustard, jalapeño pepper, ginger, garlic, black pepper, and the ¼ cup oil in a food processor and process until smooth. Transfer to a Ziploc bag, add the steak, and seal the bag. Marinate at room temperature for 30 minutes to 1 hour, turning once or twice.

2.   Heat the remaining 2 tablespoons oil in a cast-iron skillet over high heat. Remove the steak from the marinade and wipe dry with paper towels. Add to the skillet and sauté for 5 minutes, or until nicely browned. Turn over and sauté for 3 to 4 minutes longer; do not overcook. Season with salt and pepper, transfer to a cutting board, and let sit for 5 minutes before slicing.

3.   Cut crosswise on the bias into thin slices, and serve immediately.

Fillet of Beef in Tomato, Caper, and Anchovy Sauce

To prepare: 15 minutes
To cook: 20 minutes
Serves 4

....

2 tablespoons unsalted butter

2 tablespoons plus 1 teaspoon olive oil

4 beef fillet steaks, cut 1 inch thick

Salt and freshly ground black pepper

¼ cup finely minced shallots

2 large garlic cloves, peeled and finely minced

One 32-ounce can Italian plum tomatoes, drained and chopped, ½ cup juice reserved

2 teaspoons fresh oregano leaves

2 teaspoons fresh thyme leaves

4 flat anchovy fillets, drained and finely minced

1 tablespoon tiny capers, drained

Optional: 16 small black oil-cured olives, pitted

GARNISH

2 to 3 tablespoons finely minced fresh parsley

H e r e is a gutsy, flavor-packed main course that needs little in the way of a side dish. Crusty bread or buttered orzo are the best choices. The sauce is also good with pan-seared rib-eye steaks or lamb chops.

....

1. Melt the butter together with 1 teaspoon of the oil in a cast-iron skillet over high heat. Add the fillets and sauté for 3 minutes per side for medium-rare. Season with salt and pepper, transfer to a side dish, and set aside.

2. Discard the fat from the skillet. Reduce the heat and add the remaining 2 tablespoons oil. Add the shallots and garlic and cook for 1 minute. Add the tomatoes and herbs and cook for 10 minutes, or until the juices have reduced by half. Add the anchovies, capers, and optional olives and simmer 2 minutes.

3. Return the fillets to the skillet and just heat through. Correct the seasoning and serve hot, garnished with minced parsley.

T i p

....

The fillet is a pricey cut of beef, and you may substitute a 1½-inch-thick boneless rib-eye steak here if you prefer. The sauce, which is prepared separately from the beef, also works beautifully with grilled fish, pasta, or a pilaf of rice.

Veal Scaloppine in Tarragon and Lemon Cream

To prepare: 10 minutes
plus 30 minutes to rest
To cook: 35 minutes
Serves 8

....

2 tablespoons fresh lemon juice

¾ cup heavy cream

1 chicken bouillon cube or 1
    package chicken MBT

Salt and freshly ground white
    pepper

2 to 3 tablespoons finely minced
    fresh tarragon

8 large veal scaloppine (each
    about the size of your palm)

All-purpose flour for dredging

2 extra-large eggs, lightly beaten

2 cups unseasoned bread crumbs

2 teaspoons peanut oil

4 tablespoons unsalted butter

GARNISH
Sprigs of fresh tarragon

T i p

....

*Veal scaloppine can be sautéed
ahead of time, covered, and kept
warm in a 300°F oven for 25
minutes, allowing you plenty of
time to enjoy your appetizer or a
predinner drink.*

V e a l scaloppine are a wonderful Spur of the Moment cut of meat. They take only about two minutes to cook, but become exceptionally tender when baked for an additional twenty-five minutes. Try them with a side dish of broccoli rabe, escarole, or spinach, or a combination of greens quickly sautéed in olive oil with a touch of garlic and a grinding of pepper.

....

1. Combine the lemon juice, cream, and bouillon cube or MBT in a saucepan, season with salt and white pepper, and simmer for 2 minutes. Add the minced tarragon and set aside.

2. Season the veal with salt and white pepper and dredge lightly in flour, shaking off the excess. Dip in the beaten eggs, then lightly into the bread crumbs. Refrigerate, covered, in a single layer, for at least 30 minutes.

3. Preheat the oven to 350°F.

4. Sauté the scaloppine in 2 batches: For each batch, melt 2 tablespoons butter together with 1 teaspoon oil in a large skillet over medium-high heat. Add 4 scaloppine and sauté quickly until nicely browned on each side. Transfer to a well-buttered heavy baking dish in a single layer, overlapping slightly if necessary.

5. Spoon the cream sauce over the veal, cover tightly with buttered foil, and bake for 25 minutes. Serve garnished with sprigs of tarragon.

Sautéed Veal Chops in Roquefort Cream

To prepare: 15 minutes
To cook: 10 minutes
Serves 4

....

2 tablespoons Roquefort cheese

4 tablespoons unsalted butter,
    softened

4 veal rib chops, cut ¾ inch thick

Salt and freshly ground white
    pepper

All-purpose flour for dredging

2 teaspoons peanut oil

¼ cup dry vermouth or
    white wine

¾ cup Chicken Stock (page 145)
    or chicken bouillon

⅓ cup heavy cream

1 Beurre Manié (page 193)

GARNISH
Sprigs of watercress

Tip

....

*Rib veal chops are less expensive
than loin chops. They are equally
tasty and a much better buy.
Boned veal rib chops cut into ¼-
inch slices, called medallions, are
an excellent alternative when you
cannot find scaloppine.*

I am always amazed at how pricey veal chops are in most restaurants, making them a cut of meat I like to enjoy at home. They are undemanding and easy to prepare and can be teamed with herbs, a variety of mushrooms, and cheese. Be sure to look out for rib chops, which are far less expensive than loin chops and often on sale. Here, the mild blue cheese sauce nicely enhances the chops. If you cannot find a mild Roquefort, use Gorgonzola or goat cheese combined with a mincing of fresh thyme. Steamed and buttered spinach, caramelized endives, or roasted fennel are all excellent side dishes.

....

1. Mash the Roquefort together with 2 tablespoons of the butter in a small bowl. Set aside.

2. Season the chops with salt and white pepper and dust lightly with flour, shaking off the excess. Heat the remaining 2 tablespoons butter together with the oil in a cast-iron skillet over medium-high heat. Add the chops and cook for 2 to 3 minutes per side, or until nicely browned. Transfer to a serving platter and keep warm.

3. Add the vermouth or white wine to the skillet and reduce to a glaze. Add the stock or bouillon and reduce to ¼ cup. Reduce the heat, add the cream, and whisk in bits of beurre manié until the sauce lightly coats a spoon. Whisk in the Roquefort paste until smooth. Taste and correct the seasoning. Pour the sauce over the chops, garnish with watercress, and serve hot.

Sauté of Shrimp with Roasted Red Pepper and Shallot Puree

To prepare: 25 minutes
To cook: 8 to 10 minutes
Serves 4 to 5

2 large red bell peppers, roasted, peeled (see page 182), and diced (about 1½ cups)

½ cup chicken bouillon

Salt and freshly ground black pepper

4 tablespoons extra-virgin olive oil

2 small dried red chili peppers, broken

1½ pounds medium shrimp, peeled

¼ cup finely minced shallots

2 large garlic cloves, peeled and finely minced

2 teaspoons finely minced fresh ginger

¼ cup finely minced fresh cilantro or parsley

GARNISH
Sprigs of fresh cilantro or parsley

Tip

Minced shallots will keep for several months, covered with white wine, in a jar in the refrigerator. Do not mince shallots in a food processor, as this makes them bitter.

F e w foods are quicker to prepare and more versatile than shrimp. Now that excellent-quality shrimp are available almost everywhere, preparation just depends on what is in season produce-wise. Here is a terrific marriage of flavors that you can make year-round and should become a basic in your weekday cooking repertoire. Serve with Couscous with Melted Scallions (page 160) or crusty peasant bread.

1.　Puree the roasted peppers with the bouillon in a food processor. Season with salt and pepper and set aside.

2.　Sauté the shrimp in 2 batches: For each batch, heat 1 tablespoon of the oil in a heavy skillet over high heat. Add 1 chili pepper and half the shrimp and sauté until just pink. Transfer to a side dish and season with salt and pepper.

3.　Reduce the heat and add the remaining 2 tablespoons oil to the skillet. Add the shallots, garlic, and ginger and cook for 30 seconds. Add the cilantro or parsley and the pepper puree and simmer for 2 minutes, until slightly reduced. Add the shrimp and just heat through. Correct the seasoning and serve at once, garnished with sprigs of cilantro or parsley.

Pan-Seared Shrimp in a Curry Crust with Spinach and Pine Nuts

To prepare: 20 minutes
To cook: 10 minutes
Serves 4

....

3 pounds fresh spinach, stemmed and thoroughly washed

4 tablespoons olive oil

2 medium garlic cloves, peeled and thinly sliced

2 tablespoons dark raisins, plumped (see page 159)

2 tablespoons pine nuts, sautéed in a little olive oil until golden (see page 269)

Coarse salt and freshly ground black pepper

1 cup fresh bread crumbs

1 teaspoon Madras curry powder

1 teaspoon ground coriander

20 large shrimp, peeled

T i p

....

Avoid buying precooked shellfish, which tend to be tough and dry and cannot be used in any sauté preparation.

I a m always on the lookout for new and interesting ways to prepare shrimp. It is an easy search since shrimp marry so well with most herbs, spices, and seasonal vegetables. Here I lightly coat them with curry and team them with braised spinach laced with raisins and pine nuts. Carrots and turnips are equally good prepared this way and both will also enhance the crispy shrimp.

....

1. Drop the spinach into boiling salted water and cook for 2 minutes, or until just wilted. Drain and set aside.

2. Heat 2 tablespoons of the oil in a nonstick skillet over low heat. Add the garlic and cook for 30 seconds. Add the spinach and raisins and cook, stirring constantly, until all the moisture has evaporated. Add the pine nuts and season with coarse salt and pepper. Cover and keep warm.

3. Combine the bread crumbs, curry, and coriander in a shallow bowl. Dip the shrimp into the mixture to coat evenly.

4. Heat the remaining 2 tablespoons oil in a large heavy skillet over medium heat. Sauté the shrimp until nicely browned on both sides. Sprinkle with coarse salt and pepper. Place a mound of warm spinach on each plate and arrange the shrimp on top. Serve at once.

Sautéed Scallops with Root Vegetables in Mustard Cream

~~~

To prepare: 10 minutes
plus 1 hour for cream
mixture to develop
flavor
To cook: 20 minutes
Serves 4

....

¾ cup heavy cream

1 tablespoon Dijon mustard

¼ teaspoon dry mustard

5 tablespoons unsalted butter

½ cup finely diced carrot

½ cup finely diced celery root

2 tablespoons water

Salt and freshly ground white
pepper

4 teaspoons olive oil

1 pound small sea scallops, dried
on paper towels

GARNISH
2 tablespoons finely minced fresh
parsley

Tip

....

Avoid buying scallops that are sitting in a puddle of liquid, since it means they were either previously frozen or are not very fresh, or both. They will also be quite tough and chewy when sautéed.

I n this fricassee the shellfish is combined with root vegetables whose natural sweetness only enhances the delicate flavor of the scallops. A side dish is not really necessary. Instead I would opt for a hearty starter, such as Yellow Pepper and Golden Zucchini Soup (page 57). Follow the scallops with a salad and a good cheese to round off your meal.

....

1. Combine the cream and mustards in a small bowl, and let stand for 1 hour.

2. Melt 2 tablespoons of the butter in a small skillet over low heat. Add the carrot, celery root, and water, season with salt and white pepper, and simmer, covered, for 8 to 10 minutes, or until tender. Set aside.

3. Sauté the scallops in 2 batches: For each batch, heat 2 teaspoons oil in a nonstick skillet over high heat. Add half the scallops and sauté for about 2 minutes per side, or until nicely browned. Transfer to a side dish and season with salt and pepper.

4. Reduce the heat to low, add the cream mixture, and reduce slightly. Whisk in the remaining 3 tablespoons butter, add the scallops together with the vegetables, and just heat through. Sprinkle with minced parsley and serve immediately.

Seared Scallops with Asparagus and Wilted Lettuce

To prepare: 20 minutes
To cook: 20 minutes
Serves 4

....

4 tablespoons unsalted butter

1¼ pounds asparagus, trimmed, peeled, and cut on the bias into 2-inch pieces

Salt and freshly ground black pepper

2 medium garlic cloves, peeled and thinly sliced

¼ cup chicken bouillon

2 small heads Bibb lettuce, leaves separated, rinsed, and dried on paper towels

3 tablespoons crème fraîche (see page 31) or heavy cream

1 pound small sea scallops, dried on paper towels

All-purpose flour for dredging

2 teaspoons olive oil

T i p

....

Small bay scallops often release a great quantity of juices. To preserve these sweet juices, cook the scallops until they turn opaque, remove with a slotted spoon, and then cook the pan juices until they are nicely reduced and syrupy. Return the scallops to the skillet just to warm through, and season them well.

C o m e spring, I turn to this dish, which is a celebration of a great spring vegetable as well as, in some way, a farewell to a wonderful cool-weather shellfish. It is what Spur of the Moment cooking should be, a harmonious marriage of ingredients caught in their prime. Please note: Never season scallops with salt until just before sautéing. It will make them release their natural juices and render them tough.

....

1. Heat 2 tablespoons of the butter in a large skillet over medium heat. Add the asparagus and cook for 30 seconds. Season with salt and pepper, add the garlic and bouillon, and simmer, covered, for 4 to 5 minutes, or until just tender.

2. Add the lettuce to the skillet and cook, stirring constantly, until wilted. Add the crème fraîche or heavy cream and just heat through. Correct the seasoning, and keep warm.

3. Season the scallops with salt and pepper and dredge very lightly in flour, shaking off the excess.

4. Sauté the scallops in 2 batches: For each batch, melt 1 tablespoon butter together with 1 teaspoon oil in a large, nonstick skillet over medium-high heat. Add half the scallops, without crowding, and sauté for about 2 minutes per side, or until nicely browned. Add the scallops to the lettuce/asparagus mixture, and just heat through. Serve hot with crusty French bread.

Sautéed Scallops in Cumin-Scented Tomato Fondue

To prepare: 10 minutes
To cook: 30 minutes
Serves 4

....

3 tablespoons extra-virgin olive oil

3 tablespoons finely minced shallots

2 large garlic cloves, peeled and finely minced

2 large ripe tomatoes, peeled, seeded, and chopped

1 teaspoon pure chili powder

½ teaspoon ground cumin

Salt and freshly ground black pepper

½ pound large shiitake mushrooms, stemmed

1 pound small sea scallops, dried on paper towels

Juice of ½ lime, or more to taste

GARNISH
3 tablespoons tiny fresh cilantro leaves

T i p

....

Sea scallops usually have a small tough white muscle attached, which is easily removed with your fingers. If the scallops are large, slice them in half horizontally, into "scaloppine."

M u c h like shrimp, scallops can be teamed with assertive spices, but I am always careful not to mask their delicate, sweet flavor. A hint of cumin or saffron, a dicing of fresh cilantro, or a touch of curry is a nice and welcome variation in many scallop dishes. Serve with Couscous with Melted Scallions (page 160), semolina gnocchi, or crusty peasant bread.

....

1. Preheat the oven to 400°F.

2. Heat 1 tablespoon of the oil in a heavy skillet over medium-low heat. Add the shallots and garlic and cook for 1 minute. Add the tomatoes, chili powder, and cumin, season with salt and pepper, and simmer, partially covered, for 20 minutes, or until all the liquid has evaporated. Remove from the heat.

3. While the tomatoes are simmering, place the mushrooms on a baking sheet, drizzle with 1 tablespoon of the oil, and roast for 10 minutes. Cut into ¼-inch slices and set aside.

4. Heat the remaining 1 tablespoon oil in a large nonstick skillet over high heat. Add the scallops, without crowding the skillet, and sauté for about 2 minutes per side, until nicely browned. Add the tomato sauce together with the mushrooms and lime juice and just heat through. Correct the seasoning, adding more lime juice if necessary. Serve hot, garnished with tiny leaves of fresh cilantro.

Pan-Seared Salmon with Melted Leeks and Dill

To prepare: 10 minutes
To cook: 20 minutes
Serves 4

....

3 tablespoons unsalted butter

3 large leeks, trimmed of all but 2 inches of greens, cut into a fine julienne, and well rinsed

⅓ cup chicken bouillon

Coarse salt and freshly ground black pepper

½ cup heavy cream or crème fraîche (see page 31)

3 to 4 tablespoons finely minced fresh dill

4 salmon fillets (about 6 to 7 ounces each), preferably center-cut, with skin on

4 tablespoons Clarified Butter (page 103)

GARNISH
Sprigs of fresh dill

T i p

....

Fillets with the skin on are best for pan-searing since the skin will protect the flesh from becoming dry. When purchasing, look for skin that is shiny, not dull or milky.

W h e n it comes to cooking salmon, I have three favorite methods: braising, roasting and pan-searing. A salmon fillet pan-seared skin side down until crisp and still rare on the inside is indeed a great dish. Served with melted leeks and a touch of cream, it becomes a dish I never tire of: a combination of pure flavors without surprises, nothing clever, just good taste that takes only twenty minutes from skillet to table.

....

1. Melt the butter in a large skillet over low heat. Add the leeks and bouillon, season with coarse salt and pepper, and simmer, covered, for 10 minutes. Add the cream or crème fraîche and cook until it has been absorbed by the leeks. Add the minced dill and keep warm.

2. Dry the salmon on paper towels and season with coarse salt and pepper.

3. Heat the clarified butter in a large nonstick skillet over high heat. Add the fillets, skin side down, cover loosely with foil, and sauté for 2 minutes. Reduce the heat slightly and cook for 4 to 6 minutes longer, or until just opaque. Turn the fillets over and cook for 1 minute if you want them to be browned on top.

4. Place the braised leeks in the center of a serving platter. Top with the salmon fillets, skin side up, and garnish with sprigs of dill. Serve at once.

Fricassee of Salmon with Glazed Cucumbers

To prepare: 15 minutes

To cook: 15 minutes

Serves 4 to 5

....

1½ pounds fresh skinless salmon
   fillets, preferably center-cut,
   cut into 1¼-inch cubes

Coarse salt and freshly ground
   white pepper

All-purpose flour for dredging

3 tablespoons olive oil

1 large seedless (European or
   gourmet) cucumber (about
   1½ pounds), unpeeled,
   seeded and cut into pieces ½
   inch thick by 1½ inches long

⅓ cup chicken bouillon

Pinch of granulated sugar

3 tablespoons finely minced fresh
   dill, tarragon, or Italian parsley

GARNISH

Sprigs of fresh dill, tarragon, or
   Italian parsley

T i p

....

*The flesh of all fresh fish should
look almost transparent and
bright and should be firm to the
touch. Avoid fish fillets or steaks
that look opaque and have dark areas or are discolored in any way.*

H e r e the salmon fillets are cut into large cubes and sautéed until crispy, giving the finished dish the appearance of a fricassee or a stew. The crunchy, mellow taste of sautéed cucumbers further enhances this preparation. Of course, you can vary this on the Spur of the Moment with other vegetables that appeal to you in the market. Fresh peas or pan-wilted assorted greens or, especially, Belgian endives, all go well with salmon. Serve a side dish of Tangy Lemon Orzo with Red Peppers and Scallions (page 150).

....

1.   Season the salmon with coarse salt and white pepper and dredge lightly in flour, shaking off the excess.

2.   Sauté the salmon in 2 batches: For each batch, heat 1½ tablespoons oil in a large nonstick skillet over high heat. Add half the salmon, without crowding the skillet, and sauté until very crisp and browned on all sides, but still pink in the center. Set aside.

3.   Wipe out the skillet. Add the cucumber, bouillon, and sugar, season with coarse salt and pepper, and braise, covered, for 4 to 5 minutes, or until the cucumber is just tender. Remove the cover, raise the heat, and reduce the pan juices to 2 tablespoons.

4.   Add the salmon and minced dill, tarragon, or parsley and just heat through. Serve hot, garnished with sprigs of dill, tarragon, or parsley, and accompanied by orzo or boiled tiny red potatoes.

Pepper-Coated Tuna with Caviar Aïoli

To prepare: 15 minutes

To cook: 10 minutes

Serves 4

....

1 slice day-old white bread (such as toasting white)

½ cup whole milk

2 ounces red salmon caviar

Juice of 1 large lemon

2 tablespoons finely minced red onion

2 large garlic cloves, peeled and mashed

½ cup plus 4 tablespoons extra-virgin olive oil

4 tuna steaks (about 7 to 8 ounces each), cut 1¼ inches thick

1 tablespoon coarsely ground black pepper

Coarse salt

GARNISH

Tiny leaves of fresh basil or Italian parsley

Lemon wedges

Tip

....

When you refrigerate fish fillets or fish steaks, make sure that they do not touch one another, since this will cause the fish to discolor and spoil quickly.

Fresh pan-seared tuna is one of those great foods that needs little in the way of garnish. Here it is served with a garlicky caviar "aioli" that I often serve as a dip accompanied by croutons of bread fried in olive oil or brushed with oil and toasted in the oven. You can use other fish such as swordfish or mako in this preparation, but tuna stands up particularly well to the gutsy sauce. Knowing when tuna is done can be a problem since the firm texture does not change much during cooking. Your best bet is to slice into it to see if it is medium-rare, that is, still quite pink on the inside; remember that the tuna will continue to cook once it is out of the pan.

....

1. Soak the bread in the milk for 1 minute. Squeeze out the moisture and puree with the salmon caviar, lemon juice, onion, and garlic in a blender until smooth. With the machine running, add the ½ cup oil by droplets until the sauce is thick and smooth.

2. Sauté the tuna in two 10-inch nonstick skillets: Heat 2 tablespoons oil in each pan over medium to medium-high heat. Season the tuna heavily with the coarse pepper and add 2 steaks to each skillet. Sauté for 2 to 3 minutes per side, or until medium-rare; do not overcook. Season with coarse salt and transfer to individual dinner plates. Top each steak with some of the caviar aioli and garnish with tiny basil or Italian parsley leaves and lemon wedges. Serve hot, accompanied by buttered boiled new potatoes.

Seared Swordfish with a Puree of Sweet-and-Spicy Peppers

To prepare: 10 minutes
To cook: 20 minutes
Serves 4

....

1 tablespoon unsalted butter

4 tablespoons olive oil

1 medium onion, peeled and diced

1 teaspoon finely minced jalapeño pepper or 1 small dried red chili pepper, broken

3 large red bell peppers, cored, seeded, and coarsely chopped

1 large ripe tomato, peeled, seeded, and diced

Salt

4 swordfish steaks (about 7 ounces each), cut ½ inch thick

1 teaspoon coarsely ground black pepper

G A R N I S H
Tiny fresh cilantro leaves or fresh Italian parsley leaves

T i p

....

If you must buy seafood that has been prewrapped in plastic, be sure to remove it from its wrapping as soon as you get home. Place it on a shallow plate, cover loosely with foil, and keep refrigerated.

I a m always on the lookout for an "all-purpose sauce" that will go with many foods—much like a tomato sauce but different. I think this deliciously spicy yet sweet pepper sauce fills the bill. Add a touch of cream to it and serve it over pasta, or toss in a clove of crushed garlic and some minced parsley and you have the perfect accompaniment to grilled or pan-seared shrimp or scallops. I often double the recipe and add some good chicken broth for a terrific soup. So you really cannot go wrong with what is a great alternative to tomato sauce.

....

1. Melt the butter with 1 tablespoon of the oil in a heavy saucepan over medium-low heat. Add the onion and hot pepper and cook for 2 to 3 minutes, or until soft. Add the bell peppers and tomato, season with salt, and cook, partially covered, for 10 to 12 minutes, or until the vegetables are quite soft. Puree in a blender or food processor until smooth, correct the seasoning, and set aside.

2. Sauté the swordfish in two 10-inch nonstick skillets: Heat 1½ tablespoons oil in each pan over very high heat. When smoking, add 2 swordfish steaks to each pan and sauté for 2 minutes on each side. Season with salt and the coarse-ground pepper and transfer to a serving platter or individual plates. Spoon the pepper sauce over the fish, garnish with cilantro or parsley leaves, and serve immediately.

Pan-Sautéed Swordfish with Anchovies, Garlic, and Tomato Fondue

To prepare: 15 minutes
To cook: 10 minutes
Serves 4

....

4 tablespoons olive oil

1 large garlic clove, peeled and mashed through a garlic press

5 flat anchovy fillets, drained and finely minced

3 large ripe tomatoes, seeded and diced

2 to 3 tablespoons crème fraîche (see page 31)

2 tablespoons finely minced fresh Italian parsley

Salt and freshly ground black pepper

4 swordfish steaks, cut ½ inch thick, dried on paper towels

I l i k e the immediacy of "top of the stove" cooking, especially when it comes to fish steaks. Flaky fish such as snapper, grouper, or sea bass do better when oven-braised, but they too can be cooked on top of the stove as long as the skin is left on. This sauce, which takes minutes to cook, is also good on pasta or served with grilled shrimp.

....

1. Heat 2 tablespoons of the oil in a small saucepan over low heat. Add the garlic and anchovies and cook until the anchovies have melted. Add the tomatoes, crème fraîche, and parsley, season with salt and pepper, and just heat through. Keep warm.

2. Heat the remaining 2 tablespoons oil in a large nonstick skillet over medium-high heat. Add the swordfish and sauté for about 2 minutes per side, or until nicely browned but still pink in the center. Season with salt and pepper, transfer to a platter, and spoon the sauce over the fish steaks. Serve hot.

T i p

....

When buying anchovies, look for those imported from Spain or Portugal and avoid those imported from the Far East. My favorite is a Spanish brand called Duet, which is usually available in specialty stores and some supermarkets. These anchovies are "meaty," not too salty, and boneless. If you cannot get this brand, be sure to taste the anchovies you are using, and if they are very salty, soak them first in a little milk for 10 minutes, and drain.

Fricassee of Crisp-Sautéed Mako with Tomatoes, Capers, and Lemon

To prepare: 10 minutes
To cook: 15 minutes
Serves 4

....

1½ pounds mako, cut into 1-inch cubes

Salt and freshly ground black pepper

All-purpose flour for dredging

4 tablespoons olive oil

2½ ounces slab bacon, blanched and diced, about ½ cup

1 red bell pepper, cored, seeded, and cubed

¾ cup Tomato Fondue (page 109) or good-quality commercial tomato sauce

1 teaspoon dried thyme

1 teaspoon dried oregano

1 large ripe tomato, seeded and diced

GARNISH
1 tablespoon tiny capers, drained

2 teaspoons finely grated lemon zest

Tip

....

To seed tomatoes, cut them in half crosswise. The tomatoes will reveal perfect little compartments with seeds, which you can scoop out neatly with your fingers.

M a k o is a fish that is quickly gaining popularity and I am always on the lookout for it. Not only does it closely resemble swordfish in texture and appearance, but it is far less expensive. Mild-flavored, firm-fleshed, and incredibly versatile, mako is not as oily as swordfish or salmon and is at its best sautéed rather than grilled. Here, it is cut into cubes, quickly sautéed, and then simmered briefly in a full-flavored tomato fondue. Serve with plenty of crusty bread to mop up the delicious sauce.

....

1. Season the mako with salt and pepper and dredge lightly in flour.

2. Sauté the mako in 2 batches: For each batch, heat 1½ tablespoons oil in a large nonstick skillet over medium-high heat. Add half the mako and sauté until crisp and nicely browned. Transfer to a plate and set aside.

3. Add the remaining 1 tablespoon oil to the skillet and cook the bacon until lightly browned. Add the red pepper and cook for 2 minutes. Add the tomato fondue, herbs, and diced tomato and simmer for 2 minutes longer. Return the mako with any accumulated juices to the sauce and just heat through; do not overcook. Transfer to a serving dish, sprinkle with the capers and lemon zest, and serve immediately.

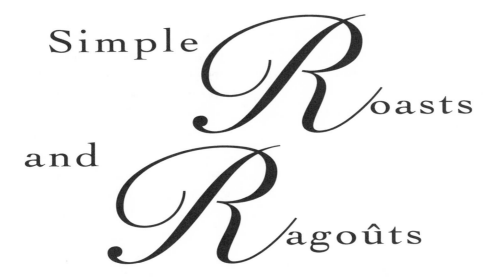

Simple Roasts and Ragoûts

For a TRULY SATISFYING MEAL, I THINK IT WOULD BE HARD TO SUR-
PASS THE SIMPLE PLEASURE OF A ROBUST, AROMATIC ROAST OR RAGOÛT.
WHILE THEIR CHARACTERS AND COOKING TECHNIQUES DIFFER, THEY BOTH
EPITOMIZE WHAT MAKES HOME COOKING SO DIFFERENT FROM RESTAURANT
FOOD: THE NATURAL LOOK OF THE INGREDIENTS, THE DEPTH OF TASTE, THE
INTENSITY OF FLAVOR, THE SIMPLICITY OF THE PRESENTATION.

A ROAST IS PERHAPS THE MORE VERSATILE—PERFECT FOR YOUR FAMILY
BUT ELEGANT ENOUGH FOR GUESTS. AT MY HOUSE, A ROAST ISN'T JUST THE
MAIN COURSE, IT'S THE CENTERPIECE. AND WHILE A ROAST GETS LOTS OF
ATTENTION, IT THRIVES ON VERY LITTLE. ONCE IT'S IN THE OVEN, ALL IT

generally needs is a glance or a light basting every ten to fifteen minutes.

What to cook with a roast? Almost inevitably, the answer is "potatoes." And while this is a natural pairing, Spur of the Moment cooks would do well to consider other ways to enhance the taste. Why not

add whole garlic cloves, cut-up onions, a dicing of celery, or chunks of parsnip to the roasting pan? The most basic vegetables will cook up wonderfully in the pan juices, give you a roast that's anything *but* basic, and help you turn a roast into a one-dish meal. Even canned legumes, like pinto beans and white kidney beans, will take on a whole new savory richness when cooked with a roast.

Does cooking a roast sound too formidable for Spur of the Moment cooking? Remember that there's a big difference between the thirty-pound Thanksgiving turkey and a nice roast pork or leg of lamb that serves six and is done in little over an hour.

Home cooking gets even homier when you take a hearty, bubbling ragoût out of the oven. It's the intensity of flavors that has made the ragoût a new bistro favorite. And that essence of flavor is what separates it from the old-fashioned stew. In a stew, the ingredients are put in together and allowed to cook for a long time, while in a properly made ragoût, each ingredient is browned first to seal in the individual flavors, and then gently braised in stock with the various vegetables added at different stages to preserve their unique taste and texture and to maximize flavor.

Ragoûts, like roasts, have all the qualities you'd look for in a friend. They're good-natured, undemanding, flexible, straightforward, uncomplicated—impossible not to like. For the Spur of the Moment cook, ragoûts make for spontaneous eating, but not for spontaneous cooking. To be really good, they should be allowed to simmer or braise gently for at least an hour, and sometimes more. And for the best possible results, they need time to "sit" in order to give the flavors time to marry—or at least develop a meaningful relationship. Which means that they're great weekend food, when you have a little more time to cook.

There's even more to like about ragoûts than their very satisfying taste. They tend to be inexpensive to make: You don't need the finest cuts of meat. They're easy to shop for: With all the basics in your vegetable bin, you probably already have most of the ingredients on hand. They are wonderfully forgiving: You can cook them ahead, you can even freeze them if you like, then reheat them at your leisure. They reheat beautifully—even overcooked, they taste good! They take happily to last-minute Spur of the Moment additions like roasted carrots or a pound of mushrooms. And unlike most people I know, they improve with age. All in all, roasts and ragoûts represent the kind of home cooking that we all look forward to hungrily and remember fondly, way after we're full!

Ragoût of Pork with Drunken Prunes and Onions

To prepare: 10 minutes
To marinate: overnight
To cook: 2 hours
Serves 6

1½ cups large prunes, preferably unpitted

¾ cup dry white wine

2 tablespoons unsalted butter

1 tablespoon peanut oil

3½ to 4 pounds boneless shoulder of pork, cut into 1½-inch cubes

Salt and freshly ground black pepper

½ pound pearl onions, peeled

Large grating of nutmeg

½ teaspoon ground ginger

2 teaspoons all-purpose flour

2 cups beef bouillon

2 tablespoons red wine vinegar

1 teaspoon granulated sugar

2 teaspoons arrowroot mixed with a little bouillon

I find that there are certain classic food marriages that are hard to improve upon and never seem to be out of style: duck with oranges, lamb with beans, pork with prunes. This delicious stew, which I consider a year-round "pantry basic," is at its best when made with unpitted prunes, which retain their shape and texture. You can use frozen pearl onions if you don't have time to peel fresh ones. Or substitute cubed turnips, which complement the prunes and add a delicious taste to the stew.

1. Combine the prunes and wine in a bowl and let soak overnight.

2. Preheat the oven to 375°F.

3. Melt the butter together with the oil in a large heavy skillet over medium heat. Sauté the pork in batches until nicely browned on all sides. Remove from the skillet, season with salt and pepper, and set aside.

4. Add the onions to the skillet and sauté until nicely browned. Return the pork to the skillet, add the nutmeg, ginger, and flour, and cook for 2 minutes, or until the onions are nicely glazed. Transfer to a large casserole or Dutch oven.

5. Drain the prunes and add the wine to the skillet. Simmer until reduced to 3 tablespoons. Add the bouillon and bring to a boil. Pour over the meat, cover tightly, and braise in the oven for 1 hour and 30 minutes. Add the prunes and braise for 15 to 20 minutes longer, or until the pork is tender but not falling apart.

6. Combine the vinegar and sugar in a small bowl.

7. Transfer the pork, prunes, and onions to a side dish and degrease the pan juices. Return the juices to the casserole, add the vinegar mixture, and bring to a simmer on top of the stove. Whisk in just enough of the arrowroot mixture so that the sauce lightly coats a spoon. Correct the seasoning, return the pork, prunes, and onions to the casserole, and just heat through. Serve hot directly from the casserole.

T i p

Peeling pearl onions is a little more time-consuming than using the peeled frozen ones, but the difference in taste and texture is enormous. A quick way to peel these little onions is to blanch them for 1 to 2 minutes. Then, while they are still warm, peel off a thick layer of the onion with a sharp paring knife, making sure not to cut through the root end, or the onion will fall apart during cooking. You will end up with a smaller onion which is, in fact, much more attractive than the large pearl onions.

Stew of Knockwurst and Summer Vegetables

To prepare: 15 minutes
To cook: 30 minutes
Serves 4

....

3 tablespoons olive oil

1 small dried red chili pepper, broken

2 large garlic cloves, peeled and finely minced

2 medium onions, peeled, quartered, and thinly sliced

1 tablespoon imported paprika

1 teaspoon dried thyme

1 teaspoon dried oregano

1 large green bell pepper, cored, seeded, and thinly sliced

2 large ripe tomatoes, peeled, seeded, and chopped

6 knockwurst or 8 to 10 frankfurters, sliced

Salt and freshly ground black pepper

1 medium zucchini, trimmed and diced

GARNISH
Finely minced fresh parsley

Sour cream

This homey stew is a dish that personifies the very essence of Viennese bistro cooking. You can sample it at every *Heurigen,* the wine bars that offer the new wine of the season. It is traditionally made with a variety of country sausages but I always make it with knockwurst, or with good old-fashioned frankfurters. Serve with a side dish of buttery mashed potatoes or just a loaf of crusty bread and a young wine.

....

1. Heat the oil in a large heavy skillet over medium-low heat. Add the chili pepper, garlic, and onions and sauté until soft and lightly browned. Add the paprika and herbs and cook for 1 minute. Add the bell pepper and tomatoes and simmer, covered, until the pepper is tender and the pan juices have reduced by half, about 10 minutes.

2. Add the knockwurst or frankfurters, season with salt and pepper, and simmer 10 minutes longer. Add the zucchini and cook until tender, 2 to 3 minutes. Correct the seasoning and serve hot, in deep bowls, garnished with parsley and a dollop of sour cream.

T i p

....

This stew can also be made with fresh Italian sweet sausage that has been sautéed in a little oil, removed from the skillet, and sliced. Discard the fat in the pan. Continue as directed, returning the sausage to the pan for the last 10 minutes. I also like to add a cup of cooked white beans or chick peas for the last 10 minutes. Instead of using sour cream, I often whisk ½ cup of yogurt into the stew just before serving.

Oxtail Ragoût in Onion Compote

To prepare: 10 minutes
To cook: 3 hours and 15
minutes to braise
Serves 5 to 6

....

4 tablespoons olive oil

5 pounds meaty oxtails, trimmed
of all fat

Coarse salt and freshly ground
black pepper

1 tablespoon unsalted butter

4 large onions, peeled, quartered,
and thinly sliced

3 large garlic cloves, peeled and
mashed

1 tablespoon imported paprika

1 teaspoon dried thyme

1½ cups beef bouillon

2 teaspoons arrowroot or potato
starch mixed with a little
bouillon

T i p

....

*Oxtails require little preparation
time and practically no attention
during their cooking. The must,
however, be thoroughly degreased,
and I therefore always cook them
a day ahead of time and refrigerate them overnight. The next
day, it is easy to degrease the oxtails, which can them be reheated
right on top of the stove, in the
oven, or in the microwave.*

A f t e r weeks of quick pasta dishes and pan-
seared fish, I crave some no-nonsense food such as this.
Oxtails need long, slow braising, so think of this dish
as weekend food that makes for delicious leftovers.
Serve the ragoût with buttered noodles, creamy mashed
potatoes, or a puree of celery root and potatoes. If you
cannot get oxtails, make the ragoût with beef shank
bones, which are equally flavorful.

....

1.   Preheat the oven to 350°F.

2.   Heat 2 tablespoons of the oil in a large skillet
over medium-high heat. Add the oxtails and brown
on all sides (do this in 2 batches). Transfer to a large
flameproof casserole, season with salt and pepper,
and set aside.

3.   Discard all but 2 tablespoons of the fat from the
skillet. Add the remaining 2 tablespoons oil together
with the butter, add the onions, and cook until soft
and brown. Add the garlic, paprika, and thyme and
stir well. Transfer to the casserole together with the
bouillon and bring to a simmer. Braise in the oven,
covered, for 2 hours and 30 minutes to 3 hours, or
until the oxtails are very tender.

4.   Transfer the oxtails to a serving dish and keep
warm. Thoroughly degrease the pan juices and return to the casserole. Whisk in the arrowroot or potato starch mixture and simmer until the sauce
lightly coats a spoon. Correct the seasoning, pour
over the oxtails, and serve hot.

Roast Leg of Lamb with Fricassee of Beans "en Persillade"

To prepare: 10 minutes
To cook: 45 minutes
Serves 4

....

3½ pounds leg of lamb (see Tip)

1 tablespoon Dijon mustard

2 teaspoons imported paprika

1 teaspoon dried thyme

1 teaspoon coarsely ground black pepper

Coarse salt

5 large garlic cloves, peeled, 2 mashed and 3 finely minced

2 tablespoons olive oil

Optional: 1 large sprig fresh rosemary

2 cups beef bouillon

One 16-ounce can red kidney beans, drained

3 tablespoons finely minced fresh parsley

A juicy, garlicky roast leg of lamb is one of my very favorite cool-weather foods. Now that you can buy just half a leg, it is easy to prepare this delicious cut in less than an hour. By adding kidney beans to the pan juices and further flavoring them with the classic Provençal "persillade" of finely minced parsley and garlic, you can enjoy a wonderful one-dish roast — with delicious leftovers for the next day's supper.

....

1. Preheat the oven to 400°F.

2. Rub the leg of lamb with the mustard and sprinkle with the paprika, thyme, pepper, and coarse salt. Make several tiny slits on the underside of the lamb and press the mashed garlic into the slits.

3. Heat the oil in a heavy roasting pan over medium heat. Add the optional rosemary and the lamb, fat side up, place in the center of the oven, and roast for 10 minutes. Lower the oven temperature to 375°F, add a little of the bouillon to the pan, and continue to roast for 35 to 45 minutes, or until an instant meat thermometer registers 135°F for medium-rare. Baste with a little of the bouillon every 10 minutes. (A rule of thumb for bone-in lamb is to count 13 minutes per pound for medium-rare.)

4. Transfer the lamb to a carving board and let sit while you finish the sauce.

5. Discard the rosemary, thoroughly degrease the pan juices, and return them to the roasting pan. Add the drained beans and simmer over low heat for 5 minutes. Taste and correct the seasoning, adding a large grinding of pepper. Stir in the minced garlic and parsley and just heat through. Keep warm.

6. Carve the lamb and place on a serving platter. Spoon the beans and pan juices around and serve hot.

T i p

When buying half a leg of lamb, you usually have the choice of either the butt or the shank end. I find the shank easier to carve, but the butt end is juicier—which is something to consider when you are going to be busy preparing other parts of the meal and do not have time to baste the roast every 10 minutes.

Roast Chicken Legs with Chili and Cinnamon Rub

To prepare: 5 minutes
To cook: 35 minutes
Serves 4 to 6

¼ cup pure chili powder

1 tablespoon plus 1 teaspoon imported paprika

1 tablespoon plus 1 teaspoon ground cumin

2 teaspoons granulated sugar

2 teaspoons all-purpose flour

1 teaspoon ground cinnamon

½ teaspoon salt

½ teaspoon freshly ground black pepper

Pinch of ground cloves

8 small chicken legs with thighs attached

2 tablespoons olive oil

H e r e is a simple, highly flavored preparation that can be put together and ready to serve in less than an hour. Once the chicken is roasting, I find that I have time to prepare a creamy polenta and a quick stir-fry of colorful peppers and tomatoes, which makes for a nice contrast of flavors and color. Other times I opt for a Viennese side dish of warm potato salad or a stir-fry of Napa cabbage.

1. Preheat the oven to 400°F.

2. Combine all the ingredients except the chicken and oil in a bowl and mix well. Rub evenly over the chicken.

3. Place the chicken in a heavy baking dish and drizzle with the oil. Roast for 30 to 35 minutes, or until the juices run pale yellow, basting often with the pan juices. Serve hot.

T i p

Good pure chili powder is not widely available in supermarkets outside the Southwest and Texas and so should be purchased in specialty stores. The pure powder does not contain cumin or other spices and is usually quite spicy and sometimes somewhat smoky. It is best to store chili powder in an airtight container in the refrigerator since the flavor dissipates rather quickly.

Ragoût of Cornish Hens with Potatoes, Onions, and Thyme

To prepare: 20 minutes

To cook: 30 minutes

Serves 4 to 6

....

2 tablespoons olive oil

2 tablespoons unsalted butter

4 Cornish hens, cut into quarters and wings removed

Salt and freshly ground black pepper

2 small onions, peeled and quartered

6 small red potatoes, unpeeled, quartered

2 teaspoons finely minced garlic

2 tablespoons finely minced fresh thyme or 1½ teaspoons dried

¾ cup Chicken Stock (page 145) or chicken bouillon

GARNISH

Finely minced fresh Italian parsley

Tip

....

This recipe can also be made with small (two-and-a-half-pound) broilers or chicken legs with the thighs attached, which will give you excellent results as well.

H e r e is a terrific dish that can be prepared and ready to serve in less than an hour. Unfortunately, in many parts of the country Cornish hens are only available frozen. Of course, if you have time, you can defrost the frozen hens; be sure to wrap them tightly in a kitchen towel for an hour before roasting to ensure proper browning.

....

1. Preheat the oven to 350°F.

2. Heat 1 tablespoon of the oil together with 1 tablespoon of the butter in a large skillet over medium-high heat. Add the Cornish hens and brown on both sides. Remove from the skillet, season with salt and pepper, and set aside.

3. Add the remaining oil and butter to the pan. When hot, add the onions and potatoes and cook for 2 minutes, shaking the skillet back and forth. Return the hens to the pan, together with the garlic, thyme, and half the stock or bouillon, and cover tightly. Braise in the oven for 20 minutes, or until the hens and vegetables are tender; do not overcook.

4. Transfer the hens to a serving platter and spoon the vegetables around them. Add the remaining stock or bouillon to the skillet and simmer until the sauce lightly coats a spoon. Correct the seasoning and spoon the sauce over the hens and vegetables. Garnish with parsley and serve hot, accompanied by braised or steamed spinach.

Garlic-Roasted Chicken with Fennel and Onions

To prepare: 15 minutes
To cook: 1 hour and 15
minutes
Serves 4

....

1 pound fennel (about 2 medium
bulbs), tops and stalks removed; do not core

1 whole chicken (about 3½
pounds)

2 large garlic cloves, peeled and
mashed, plus 3 cloves,
peeled

2 teaspoons dried thyme

Coarse salt and freshly ground
black pepper

Optional: Sprig of fresh rosemary

2 tablespoons unsalted butter

1 tablespoon extra-virgin olive oil

4 to 6 small yellow onions, unpeeled, cut in half crosswise

1¼ cups Chicken Stock (page
145) or chicken bouillon

1 teaspoon arrowroot or potato
flour mixed with a little stock

GARNISH
2 to 3 tablespoons finely minced
fennel tops or fresh parsley

R o a s t i n g a chicken properly is a bit like knowing how to hard-boil an egg. Simple as it seems, there is tremendous room for error, and a good roast chicken is ultimately not that easy to find either in res-taurants or in the home. Here is a recipe that couldn't be simpler. Its success depends on the quality of the raw materials and on your willingness to keep an eye on the chicken and baste it frequently so that it does not dry out. Since the vegetables here are roasted right along in the pan, this is in fact a terrific one-dish meal. If you are happy just with crusty bread for mopping up the delicious sauce, dinner can be on the table in a little over an hour—during which time you can make a salad or simply relax with a glass of wine.

....

1. Preheat the oven to 425°F.

2. Discard any brownish outer layers from the fen-nel bulbs. Cut into quarters through the core, or, if large, into eighths. Set aside.

3. Rub the chicken with the mashed garlic and the thyme and season with coarse salt and pepper. Place the optional rosemary and the whole garlic cloves in the chicken cavity.

4. Melt the butter together with the oil in a large heavy flameproof baking dish over medium-high heat. Add the chicken and brown nicely on all sides.

Add the fennel and onions, cut side down, to the baking dish and season lightly with salt and pepper. Add ¼ cup of the stock or bouillon and roast in the oven for 45 minutes to 1 hour, adding a little more stock to the dish as necessary and basting with the pan juices every 10 minutes, until the juices run yellow; do not let pan juices run dry. Turn the fennel 2 or 3 times during roasting.

5. When the chicken is done, transfer to a serving platter together with the vegetables. Add the remaining stock or bouillon to the baking dish, bring to a simmer, and whisk in just enough of the arrowroot or starch mixture so that the sauce lightly coats a spoon. Taste and correct the seasoning. Spoon the sauce over the vegetables, garnish with the fennel or parsley, and serve hot.

T i p s

The onions are wonderful served in their "jackets." They can easily be squeezed out of their peels before serving, but the beauty of this dish is this rather "peasant-like" presentation.

For roasting, always choose small birds. One 3½-pound chicken takes no more than 45 minutes to roast at 425°F. Trussing a bird this size is not necessary, but be sure to baste it every 10 minutes with bouillon. If you want to roast a larger bird (4 to 5 pounds), always truss it, and roast it on its side, turning once during roasting. This keeps the chicken breast moist.

Roast Cornish Hens
in Rosemary-Lemon Essence

To prepare: 10 minutes
To cook: 50 minutes
Serves 4

....

4 Cornish hens (about 1¼ pounds each)

1½ teaspoons dried thyme

1½ teaspoons dried marjoram

1 tablespoon Dijon mustard

1½ teaspoons imported paprika

1 large garlic clove, peeled and mashed

Coarse salt and freshly ground black pepper

2 tablespoons unsalted butter

1 tablespoon olive oil

1¼ cups chicken bouillon or Chicken Stock (page 145)

Juice of 1 lemon

¾ cup heavy cream

1 Beurre Manié (page 193)

1 tablespoon fresh rosemary leaves

Optional: 8 double-poached large garlic cloves (see page 41)

GARNISH
Sprigs of watercress

For the Spur of the Moment cook, Cornish hens are a terrific buy. The hens roast in only forty-five minutes, just enough time to prepare a salad or a simple vegetable side dish. I usually use a roasting pan large enough so I can braise a mixture of carrots, turnips, and/or parsnips right alongside the hens. Other vegetables, especially fennel cut into small wedges, whole Belgian endives, or small whole shallots and pearl onions also work well and make for a delicious accompaniment.

1. Preheat the oven to 400°F.

2. Dry the Cornish hens thoroughly with paper towels and truss them.

3. In a small bowl, combine the thyme, marjoram, mustard, paprika, and mashed garlic and mix well to form a paste. Rub the paste all over the hens, and season with coarse salt and pepper.

4. Melt the butter together with the olive oil in a large heavy flameproof baking dish over medium heat. Add the hens and brown on all sides, regulating the heat as necessary so as not to burn them. Add ¼ cup of the bouillon or stock and place the baking dish in the center of the oven and roast for 35 to 40 minutes, or until the juices run pale yellow and the internal temperature of a thigh reaches 180°F on a meat thermometer. Every 10 minutes, add a little stock to the pan and baste the hens with the pan juices.

5. When the hens are done, transfer them to a cutting board and discard the trussing strings.

6. Thoroughly degrease the pan juices and return them to the baking dish together with the remaining stock. Bring to a boil and reduce to 3 tablespoons. Add the lemon juice and heavy cream and reduce slightly. Then whisk in bits of the beurre manié and simmer until the sauce lightly coats a spoon. Add the rosemary and optional double-poached garlic, and correct the seasoning. Keep warm.

7. Cut the hens in half and place on individual serving plates. Spoon the lemon sauce around the hens and garnish with sprigs of watercress. Serve at once.

T i p

....

You can now buy peeled garlic cloves packed in jars in many supermarkets. These are great time-savers, especially for such preparations as a garnish of double-poached or caramelized garlic. Since they are quite mild, you can use as many as 16 to 20 as an accompaniment to the Cornish hens.

Roast Turkey with Golden Raisin Chutney

To prepare: 15 minutes

To roast: 1 hour and 50 minutes

Serves 8

....

1 fresh turkey (about 10 to 12 pounds)

1 tablespoon dried thyme

Coarse salt and cracked black pepper

2 tablespoons unsalted butter

1 teaspoon peanut oil

2½ cups Chicken Stock (page 145) or chicken bouillon

RAISIN CHUTNEY

1 medium onion, peeled and quartered

One 2-inch piece fresh ginger, peeled and coarsely chopped

2 large garlic cloves, peeled

2 tablespoons olive oil

2 small dried red chili peppers, broken

½ pound golden raisins, plumped (see page 159)

1½ teaspoons ground cumin

1 teaspoon coriander

½ teaspoon cardamom

2 teaspoons dark brown sugar

½ cup fresh tangerine juice

1½ tablespoons red wine vinegar

Salt and freshly ground black pepper

M o s t people assume that roasting a turkey is time-consuming. Not so! A small (nine- to ten-pound) turkey, roasted according to the high-temperature method, is ready under two hours—and you have the added benefit of wonderful leftovers that provide you with many delicious possibilities. I love roasting a whole turkey on a covered charcoal grill with some green lilac or apple wood for a slightly smoky taste but I also enjoy it roasted at a high temperature in the oven, which results in irresistibly crisp skin. Either way, with a side dish of this sweet annd spicy chutney, roast turkey is perfect for the weekend cook. Served with Sweet Potato and Carrot Puree (see page 260) or one made with rutabagas and topped with crispy on-ions, it makes a superb, comforting meal that need not be reserved exclusively for holiday entertaining.

1. Preheat the oven to 425°F.

2. Dry the turkey thoroughly with kitchen towels. Season with the thyme and coarse salt and pepper, and truss the legs.

3. In a large heavy flame-proof roasting pan, melt the butter together with the oil over medium heat. Add the turkey, breast side up, and ¼ cup of the stock or bouillon. Place in the center of the oven and roast for 1 hour 30 minutes to 1 hour 45 minutes, or until the internal temperature of a thigh registers 180°F on a meat thermometer and the juices run pale yellow. Every 10 to 15 minutes, add a little more stock to the pan and baste with the pan juices. If the turkey becomes too dark before it is done, tent loosely with foil.

4.   While the turkey is roasting, prepare the chutney: In the workbowl of a food processor, combine the onion, ginger, and garlic. Process to a smooth paste.

5.   In a heavy skillet, heat the olive oil over medium heat. Add the chili peppers and heat until they darken; discard. Add the onion paste and cook, stirring, until softened and lightly browned. Reduce the heat, add the raisins, cumin, coriander, and cardamom, and cook for 3 minutes, stirring constantly. Add the brown sugar, tangerine juice, and vinegar. Season with salt and pepper to taste. Cook for another 5 to 8 minutes, or until the cooking juices are reduced and syrupy. Set aside.

6.   When the turkey is done, remove from the oven and transfer to a carving board. Discard the trussing string and let sit for 5 to 10 minutes before carving.

7.   Degrease the pan juices thoroughly and return them to the baking dish together with the remaining stock or bouillon. Bring to a boil over high heat and reduce to ¼ cup. Add the chutney and correct the seasoning. Remove from the heat and keep warm.

8.   Carve the turkey, place on a large serving platter, and serve hot, with the chutney on the side.

Ragoût of Calamari with Tubettini and Onion-Tomato Compote

To prepare: 15 minutes
To cook: 45 minutes
Serves 4

....

2 tablespoons extra-virgin olive oil

1 small dried red chili pepper, broken

2 medium red onions, peeled, quartered, and thinly sliced

2 large garlic cloves, peeled and finely minced

3 large ripe tomatoes, peeled, seeded, and chopped

1 teaspoon dried oregano

1 teaspoon dried thyme

1 pound fresh calamari, cleaned and cut into 1-inch pieces

Salt and freshly ground black pepper

1½ cups imported tubettini

GARNISH
Finely minced fresh Italian parsley

1 large garlic clove, peeled and finely minced

I g r e w up in Barcelona, where calamari was a staple that my mother served at least twice a week. I had a passion for fried calamari as a child and to this day consider it one of my very favorite foods. But other calamari preparations are also high on my list, and this is one of them.

I was amazed on a recent visit to Barcelona to see how many cooks were buying frozen calamari. I was assured that when it is braised, one cannot tell the difference, which makes this dish more accessible for those cooks who cannot get fresh calamari. The addition of tiny pasta turns the ragoût into a light main course, but without the tubettini it makes a lovely starter, followed by a simple main course such as sautéed chicken breasts or veal scaloppine.

....

1. Heat the oil in a large heavy skillet over medium heat. Add the chili pepper and onions and cook, stirring often, until the onions are soft and lightly browned, about 15 minutes.

2. Add the garlic, tomatoes, herbs, and calamari, season with salt and pepper, and simmer, covered, until the juices have reduced and the calamari is tender, about 20 minutes. Keep warm.

3. Drop the tubettini into a large pot of boiling salted water and cook until just tender, or al dente. Drain well.

4.   Add the pasta to the calamari sauce. Correct the seasoning and just heat through. Serve hot, directly from the skillet, garnished with parsley and the optional minced garlic.

T i p

....

When there is a choice between cleaned calamari versus uncleaned, I prefer buying it uncleaned. Cleaning calamari takes only minutes and there is usually quite a price difference. Once it is cleaned, be sure to dry it thoroughly on several layers of paper towels before sautéing.

Catalan Roasted Bluefish with a Gratin of New Potatoes and Onions

To prepare: 20 minutes
To cook: 55 minutes
Serves 4 to 5

....

5 tablespoons extra-virgin olive oil

2 large red onions, peeled, quartered, and thinly sliced

2 large garlic cloves, peeled and thinly sliced

3 tablespoons finely minced fresh thyme

1 pound small red new potatoes, unpeeled, cut into ¼-inch slices

Salt and freshly ground black pepper

½ to ¾ cup fish bouillon

3 medium ripe tomatoes, sliced

1½ to 1¾ pounds fresh bluefish fillet, in one piece

⅓ cup dry white wine

GARNISH
½ cup finely minced fresh parsley

1 large garlic clove, peeled and finely minced

3 to 4 tablespoons fresh bread crumbs

Extra-virgin olive oil

½ cup small black oil-cured olives, pitted and cut in half

T h e oily texture of bluefish is ideal for this Mediterranean preparation in which the potatoes form a bed for the fish, which essentially cooks in its own juices. Since bluefish is really at its best in the Northeast, where it is most plentiful, you may have a hard time getting it in your area, but Spanish mackerel will do equally well.

....

1. Preheat the oven to 350°F.

2. Heat 3 tablespoons of the oil in a large heavy skillet over medium heat. Add the onions, garlic, and 2 tablespoons of the thyme and cook for 3 to 4 minutes, or until the onions begin to soften. Add the potatoes and season with salt and pepper.

3. Spoon the potato mixture into a rectangular or oval baking dish, add ½ cup bouillon, and top with overlapping slices of tomatoes. Sprinkle with the remaining 1 tablespoon thyme and drizzle with the remaining 2 tablespoons oil. Bake for 15 to 20 minutes, or until the potatoes are almost tender; you may need to add more bouillon, depending on the juiciness of the tomatoes. Then place the bluefish on top, season with salt and pepper, and add the white wine. Bake until just done, about 30 minutes.

4. While the fish is baking, prepare the garnish: Combine the parsley, garlic, and bread crumbs in a small bowl and add enough oil to moisten.

5. Top the baked bluefish with the bread-crumb mixture and the olives and run under a preheated broiler for 2 minutes, or until crusty and lightly browned. Serve at once directly from the baking dish.

T i p

Even more so than any other seafood, oily fish such as bluefish and mackerel require utmost freshness to be truly good without any aftertaste. Since very fresh fish may be hard to obtain for anyone living away from the shore, a simple marinade of lemon juice, olive oil, and fresh herbs will refresh the fish and rid it off any oily aftertaste. Do not marinate the fish for more than twenty minutes, or it will "cook" in the marinade.

Oven-Braised Salmon Fillets in Lemon Crème Fraîche

To prepare: 10 minutes
To cook: 25 minutes
Serves 4

Juice of 1 large lemon

1½ cups crème fraîche (see page 31)

Salt and freshly ground white pepper

6 tablespoons unsalted butter

2 tablespoons finely minced shallots

½ cup dry vermouth

4 salmon fillets (about 6 to 7 ounces each), preferably center-cut

GARNISH
Finely minced fresh dill or chives

E v e n those people whose idea of eating fish was once limited to some kind of baked or broiled flounder have discovered the wonderful taste of salmon. Farm-raised and fresh, it is available everywhere, and I find myself serving it once or twice a week since it is as versatile as chicken.

Braised in the oven with a touch of lemon cream, a dicing of shallots, and some vermouth, salmon makes an ideal main course. What's more, it allows for an endless choice of quick and effortless side dishes. While the fish is in the oven, you can steam some fresh asparagus, sauté some zucchini, or skillet-braise a root vegetable mixture of carrots and turnips, all of which go nicely with the fish.

1.   Preheat the oven to 350°F.

2.   Combine the lemon juice and crème fraîche in a small bowl, season with salt and white pepper, and set aside.

3.   Melt 2 tablespoons of the butter in a large flameproof baking dish over low heat. Add the shallots and vermouth and reduce to a glaze. Remove from the heat.

4.   Season the salmon with salt and white pepper and place in a single layer in the baking dish. Pour the crème fraîche mixture over the salmon, cover with buttered foil, and bake for 15 to 20 minutes, or until the fish is just opaque; do not overcook.

5. Transfer the fillets to a serving platter and keep warm. If the pan juices seem thin, reduce over medium heat until the sauce lightly coats a spoon, and remove from the heat. Whisk in the remaining 4 tablespoons butter and correct the seasoning. Wipe any accumulated juices from the platter and spoon the sauce over the fillets. Garnish with dill or chives and serve hot.

T i p

When buying salmon fillets, choose only the center cut, versus the end part, which is usually so thin that it is difficult not to overcook it. Usually, a nice fish-monger will slice off the first 2 inches from several sides of salmon, which will make the fillets all uniform in size—so they will cook evenly.

Braised Halibut with Pinto Beans and Saffron Sofrito

To prepare: 20 minutes
To cook: 30 minutes
Serves 4 to 5

....

½ teaspoon saffron threads

3 cups water

2 fish bouillon cubes

1 medium zucchini, trimmed and cut into ⅓-inch cubes (discard most of the seedy pulp)

3 tablespoons olive oil

1 small dried red chili pepper, broken

1 large onion, peeled, quartered, and thickly sliced

2 large garlic cloves, peeled and thinly sliced

1 teaspoon dried thyme or 1 tablespoon fresh thyme leaves

1 Turkish bay leaf

½ teaspoon imported paprika

2 cups drained canned pinto beans

1 large red bell pepper, roasted, peeled and thinly sliced

1½ pounds trimmed halibut fillets or steaks, cut into 1½-inch cubes

Salt and freshly ground pepper

GARNISH

2 to 3 tablespoons coarsely chopped fresh Italian parsley

T h e firm texture of halibut makes it perfect for braising both in the oven and on top of the stove. I particularly love this earthy Catalan preparation in which chunks of the fish are simmered in a shallow terra-cotta pan in an onion and paprika *sofrito*. Many pantry basics can be added to this fish "ragoût," making it a perfect quick one-dish meal. Cubed boiled potatoes, and blanched carrots, turnips, or other legumes all work well. If you substitute other canned beans for the pintos, I suggest you go with chick peas or red kidney beans, which retain their texture well.

....

1. Combine the saffron, water, and bouillon cubes in a small saucepan and bring to a simmer. Simmer, partially covered, for 15 minutes. Set aside.

2. Steam the zucchini, covered, over simmering water until barely tender. Set aside.

3. Heat the oil in a large casserole over medium heat. Add the chili pepper and cook until dark; remove and discard. Add the onion and garlic and cook until soft but not browned. Add the thyme, bay leaf, and paprika and cook for 1 minute longer, stirring constantly.

4. Add the pinto beans, zucchini, and roasted pepper. Top with the halibut, season with salt and pepper, and cover with the saffron broth. Simmer for 3 minutes, or until the halibut is just opaque; do not overcook. Immediately remove from the heat. Serve in deep soup bowls, garnished with the parsley.

Side ishes That Steal the Show

I have RECENTLY NOTICED A DINING EXPERIENCE I CALL "THE SIDE DISH PHENOMENON." IT OCCURS WHEN YOU'VE GONE OUT TO DINNER, COME HOME, AND THEN FIND YOURSELF THINKING MORE ABOUT HOW DELICIOUS AND MEMORABLE THE SIDE DISH WAS THAN THE ENTRÉE IT ACCOMPANIED.

OVER AND OVER I FIND MYSELF RECALLING THE CRISPY FRIED POTATOES THAT ACCOMPANIED THE LEMON-SPIKED SCALOPPINE OR THE RICH AND CREAMY POLENTA THAT ECLIPSED A PEPPER-RUBBED ROAST. EVEN SIMPLE SIDE ORDERS STAND OUT IN MY MIND: A TART COLESLAW FROM A ROADSIDE STAND IN NEW YORK STATE, THE CRUNCHY HUSHPUPPIES AT A DINER IN ALABAMA, THE QUINTESSENTIAL CORN BREAD IN ATLANTA.

I am more and more interested in the spectacular potential of side dishes that go beyond the familiar, through either new interpretations or new ingredients. And I find that top chefs are discovering the same satisfaction of working with simple, unsung vegetables like carrots, po-tatoes, turnips, and parsnips, along with basic grains like rice, couscous, and bulgur, and transforming them into simple but show-stopping side dishes.

Clearly, we all share the same goal: no more boring side dishes. With an equal amount of planning and creativity, I think it's relatively easy to take any ordinary fruit or vegetable out of the ordinary. Why settle for baked acorn squash when you can serve a sublime acorn squash and roasted pear puree? Why make plain green peas when you can knock their socks off with a puree of peas teamed up with velvety sour cream and an unexpected hit of mint?

For the Spur of the Moment cook, the right side dish can enliven and ennoble even the simplest main course. The rules are simple and the caveats are few. Push a little, experiment, don't worry about making mistakes. Wonderful new combinations of ingredients are possible if you think beyond the expected. For example, fruits and vegetables are now being served together, in intriguing new relationships. Pears with squash, tomatoes with lemon, apples with onions, or leeks with raisins can all harmonize beautifully. But remember to keep it balanced. With side dishes, a well-conceived simplicity is the goal.

Think of yourself as a fashion designer creating separates that have to go together and complement each other. And as with accessorizing, it's the small things that can make a dramatic difference. Some diced unpeeled tomato, a touch of fruity olive oil, or a couple of sprigs of fried parsley can be sublime additions. Beware the overdramatic and overreaching. Steer clear of woefully undercooked nouvelle vegetables and of old-fashioned overcooked vegetables that taste as if they've been sitting for hours on the steam table. Be careful not to overbutter, overherb, or overblend. Think of yourself as an elegantly basic purist rather than the kind of designer who keeps adding and embellishing.

And don't forget that you can't give every dish equal time. Some days you feel like doing an ambitious side dish and serving it with a hamburger. Some days you'll knock yourself out on a major entrée and only feel like steaming some fresh beans to round it out. And other days, you'll be too busy to give anything much time at all. Which is a good time to try someone else's fabulous coleslaw, hushpuppies, or corn bread!

Honey-Glazed Beets with Balsamic Vinegar

To prepare: 10 minutes
To cook: 6 to 8 minutes
Serves 4

....

2 tablespoons pure honey

1½ tablespoons balsamic vinegar

One ½-inch piece fresh ginger, peeled and passed through a garlic press

3 tablespoons unsalted butter

2 pounds cooked beets, peeled and cut into ¼-inch julienne

Salt and freshly ground black pepper

T i p

....

When testing cooked beets for doneness, do not prick with a fork, which would release the beet juices and make them lose their color. Instead, use the tip of a sharp knife.

B e e t s are a seasonal gem, and who can resist picking up a fresh bunch at the farm market? Although they are available practically year-round, they are at their best during the summer and early fall months. At that time, small beets will take only fifteen to twenty minutes to cook. At other times you can use store-bought jarred beets, which work well in most recipes. Beets can also be baked, or cooked in the microwave. Always be sure to keep the roots and an inch of the beet tops attached so they don't bleed.

....

1.   Combine the honey, vinegar, and ginger juice in a small bowl and set aside.

2.   Melt the butter in a large skillet over medium heat, add the beets, and cook for 3 to 4 minutes, or until just heated through. Add the honey mixture, season with salt and pepper, and cook for another 3 to 4 minutes, or until the beets are nicely glazed. Serve at once.

Brussels Sprouts with Bacon, Pine Nuts, and Sour Cream

To prepare: 10 minutes
To cook: 20 minutes
Serves 4

....

3 tablespoons olive oil

2½ ounces slab bacon, blanched and cut into ¼-inch dice, about ½ cup

3 tablespoons pine nuts

1 pint Brussels sprouts, trimmed and cut into ¼-inch slices

½ to ¾ cup chicken bouillon

Salt and freshly ground black pepper

½ cup sour cream

1 large garlic clove, peeled and mashed

T i p

....

A lovely way to use Brussels sprouts is to separate them into individual leaves. This is easily done by blanching the sprouts first for 2 minutes and then separating the leaves, discarding the inside core.

F o r anyone who has grown Brussels sprouts or had the good fortune of sampling them truly fresh, the cool-weather kitchen would not be complete without this fall vegetable. Brussels sprouts are around in the supermarket for a very long time, which makes them an excellent Spur of the Moment choice. Brussels sprouts can be prepared in the simplest of ways, but they should always be just tender, not overcooked. The sprouts, however, do like company—especially that of bacon and pine nuts. Smoked turkey breast or ham can be substituted for the bacon in this recipe. Serve the sprouts as an appetizer or as a side dish to a simple roast chicken (see page 228) or Skillet-Seared Flank Steak in Spicy Ginger Marinade (page 202).

....

1. Heat the oil in a cast-iron skillet over medium-low heat. Add the bacon and pine nuts and sauté until lightly browned. Add the sprouts together with ½ cup bouillon, season with salt and pepper, and simmer, partially covered, for 12 to 15 minutes, or until the sprouts are crisp-tender, adding more bouillon if necessary.

2. Fold in the sour cream and garlic and cook until reduced to a glaze. Correct the seasoning and serve hot.

Gratin of Eggplant with Tomatoes and Basil Vinaigrette

To prepare: 15 minutes
To cook: 20 minutes
Serves 4 to 5

....

2 medium eggplants, unpeeled, cut crosswise into ½-inch slices

Coarse salt and freshly ground black pepper

All-purpose flour for dredging

About 1 cup extra-virgin olive oil

2 medium ripe tomatoes, sliced

2 large garlic cloves, peeled and thinly sliced, plus 1 large clove, peeled and mashed

1 cup fresh basil leaves

1½ tablespoons red wine vinegar or a mixture of red wine vinegar and balsamic vinegar

GARNISH

Small fresh Italian parsley leaves or 2 tablespoons minced parsley

W h e n I first had this dish at a friend's house in Tuscany, I thought it was exquisite. The tender sautéed eggplant was interlaced with slices of ripe tomatoes, then briefly reheated to warm the tomatoes. It was served simply sprinkled with superb extra-virgin olive oil, some coarse salt, and a shower of tiny basil leaves.

I have since made this dish in many different ways. Depending on the amount of time I have, I often leave the tomatoes raw and drizzle the whole dish with the basil vinaigrette. You may also add slices of mozzarella and thinly sliced red onions, turning the dish into a flavorful luncheon or supper main course.

....

1. Preheat the oven to 350°F.

2. Season the eggplant with coarse salt and pepper and dredge very lightly in flour.

3. Heat ¼ cup oil in a large nonstick skillet over medium heat. Add a few eggplant slices and sauté until browned on both sides. Drain on paper towels. Continue to sauté the remaining eggplant, adding more oil to the skillet when necessary.

4. Transfer the eggplant to a large baking dish, alternating with the tomatoes and thinly sliced garlic in a single layer. Season with salt and pepper, and bake for 10 minutes, or until the tomatoes are heated through.

5. While the gratin is in the oven, make the vinaigrette: Puree the basil with the mashed garlic, vinegar, and 6 tablespoons oil in a blender. Season with salt and pepper. If the vinaigrette is too sharp, add a little more olive oil.

6. Drizzle the gratin with the vinaigrette, garnish with parsley, and serve warm or at room temperature.

T i p

Fresh basil is an extremely delicate herb that has a short shelf life once refrigerated. To keep the leaves from turning dark, place the bunch in a glass full of cold water and cover the leaves loosely with a plastic bag. Store in refrigerator.

Mascarpone and Chive Mashed Potatoes

To prepare: 5 minutes
To cook: 20 minutes
Serves 4

3 medium all-purpose potatoes
(about 1½ pounds), peeled
and cut into eighths

4 tablespoons unsalted butter

2 tablespoons sour cream

¼ cup mascarpone

2 to 3 tablespoons finely minced
fresh chives

Salt and freshly ground black
pepper

T i p

Mascarpone is now available in many supermarkets. The container is usually stamped with a sell-by date. Even so, mascarpone can often be just past its prime, so I recommend that you taste it before using. The taste must be sweet and that of very fresh heavy cream. If it is even slightly sour, do not use it, since it will change the taste of any preparation in which it is used.

T h e good news is that homey mashed potatoes are back in vogue. You can now sample a variety of interpretations in three-star restaurants as well as casual bistros on both sides of the Atlantic. The bad news is that mashed potatoes really taste good only when enriched with butter, sour cream, or mascarpone—and the more the better. Is it worth it? To me it is. Serve this version with just about any main course in the book. I like to double the recipe and have leftovers. Mashed potatoes heat up beautifully in a low oven or the microwave. In addition, leftovers can be turned into the gnocchi on page 129 or mixed with finnan haddie and an egg or two to make the most wonderful fritters.

1. Drop the potatoes into boiling salted water and cook until tender; drain. Pass through a food mill, and transfer to the top of a double boiler set over simmering water.

2. Add the butter, sour cream, mascarpone, and chives and mix well. Season with salt and pepper and serve hot.

Red Onion Jam with Red Wine and Cassis

To prepare: 10 minutes
To cook: 40 minutes
Serves 6

6 tablespoons unsalted butter

2 pounds red onions, peeled, quartered, and thinly sliced

¼ cup granulated sugar

3 cups dry red wine

¼ cup Cassis

1½ tablespoons sherry vinegar

Salt and freshly ground black pepper

T i p

You can also make this onion jam with Spanish onions and tint it red by adding 2 to 3 tablespoons of grenadine.

W h e t h e r made with red onions or Spanish onions, an onion jam is a terrific pantry basic that goes well with all grilled foods. I particularly like this slightly sweet version, to which the Cassis gives a nice fruity taste. Serve it as a side dish to a simple roast turkey, grilled chicken, or, especially, Grilled Salmon with Cracked White Pepper and Dill Rub (page 177). I usually double or even triple the recipe since it keeps, refrigerated, for up to two months. Onion jams can be served warm, at room temperature, or slightly chilled, and as a wonderful topping to a bruschetta or as a filling for an omelette.

1. Melt the butter in a cast-iron skillet over medium heat. Add the onions and sugar and cook, stirring often, until the onions begin to brown.

2. Reduce the heat, add the wine, Cassis, and vinegar, and simmer for 30 to 40 minutes, or until all the liquid has evaporated. Season with salt and pepper and serve warm or at room temperature.

Remarks: For an interesting variation with a more unusual taste and texture, add ½ cup plumped dark raisins (see page 159) and ¼ cup pine nuts, sautéed until golden in a little olive oil (see page 269), to the jam.

Caramelized Corn, Mango, and Bacon Medley

To prepare: 15 minutes
To cook: 15 minutes
Serves 4 to 6

....

6 ears of fresh corn, shucked

2 tablespoons unsalted butter

2½ ounces slab bacon, blanched and diced, about ½ cup

1 medium onion, peeled and finely minced

4 to 5 tablespoons pure maple syrup

Salt and freshly ground black pepper

2 to 4 tablespoons finely minced fresh cilantro

1 large ripe mango, peeled and finely cubed

T i p

....

The best mangoes are the large Mexican ones that start appearing in the markets in late spring and are available throughout the summer. For a variation you can use papaya in this recipe together with the juice of ½ lime.

E v e r y o n e has a particular favorite way with fresh corn. Mine is to leave three or four ears in the cooking water overnight and munch on the cold ears the next day. True, the corn is somewhat soggy, but that is exactly what I love about it. I am also addicted to this corn medley, which can be served like a chutney or side dish to grilled meats, seafood, and poultry. If you cannot find a ripe mango, half a cup of plumped golden raisins is a nice substitute. Just be sure to cut down on the amount of maple syrup so the mixture is not too sweet.

....

1. Drop the corn into boiling water and cook for 4 minutes; drain. Cut off the kernels with a sharp knife and set aside.

2. Melt the butter in a 10-inch skillet over medium heat. Add the bacon and cook until almost crisp. Add the onion and cook until soft but not browned. Add the corn and maple syrup and cook for 3 to 4 minutes, or until the corn is nicely glazed. Remove from the heat, season with salt and pepper, and fold in the cilantro and mango. Serve warm or at room temperature, with pan-seared chicken breasts or grilled Cornish hens.

Tuscan Fricassee of Savoy Cabbage and Pancetta

To prepare: 10 minutes
To cook: 25 minutes
Serves 4

....

One 1-pound Savoy cabbage, quartered

3 tablespoons extra-virgin olive oil

2½ ounces pancetta or meaty slab bacon, blanched and diced, about ½ cup

2 large garlic cloves, peeled and finely minced

1 large shallot, peeled and finely minced

3 tablespoons finely minced fresh parsley

¾ to 1 cup beef bouillon

Salt and freshly ground black pepper

Tip

....

If you cannot get pancetta or slab bacon, you can use smoked pork shoulder butt or even finely diced smoked ham.

When I am in Florence in the winter, I often order this simple fricassee as a side dish to sautéed veal scaloppine or a steak alla Fiorentina. Considering the fact that Italians certainly know how to cook vegetables, it's odd that the cabbage in this dish is almost invariably overcooked. But that's OK, I rather like it like that. It is quite "cabbagey"-tasting but still delicious and very homey. Serve as a side dish to pan-seared pork tenderloin or sautéed Italian sausage.

....

1. Drop the cabbage into boiling salted water and cook for 3 minutes. Drain. When cool enough to handle, cut crosswise into ½-inch julienne. Set aside.

2. Heat the oil in a large cast-iron skillet over low heat. Add the pancetta or bacon and sauté until almost crisp. Add the garlic, shallot, and parsley and cook for 1 minute. Add the cabbage and ½ cup bouillon, season lightly with salt and pepper, and simmer, covered, for 15 to 20 minutes, or until tender, adding more bouillon as necessary after 10 minutes. Correct the seasoning and serve.

Sautéed Snow Peas in Shallot and Parsley Butter

To prepare: 15 minutes
To cook: 4 to 5 minutes
Serves 4 to 5

....

3 tablespoons unsalted butter, softened

1½ tablespoons finely minced shallots

2 tablespoons finely minced fresh parsley

2 tablespoons extra-virgin olive oil

1 pound snow peas trimmed

2 large garlic cloves, peeled and sliced

2 tablespoons dry sherry

¼ cup chicken bouillon

Coarse salt and freshly ground black pepper

T i p

When buying snow peas, look for those that are very crisp with bright green tips. Avoid any that are limp and with brown and wilted-looking tips. Snow peas will keep for up to 10 days when stored in a plastic bag in the vegetable bin. Leftover snow peas can be heated successfully in the microwave if not overcooked.

C e r t a i n vegetables are so strongly identified with a specific cuisine that it takes a while to see all their creative possibilities. Such has been the fate until recently of the crisp and flavorful snow pea. It seems to belong in Chinese and other Far Eastern preparations, much like bok choy and shiitake mushrooms. But snow peas are amazingly versatile, and I like to team them with shallots and parsley in this Spur of the Moment side dish. They also go well with other herbs, especially mint, dill, and chives. Take advantage of their bright green color to enhance a plateful of oven-roasted peppers. Caramelized garlic cloves add a nice taste and interesting texture to this lively sauté.

1. Combine the butter, shallots, and parsley in a small bowl and blend with a fork into a smooth paste. Cover and refrigerate.

2. Heat the oil in a large nonstick skillet over medium-high heat. Add the snow peas and sauté quickly until they just begin to brown. Add the garlic and sherry and continue to cook until nicely browned, shaking the skillet back and forth to prevent the peas from burning.

3. Reduce the heat, add the bouillon, season with salt and pepper, and simmer, covered, for 2 to 3 minutes, or until just tender. Add the shallot butter and let it melt into the peas. Serve immediately.

Acorn Squash and Roasted Pear Puree

To prepare: 5 minutes
To cook: 1 hour
Serves 4

....

2 medium acorn squash

1 medium ripe Bosc pear, peeled, cored, and cut into eighths

2 teaspoons granulated sugar

¼ cup water

3 tablespoons unsalted butter

Salt and freshly ground white pepper

Large grating of nutmeg

T i p

....

Although you can cook acorn squash in the microwave with good results, the taste of the oven-roasted squash is far superior and well worth the extra time. Baking the squash produces nutty-sweet and evenly tender flesh, which is not possible when using the microwave.

W i n t e r **squash is traditionally paired with brown sugar and spices, and in fact, I find a baked acorn squash, its cavity filled with butter and brown sugar, a hard act to follow. Still, I am very fond of this rather different late-harvest marriage of flavors. If you are pressed for time, use canned Bartlett pears, with some of their syrup, when preparing the squash. Serve the puree with the Skillet Steak in Tarragon and Green Peppercorn Sauce (page 201) or Ragoût of Cornish Hens with Potatoes, Onions, and Thyme (page 227).**

....

1.   Preheat the oven to 375°F.

2.   Place the acorn squash in a small baking dish and roast, turning once, for 1 hour, or until tender when pierced with a fork. Place the pear in another baking dish, sprinkle with the sugar, add the water and 1 tablespoon of the butter, and roast alongside the squash for 20 to 25 minutes, or until tender and lightly browned.

3.   Cut the squash in half and discard the seeds. Scoop out the pulp and puree in a food processor, together with the pear, until smooth. Add the remaining 2 tablespoons butter, season with salt and white pepper and nutmeg, and serve hot.

Sauté of Zucchini Milanese

To prepare: 10 minutes
To cook: 10 to 12 minutes
Serves 4 to 5

....

5 tablespoons unsalted butter, softened

2 tablespoons finely minced fresh parsley

1 large garlic clove, peeled and finely minced

Salt and freshly ground black pepper

6 small zucchini, trimmed and cut crosswise into ½-inch slices

¼ cup chicken bouillon

Tip

....

If you can get only large zucchini, use the skin, avoiding the seedy center, since most of the taste is in the skin and the layer of flesh closest to it. The best way to prepare large zucchini is to cut off the skin in strips with about ¼ inch of the pulp. Cut these strips into cubes and discard the seedy and watery inside pulp.

A n y o n e who has even grown zucchini has ended up with too many, no matter how well the garden was planned. I am faced with the same dilemma every summer—what to do with this vegetable that seems so versatile but is still at its best when prepared simply. I recently sampled this preparation at the house of a friend in Umbria. She makes a large batch of herb butter, adding fresh basil, tarragon, or another herb from her garden and drops one or two tablespoons of this delicious fragrant butter into braised zucchini. Nothing could be simpler, yet it is a wonderful combination of flavors that never fails to please.

....

1. Combine 3 tablespoons of the butter with the parsley and garlic in a small bowl. Season with salt and pepper and mix well. Refrigerate while you sauté the zucchini.

2. Melt the remaining 2 tablespoons butter in a large skillet over medium heat. Add the zucchini and sauté quickly until lightly browned. Season with salt and pepper, add the bouillon, and simmer, covered, for 3 to 4 minutes, or until tender.

3. Remove from the heat, fold in the parsley butter, and correct the seasoning. Serve at once.

Wilted Spinach with Red Peppers, Prosciutto, and Leeks

To prepare: 15 minutes

To cook: 10 minutes

Serves 4 to 6

....

2 pounds fresh spinach, stemmed and well rinsed

3 tablespoons olive oil

2 large garlic cloves, peeled and thinly sliced

½ cup diced prosciutto or smoked ham

1 cup finely diced red bell pepper

1½ cups diced leeks (white part only), well rinsed and drained

3 tablespoons water

Salt and freshly ground black pepper

T i p

....

Spinach can be stir-fried in a skillet without preliminary blanching. However, I find that the spinach retains a prettier deep-green color when blanched briefly. Be sure not to overcook the spinach, and drain immediately under cold running water. Blanched spinach will keep for 3 to 4 days in the refrigerator.

H e r e is a side dish that brings to life the simplest main course. If you keep leeks and a couple of red peppers on hand at all times, you can cook up a quick vegetable fricassee on a moment's notice. Add a few tender spinach leaves and you are on your way. If you happen to see nice, fresh plump sea scallops at your fish market, sauté them to serve with this colorful dish. Or be adventurous and use other seafood, such as monkfish scaloppine, skate, or soft-shell crabs.

....

1. Drop the spinach into boiling salted water and cook for 1 minute. Drain immediately and set aside.

2. Heat the oil in a large skillet over low heat. Add the garlic and prosciutto or ham and cook for 1 minute. Add the red pepper, leeks, and water and cook for 2 to 3 minutes, or until the vegetables are tender. Fold in the spinach, season with salt and pepper, and serve hot.

Marmalade of Fennel and Tomatoes

To prepare: 10 minutes
To cook: 30 minutes
Serves 4

....

2 tablespoons extra-virgin olive oil

2 pounds fennel (about 4 small bulbs), trimmed and cut into eighths through the core

1 large garlic clove, peeled and thinly sliced

1 teaspoon fennel seeds

2 large ripe tomatoes, peeled, seeded, and cubed

Salt and freshly ground black pepper

GARNISH
About 1 tablespoon extra-virgin olive oil

12 small black oil-cured olives

Tip

....

When buying fennel, look for small bulbs that still have their feathery greens attached. Pre-trimmed fennel bulbs will still give you excellent results but they are less fresh and may be woody in texture. Always remove the outer layer of the fennel bulb, which is fibrous and will not cook evenly.

T h i s "compote" has always been in the top ten of my favorite vegetable dishes, one that I grew up with and never seemed to tire of. For years, however, it was virtually impossible to make it in the Northeast since the two main ingredients, fresh fennel and ripe tomatoes, are not in season at the same time. Now, however, with good tomatoes coming from Israel and fennel available even in the summer, you can easily prepare this simple dish with excellent results. Serve as a simple starter or as a side dish to roast chicken or pan-seared salmon or tuna.

....

1. Heat the oil in a heavy skillet over medium heat. Add the fennel and garlic and sauté until the fennel is nicely browned on all sides, about 5 minutes.

2. Reduce the heat, add the fennel seeds and tomatoes, and season with salt and pepper. Simmer, covered, for 15 to 20 minutes, or until the vegetables are very tender and most of the liquid has evaporated.

3. Correct the seasoning and serve hot or at room temperature, drizzled with a little olive oil and garnished with black olives.

Curried Leek and Raisin Chutney

To prepare: 15 minutes
To cook: 12 minutes
Serves 4 to 6

....

1½ teaspoons Madras curry
  powder

1½ teaspoons granulated sugar

1 tablespoon balsamic vinegar

¼ cup extra-virgin olive oil

Salt and freshly ground black
  pepper

4 medium leeks, trimmed of all
  but 1 inch of greens

3 tablespoons unsalted butter

¼ cup water

½ cup golden raisins, plumped
  (see page 159)

¼ cup pine nuts, sautéed in a
  little olive oil until golden
  (see page 269)

T i p

....

*After buying leeks, immediately
remove all but 1 inch of the greens
and place separately in a plastic
bag. Do not rinse or wash leeks
until you are ready to use them.
Leek greens are great for stocks
and the tender light part can also
be used in soups. Choose leeks of
even size and preferably no more
than ½ to ¾ inch in diameter.*

I l i k e most vegetables, I love some, but I adore leeks. I use them in everything—soups, sauces, appetizers, omelettes, and pasta and rice dishes—and serve them as a side dish to braised fish. Here they are gently stewed and enhanced by mild curry and raisins.

A word of warning: This compote is addictive and you may end up eating the whole bowl before it ever gets to the table! Serve the chutney with Shallot and Herb–Infused Lamb Chops (page 199) or Grilled Chicken in Lemon-Cumin Marinade on (page 165).

....

1. Combine the curry powder, 1 teaspoon of the sugar, and the vinegar in a small bowl and whisk until well blended. Add the oil in a slow, steady stream, whisking constantly until the vinaigrette is smooth and emulsified. Season with salt and pepper and set aside.

2. Cut the leeks in half lengthwise and then crosswise into ½-inch slices. Place in a colander and rinse under warm water to remove all sand.

3. Melt the butter in a nonstick skillet over low heat. Add the leeks, the remaining ½ teaspoon sugar, and the water, season with salt and pepper, and simmer, covered, for 10 minutes, or until tender. Remove the cover, raise the heat, and cook until all the water has evaporated. Transfer to a serving bowl, add the raisins, pine nuts, and curry vinaigrette, and mix well. Correct the seasoning and serve at room temperature.

Pepper, Tomato, and Onion Compote

To prepare: 20 minutes
To cook: 30 minutes
Serves 4 to 5

....

¼ cup extra-virgin olive oil

2 large onions, peeled, quartered, and thinly sliced

1 small dried red chili pepper, broken

2 large bell peppers (1 green and 1 red), cored, seeded, and thinly sliced

2 large garlic cloves, peeled and thinly sliced

4 large ripe tomatoes, peeled, seeded, and chopped

1 tablespoon fresh oregano leaves

1 tablespoon fresh thyme leaves

Salt and freshly ground black pepper

2 tablespoons finely minced fresh parsley

T i p

A quick way of peeling tomatoes is to hold them with a fork over a gas flame until the skin blisters and peels off. This method also gives the tomatoes a light smoky flavor.

C o m e summer, this simple stew of onions, peppers, and vine-ripened tomatoes is my favorite accompaniment to just about everything: grilled monkfish scaloppine, a bowl of steamed mussels, or grilled lamb chops, or as a topping to a bowl of nicely cooked tubular pasta. Flavor the compote with an herb of your choice such as basil, rosemary, thyme, or mint. If peppers and tomatoes are particularly plentiful in your farm market or at a local stand, double the recipe. Topped with some olive oil and refrigerated, the compote will keep for a week to ten days.

....

1. Heat the oil in a large skillet over medium heat. Add the onions and chili pepper and cook for 5 minutes, or until lightly browned, stirring often. Add the bell peppers and garlic and cook for 5 minutes longer.

2. Add the tomatoes, oregano, and thyme, season with salt and pepper, and simmer, partially covered, for 15 to 20 minutes, or until the liquid has evaporated and the vegetables are tender. Sprinkle with the parsley and serve warm or at room temperature.

Fricassee of Peppers in Spicy Crème Fraîche

To prepare: 10 minutes
To cook: 8 to 10 minutes
Serves 4 to 6

....

3 tablespoons extra-virgin olive oil

2 large garlic cloves, peeled and
sliced

2 teaspoons finely minced jalapeño pepper

4 bell peppers (2 red, 1 yellow,
and 1 orange), cored, seeded,
quartered, and cut into fine
julienne

⅓ to ½ cup chicken bouillon or
water

2 to 3 tablespoons crème fraîche
(see page 31) or sour cream

Coarse salt and freshly ground
black pepper

T i p

....

When making crème fraîche (see
page 31), always choose a porce-
lain or ceramic jar, either of which
is an excellent conductor of heat.
Warm the jar over a pilot light or
in a 150°F oven; it should just be
warm, not hot.

T h e pepper revolution continues, and there seems
to be no end to the variety of dishes in which a red,
yellow, purple, or green pepper appears in one way or
another. Personally, I like them best when they are allowed to shine on their own, as in this medley. Serve
a spoonful of the mildly spicy peppers as a bed for pan-
seared monkfish medallions or heap them onto a well-
seared juicy "kebab-burger" (see page 169). For a
flavor-packed variation that requires only five more
minutes of your time, caramelize or double-poach sixteen to twenty garlic cloves (see page 41) and add to
the fricassee.

....

1. Heat the oil in a large cast-iron-skillet over medium-high heat. Add the garlic and jalapeño pepper
and cook for just 1 minute. Add all the bell peppers
and sauté for 2 minutes, or until they just start to
brown.

2. Add ⅓ cup bouillon or water, reduce the heat,
and simmer for 3 minutes, or until the peppers are
almost tender, adding additional liquid if needed.

3. Add 2 tablespoons crème fraîche and cook until
absorbed by the peppers. If you prefer a creamier
mixture, add another tablespoon of crème fraîche.
Season with coarse salt and pepper and transfer to
a shallow serving bowl. Serve hot as an accompaniment to roast or grilled meats, fish, or shellfish.

Sweet Potato and Carrot Puree

To prepare: 10 minutes
To cook: 15 minutes
Serves 4

....

3 medium sweet potatoes, peeled
and cut into 1-inch pieces

5 large carrots, peeled and cut
into 1-inch pieces

3 tablespoons sour cream

2 to 4 tablespoons unsalted
butter

2 tablespoons dark brown sugar

Salt and freshly ground black
pepper

Tip

....

*For a variation, add 1 peeled
Golden Delicious apple or Bartlett
pear to the puree for both texture
and taste. Dice the fruit and sauté
in a little butter with a touch of
sugar before adding to the finished
puree.*

C o m e fall, I go right back to some of my per-
ennial easy Spur of the Moment side dishes, and this
one is on top of my list. Trust me: Not only is it quick
and delicious, but it reheats beautifully. For an interesting variation, use parsnips instead of carrots. Either
way the puree is a perfect side dish to Pan-Seared
Shrimp in a Curry Crust with Spinach and Pine Nuts
(page 207), Garlic-Roasted Chicken with Fennel and
Onions (page 228), or Skillet Steak in Tarragon and
Green Peppercorn Sauce (page 201).

....

1.   Combine the potatoes and carrots in a large
saucepan, add salted water to cover, and simmer until very tender.

2.   Drain the potatoes and carrots well and pass
through a food mill into a large bowl. Add the sour
cream, butter, and sugar and mix well. Season with
salt and pepper. Serve hot.

Puree of Peas with Sour Cream and Mint

To prepare: 5 minutes
To cook: 10 minutes
Serves 6 to 8

....

3 packages (10 ounces each)
   frozen peas

¼ cup water

1 tablespoon granulated sugar

2 tablespoons unsalted butter

2 tablespoons all-purpose flour

¼ to ½ cup sour cream

Salt and freshly ground white
   pepper

3 tablespoons finely minced
   fresh mint

T i p

....

You can keep the puree warm, covered, in a double boiler until serving time.

Every once in a while, even the most avid seasonal cook will reach for a canned or frozen vegetable. When it comes to this flavorful puree, I always use frozen peas with excellent results. A mixture of minced dill and chives makes for a nice change, but the pairing of peas with just mint is really an unbeatable combination. Serve this puree with any one of the salmon dishes or other simple fish preparations in this book or with Sautéed Veal Chops in Roquefort Cream (page 205).

....

1. Combine the peas, water, and sugar in a saucepan and simmer, covered, for 5 to 6 minutes, or until tender. Drain and puree in a food processor until smooth.

2. Melt the butter in a skillet over medium heat. Add the flour and cook, whisking constantly, until the mixture turns a hazelnut brown. Add to the pea puree together with the sour cream, season with salt and white pepper, and process until smooth. Add the mint and serve hot.

Wild Mushrooms Roasted with Rosemary and Thyme

To prepare: 15 minutes
To cook: 15 minutes
Serves 4

....

2 tablespoons balsamic vinegar

1 teaspoon coarse salt

Freshly ground black pepper

4 tablespoons extra-virgin olive oil

4 large garlic cloves, peeled and thinly sliced

2 tablespoons fresh rosemary leaves

2 tablespoons fresh thyme leaves

4 cups fresh mushrooms, such as a mixture of shiitake, cremini, chanterelle, and oyster, stemmed and wiped

Tip

....

Mushrooms absorb a great deal of oil when sautéed in a skillet. I now find that I prefer oven-roasting them, which is both quick and greaseless. If you do cook mushrooms in a skillet, transfer them to a colander over a bowl and let them release the oil they have absorbed during cooking.

Now that "wild" mushrooms such as shiitake, cremini, and oyster are available in supermarkets everywhere, they can be used with great creativity by the Spur of the Moment cook. Here, any combination of these mushrooms work well. Serve as an accompaniment to grilled meat or poultry, with peasant bread as a starter, or even as a topping to a mixed green salad.

....

1. Preheat the oven to 425°F.

2. Combine the vinegar, salt, and a large coarse grinding of pepper in a large bowl. Add the oil in slow stream and whisk until well blended. Add the garlic, herbs, and mushrooms and toss to coat well. Transfer to a heavy baking sheet and roast for 15 minutes, or until the mushrooms are tender and lightly browned, turning once. Serve hot.

Sweet Yellow Corn Pudding

To prepare: 5 minutes
To cook: 35 to 45
minutes
Serves 10 to 12

....

Two 16-ounce cans whole kernel corn, drained

One 16-ounce can cream-style corn

10 tablespoons unsalted butter, melted

¼ cup granulated sugar

5 extra-large eggs, lightly beaten

1 cup all-purpose flour

2 teaspoons baking powder

Salt and freshly ground black pepper

T i p

....

You can give this dish extra flavor by adding 1 cup finely diced red bell pepper and 1 to 2 teaspoons finely minced jalapeño pepper to the mixture before baking.

Y e s , canned corn is the basis for this buttery moist pudding. The recipe was given to me by a friend just prior to one Thanksgiving when I was searching for a quick and easy side dish to the holiday meal. It has since become a favorite, and while it is a good accompaniment to many main courses, I like it best with roast turkey, a crispy roasted duck, or with juicy pan-seared veal chops.

You can also bake small acorn squashes, remove the seeds, and fill the cavities with the corn pudding. Then bake the stuffed acorn squashes with a sprinkling of brown sugar and butter until the pudding is set, and you will have a delicious and memorable dish.

....

1. Preheat the oven to 350°F.

2. Combine the corn, butter, sugar, eggs, flour, and baking powder in a large bowl. Season with salt and a large grinding of pepper, and mix well. Pour into a buttered au gratin dish or baking dish and bake for 35 to 45 minutes, or until a knife comes out clean. Serve warm.

Braised Belgian Endives
with Balsamic-Garlic Vinaigrette

To prepare: 15 minutes

To cook: 20 minutes

Serves 6 to 8

....

1 tablespoon balsamic vinegar

1 large garlic clove, peeled and mashed

Optional: 1 tablespoon finely minced shallot

Salt and freshly ground black pepper

8 tablespoons extra-virgin olive oil

6 to 8 Belgian endives, cut in half

1 teaspoon granulated sugar

⅓ cup chicken bouillon

T i p

....

Many supermarkets package Belgian endives in cellophane-wrapped packages, which expose the endives to light and eventually turn them green. Be sure to avoid any endives that are not completely white with just a tinge of yellow at the tips. Greenish endives are bitter and will remain so even after being braised.

B e l g i a n endives cut in half, seasoned with salt, pepper, and a touch of sugar, and then braised in a little butter and broth need no further enhancement. For a more unusual version, one that is especially good with pan-seared fish, lamb chops, or chicken breasts, I like to dress the endives in this vinaigrette. Left to cool to room temperature, the endives make a lovely cool starter, topped with some finely sliced prosciutto and served with crusty bread.

....

1. Make the vinaigrette: Combine the vinegar, garlic, and optional shallot in a small bowl and season generously with salt and pepper. Slowly add 5 tablespoons of the oil, whisking constantly until creamy. Set aside.

2. Heat the remaining 3 tablespoons oil in a cast-iron skillet over medium heat. Add the endives, season with salt and pepper and the sugar, and sauté until nicely browned. Add the bouillon and braise, covered, until tender and caramelized, about 10 to 15 minutes.

3. Transfer the endives to a serving dish, spoon the vinaigrette over them, and serve at room temperature.

Zucchini and Tomatoes in Pesto Sour Cream

To prepare: 10 minutes
To cook: 10 minutes
Serves 4

....

1 packed cup of fresh basil
leaves

2 large garlic cloves, peeled and
finely minced

4 tablespoons extra-virgin olive oil

⅓ cup crème fraîche (see
page 31)

4 medium zucchini, trimmed and
cubed

4 large ripe Italian plum tomatoes, cubed

Salt and freshly ground black
pepper

T i p

....

*Change the recipe from crème
fraîche to sour cream and then use
this tip: You can often substitute
sour cream in recipes that call for
crème fraîche. However, beware:
sour cream curdles in cooking.
This will not affect the taste of the
dish, only its appearance, but you
can add ½ teaspoon of flour per
⅓ cup of sour cream to keep it
from curdling.*

E v e n though fresh basil is now available practically year-round, the best results are still achieved
when using the garden-grown fresh herb in the summer
and early fall. If you do think about it, make several
batches of a simple basil paste during the height of the
season and freeze in small containers: Puree the basil
leaves in a food processor with olive oil to form a thick
paste, pack in small jars, and cover with oil.

....

1. Puree the basil with the garlic and 2 tablespoons
of the oil in a food processor or blender. Add the
crème fraîche and process until smooth. Set aside.

2. Heat the remaining 2 tablespoons oil in a heavy
skillet over medium heat. Add the zucchini and sauté
quickly until lightly browned. Add the tomatoes,
season with salt and pepper, and sauté for 2 to 3
minutes longer.

3. Add the basil mixture, fold in gently but thoroughly, and just heat through. Correct the seasoning, and serve warm or at room temperature.

Napa Cabbage and Endive Slaw

To prepare: 15 minutes

To marinate: 1 hour

Serves 4

....

2 tablespoons sherry vinegar

1 large garlic clove, peeled and mashed

2 teaspoons finely grated fresh ginger

1 tablespoon light soy sauce

1 to 2 teaspoons granulated sugar

2 tablespoons Chinese sesame seed oil

3 tablespoons extra-virgin olive oil

1 pound Napa cabbage, cut into a fine julienne

2 medium Belgian endives, cored and cut into a fine julienne

1 large red bell pepper, cored, seeded, and cut into a fine julienne

½ cup finely minced scallions

Salt and freshly ground black pepper

I w a s never much of a fan of Napa cabbage until I decided to give it a serious try. Now I find it refreshing and versatile. With its delicate flavor, the cabbage takes well to an assertive vinaigrette. The endives add additional texture and character to this salad. Serve the slaw as a side dish to the Spicy Grilled "Kebab-burgers" (page 169) or grilled sausages. The slaw will be equally good after a day or two, so plan on leftovers if you can.

....

1.   Combine the vinegar, garlic, ginger, soy sauce, and 1 teaspoon sugar in a large serving bowl. Slowly whisk in both oils until well blended. Add the cabbage, endives, bell pepper, and scallions and toss lightly. Let marinate at room temperature for 1 hour.

2.   Season with salt and pepper, and add more sugar if necessary. Serve lightly chilled.

T i p

....

Napa cabbage is often sold as Peking cabbage or celery cabbage. Raw, it has a very mild taste that teams well with almost any vinaigrette, but especially those that include soy sauce and garlic. In cooking, Napa cabbage is almost interchangeable with bok choy. Both release a great deal of water during cooking and should be seasoned with salt only after they are done.

Union Square Café's Slaw of Two Cabbages with Mustard and Champagne Vinaigrette

To prepare: 15 minutes
plus 1 hour to drain
cabbage
To marinate: 1 hour
Serves 6

....

⅓ pound red cabbage, cored and finely shredded

⅔ pound Savoy cabbage, cored and finely shredded

Coarse salt

1¼ cups crème fraîche (see page 31)

3 tablespoons Dijon mustard

2 teaspoons yellow mustard seeds

2 tablespoons Champagne vinegar

3 tablespoons granulated sugar

Freshly ground black pepper

1 small red onion, peeled, quartered, and thinly sliced

1 large carrot, peeled and finely shredded

Whenever I have lunch at Union Square Café, one of my favorite restaurants in New York City, I order either the hamburger or tuna burger with a large side dish of their excellent slaw. This recipe makes a good amount, but it is so delicious, chances are it will be gone before you know it. The slaw is also wonderful with roast turkey, grilled lamb chops, chicken wings, and especially Smoked Cod, Potato, and Parsley Fritters (page 82).

....

1. Sprinkle the cabbages with coarse salt and drain in a colander for 1 hour.

2. Combine the crème fraîche, mustard, mustard seeds, vinegar, and sugar in a large bowl and whisk until well blended. Season with salt and pepper.

3. Gently squeeze the excess moisture from the cabbages with your hands. Add to the vinaigrette together with the onion and carrot. Let stand at room temperature for 1 hour, then cover and chill until serving time.

4. Correct the seasoning and serve lightly chilled.

T i p

If you cannot find Savoy cabbage but feel like making this delicious slaw, you can use any fresh white cabbage. And you can substitute sour cream mixed with a little heavy cream for the crème fraîche — the result may not be quite as delicate but will still be delicious.

Beet Salad in a Sweet Mustard Vinaigrette

To prepare: 15 minutes

To marinate: 2 to 3 hours

Serves 6

....

2 teaspoons Dijon mustard

2 teaspoons granulated sugar

Juice of ½ lemon

6 tablespoons olive oil

Salt and freshly ground black pepper

3 to 4 tablespoons finely minced fresh dill

4 to 6 cups diced cooked beets

A s i m p l e quick beet salad is a good accompaniment to cold roast chicken, a piece of quickly poached salmon, or a nicely grilled turkey breast. You can use canned beets in this preparation with good results.

....

1.   Combine the mustard, sugar, and lemon juice in a serving bowl. Add the oil in a slow stream, whisking constantly until the mixture is smooth and creamy. Season with salt and pepper to taste.

2.   Add the dill and beets to the vinaigrette and toss gently but thoroughly. Marinate for 2 to 3 hours before serving.

3.   Taste and correct the seasoning, and serve lightly chilled or at room temperature.

T i p

....

Drop cooked beets into ice water to stop them from further cooking. Then their skins will slip right off. Cooked beets will keep refrigerated for 3 to 5 days.

Stir-fry of Escarole with Pine Nuts and Garlic

To prepare: 5 minutes
To cook: 3 to 5 minutes
Serves 4

....

5 tablespoons olive oil

2 tablespoons pine nuts

3 large garlic cloves, peeled and thinly sliced

1 large head escarole, washed, dried, and torn into 1-inch pieces

Salt and freshly ground black pepper

W h i l e I am not a fan of escarole as a salad green, it is one of my favorite vegetables for a quick sauté. This gutsy stir-fry is good with seafood as well as roast Cornish hens. It can also be tossed into cooked pasta, with some additional extra-virgin olive oil, or served as a bed for grilled or pan-seared portabello or shiitake mushrooms.

1. Heat 1 tablespoon of the oil in a small skillet over medium-low heat. Add the pine nuts and sauté, stirring constantly, until lightly browned. Reserve.

2. In a large skillet, heat 2 tablespoons of the olive oil over medium heat. Add half of the garlic and half of the escarole and cook, tossing in the oil, until just wilted. Transfer to a side dish and season with salt and pepper.

3. Add the remaining 2 tablespoons oil to the skillet and cook the remaining escarole with the remaining garlic in the same manner. Return the first batch of escarole to the skillet together with the pine nuts, correct the seasoning, and just heat through. Serve hot with roast Cornish hens, grilled pork tenderloins, or pan-seared steaks.

T i p

When you buy escarole, cut ½ inch off the root ends and tear the leaves into 2-inch pieces. Stored unwashed in a zip-lock bag, escarole will keep for a week to ten days.

Sweet Endings

When Oscar Wilde quipped, "I can resist everything except temptation," he must have been thinking about dessert. Of course, these days, the pleasure of even contemplating something sweet and satisfying tends to be immediately outweighed by all sorts of guilty feelings (and nightmares about Stairmasters and advanced step aerobics classes).

Giving in to the temptation of dessert is not only perfectly understandable, it's perfectly easy for the Spur of the Moment cook, who need only consider the delicious possibilities of naturally sweet seasonal fruits. Fruits have been providing pleasur-

able endings to meals throughout the Mediterranean for centuries. To this day, even the finest restaurants in Italy and Spain rarely feature any dessert other than a thinly sliced orange or ripe berries served with a bowl of sugar on the side. When I was growing up in Barcelona, a re-freshing glass of freshly squeezed orange juice often ended our meals.

Now that so many imported and exotic fruits have leapt from the specialty stores to the shelves of our local supermarkets, a craving for a particular seasonal fruit can be satisfied most any time of year. However, for me, these will never replace the harmonious and traditional pleasure of a fresh ripe autumn pear, tart winter citrus, berries in springtime, and the sweet cherries and plums of summer. A freshly picked melon, jewel-like and sweet, a messily juicy white summer peach, blueberries and plump nectarines in a cut-glass bowl—all of these need no adornment to satisfy a craving for sweets. And when these are teamed with a light sauce of fresh blueberries with Cassis or a gingered-wine syrup, the results can be transcendent, transforming a simple fruit into an irresistibly elegant and enticing dessert.

There are times, however, when even the most tempting fruit is not quite enough. As the daughter of a Viennese mother, I am no stranger to the siren call of the sweet tooth. But it was only after coming to America—where desserts are richer, sweeter, and more complex than in Europe—that I realized I was only an amateur in the dessert league!

None of the desserts in this book approach the major-league "death-by-chocolate" school of seriously wicked sweets, but they will satisfy your desire to indulge. Having a good store-bought ice cream on hand, along with some imported chocolate and fresh nuts for Spur of the Moment sauces and finishing touches, will make it easy to whip up anything from a simple vanilla pot de crème to a bittersweet chocolate tart.

If time is an issue, remember that many of these desserts and dessert sauces can be made a few hours, or even several days, before you plan to serve them. Then all you need is the willpower to leave some for your company! And if dessert is going to be more ambitious than just fresh, ripe fruit, make the main course simple and light. Finally, of course, make sure you don't invite anybody on a serious diet. I find that a passion for sweets, like all major passions, is best shared by like-minded souls.

Gratin of Roasted Cherries in Red Wine

To prepare: 15 minutes
To cook: 40 minutes
Serves 6

....

1½ cups dry red wine

¾ cup granulated sugar

One 3-inch cinnamon stick

2 whole cloves

One 3-inch strip of lemon zest

2 pounds Bing cherries, stemmed
and pitted

T i p

....

*Many fruits can be roasted in a
red wine or white wine syrup with
excellent results. I especially like
nectarines, peaches, Italian plums,
and pears; for best results, these
should be only semiripe.*

If you are lucky enough to be in Oregon in mid-July when cherries are in full season, this is indeed a Spur of the Moment dessert. But even for those of us who don't live in "cherry country," a bowl of this ripe fruit is a perfect way to end a meal. Every once in a while, when I can get hold of some overripe cherries at a good price, I love "roasting" them in a cinnamon-infused red wine syrup. Serve the cherries with sweetened crème fraîche for a light and refreshing summer dessert.

....

1. Preheat the oven to 350°F.

2. Combine all the ingredients except the cherries in a saucepan and simmer until the sugar is dissolved. Place the cherries in a gratin dish or shallow baking dish, pour the wine syrup over, and "roast" in the oven for 30 to 35 minutes, or until tender.

3. Let the cherries cool in the liquid. Serve with good-quality ice cream or sugared crème fraîche (see page 31).

Crisp Almond Phyllo Cookies

To prepare: 10 minutes
To cook: 12 to 13
minutes
Serves 6

....

3 sheets frozen phyllo dough,
   thawed

4 to 5 tablespoons unsalted
   butter, melted

2 tablespoons granulated sugar

⅔ cup sliced almonds

T i p

....

Phyllo dough and puff pastry should always be stored in the freezer. To thaw them evenly and with best results, place them in the refrigerator, not on the countertop.

I k e e p a box of phyllo dough in my freezer at all times but I have found that once I open a box, I never seem to need the whole batch. So these quick and buttery cookies, which can be made from a few sheets of the dough, come in very handy. Serve them for dessert with a cup of espresso or good store-bought ice cream. Or serve as "sandwiches," with chocolate mousse or ice cream in the center.

....

1. Preheat the oven to 350°F.

2. Place 1 sheet of phyllo on a large cookie sheet. Brush the entire surface with melted butter and sprinkle with 2 teaspoons of the sugar and ⅓ cup of the almonds. Top evenly with another sheet of dough, brush with butter, and sprinkle with 2 teaspoons sugar and the remaining almonds. Top with the remaining sheet of dough, brush with butter, and sprinkle with the remaining 2 teaspoons sugar.

3. Cut out 12 circles from the layered dough with a 2½-inch round cookie cutter, but do not remove the circles from the sheet of dough. Bake for 12 to 13 minutes or until golden brown and crisp. Cool completely on the baking sheet, then carefully lift the cookies from the sheet with a spatula.

Pink Grapefruit Sabayon with Strawberry Sauce

To prepare: 15 minutes

To cook: 10 minutes

Serves 6

....

6 large pink grapefruit

¾ cup granulated sugar

4 extra-large egg yolks

¾ cup frozen grapefruit juice
    concentrate, thawed

½ cup crème fraîche (see
    page 31)

1½ cups heavy cream, whipped

1 recipe Strawberry and Red
    Currant Sauce (page 291)

GARNISH
Tiny leaves of fresh mint

Optional: Fresh raspberries

Tip

....

Lightly chilled fresh, ripe fruit is the Spur of the Moment cook's best dessert solution, and grapefruit segments are one of my favorites.

Grapefruit, orange, and pineapple concentrates are three of the most useful freezer basics. They lend themselves to a variety of quick desserts and light fruit sauces and are especially good when teamed with fresh citrus fruit. Serve this sabayon following a hearty stew, ragoût, or pasta dish. You can omit the strawberry sauce if you are pressed for time — or even the sectioned grapefruit garnish. Just heap the sabayon into ramekins and garnish with mint leaves.

....

1. Using a sharp knife, remove the grapefruits' rind together with all of the white pith, completely exposing the pulp. Cut into the pulp between the connecting white membranes to remove the segments without including any of the membrane. (Be sure to squeeze out and save the juice that remains in the membranes.) Set the segments aside.

2. Combine the sugar, yolks, grapefruit concentrate and any juice, and crème fraîche in the top of a double boiler. Place over simmering water and whisk constantly until the mixture heavily coats a spoon. Immediately transfer to a bowl and refrigerate until completely cool. Fold in the whipped cream, cover, and refrigerate until serving.

3. To serve, arrange the grapefruit segments in the center of individual shallow soup or dessert plates. Top each portion with a large dollop of the sabayon and drizzle the strawberry sauce around each. Garnish with mint and the optional raspberries and serve at once.

Mascarpone Yogurt Cream with Grated Orange and Spring Berries

To prepare: 15 minutes
plus 30 minutes to chill
Serves 6

....

8 ounces mascarpone

3 tablespoons goat's milk yogurt or plain yogurt

2 tablespoons confectioner's sugar

1 tablespoon finely grated orange zest

6 cups mixed berries, such as blueberries, raspberries, and strawberries

¼ cup superfine sugar

GARNISH
Tiny leaves of fresh mint

T i p

....

To intensify their bright red color and flavor, sprinkle raspberries and strawberries with sugar several hours before serving.

N o w that good-quality mascarpone is widely available, it has greatly enhanced the repertoire of the busy cook. Delicious with berries, coffee, and certain citrus fruits, mascarpone provides the possibility of creating an almost instant elegant dessert. Be sure to taste the cheese as soon as you open the container, since the sell-by date can be misleading. If it does not have the taste of very fresh heavy cream, do not use it. It is impossible to mask the taste of the mascarpone that is even very slightly off.

....

1. Combine the mascarpone, yogurt, confectioner's sugar, and orange zest in a bowl and whisk until well blended. Chill for 30 minutes.

2. Toss the berries with the superfine sugar and divide among 6 individual serving bowls. Top with the mascarpone yogurt cream, garnish with mint, and serve lightly chilled.

Compote of Gingered Blueberries and Nectarines

To prepare: 10 minutes
To cook: 10 minutes
Serves 6 to 8

....

6 to 8 nectarines, pitted and cut into eighths

2 pints fresh blueberries, rinsed

¾ to 1 cup granulated sugar

5 thin slices peeled fresh ginger

GARNISH
Crème fraîche (see page 31)

1 cup fresh blueberries

Tiny leaves of fresh mint

T i p

....

When you make a compote of fresh fruit, be sure to include some unripe fruit. Unripe fruit contains more natural pectin and will produce a thicker compote with a better texture.

I l o v e fruit compotes, especially in the summer when so much fresh fruit is around and affordable. Compotes in general should be high on every cook's list since they take only minutes to prepare and can be used in many wonderful ways. Instead of nectarines, you can use peaches or a mixture of both in this dish. Or, if you live in an area where apricots are good, by all means use them instead. Later in the season, around the end of August, I love to combine pears, plums, and blueberries.

....

1. Combine the nectarines, blueberries, sugar, and ginger in a large casserole and simmer for 5 to 10 minutes, or until the nectarines are just tender. Do not cook too long, or the compote will turn to jelly. Cool completely.

2. Serve lightly chilled, but not too cold, with a dollop of crème fraîche on each serving and a garnish of a few fresh blueberries and tiny leaves of mint.

Peach Gratin with Creamy Pecan Crumble

To prepare: 10 minutes
To cook: 25 to 30
minutes
Serves 6

....

6 large ripe peaches, preferably
   freestone

2 tablespoons granulated sugar

Large grating of nutmeg

1 teaspoon ground cinnamon

6 tablespoons unsalted butter,
   softened

1 tablespoon all-purpose flour

⅓ cup dark brown sugar

½ cup diced pecans or walnuts

¾ cup heavy cream

OPTIONAL GARNISH
Good-quality vanilla ice cream

Tip

....

I like to stock up on a variety of nuts and have found that it is best to keep the oily ones, such as walnuts, pecans, almonds, and hazelnuts, in the freezer. Before using frozen nuts, be sure to toast them on a cookie sheet at 350°F for 10 minutes, or until fragrant. Then let them cool completely.

Although this may not be a dessert that you will throw together on the Spur of the Moment, it is the perfect ending to a weekend meal. You can bake the peaches at your leisure and then reheat the dessert in a low oven or the microwave. The peaches are not a must: Nectarines, which do not require peeling, will do as well. I usually double or triple the recipe for the topping and keep it refrigerated for later use on Italian plums and pears and as a filling for baked apples.

....

1.   Preheat the oven to 375°F.

2.   Drop the peaches into boiling water for 30 seconds. Peel, cut into eighths, and place in a baking dish. Sprinkle with the granulated sugar, nutmeg, and ½ teaspoon of the cinnamon and toss lightly.

3.   Combine the butter, flour, brown sugar, pecans or walnuts, and remaining ½ teaspoon cinnamon in a small bowl, and blend with a fork into a coarse paste. With a teaspoon, drop the mixture over the peaches. Add the cream to the baking dish and bake for 25 to 30 minutes, or until the topping is nicely browned and the mixture is bubbly.

4.   Remove from the oven and let cool slightly. Serve warm, garnished with optional scoops of vanilla ice cream.

Pineapple Custard Mousse with Sauternes

To prepare: 10 minutes
plus 1 hour to macerate
To cook: 10 minutes
Serves 4

....

1 large ripe pineapple

4 tablespoons good-quality kirsch

½ cup plus 2 tablespoons granulated sugar

4 extra-large egg yolks

½ cup frozen pineapple concentrate, thawed

2 tablespoons Sauternes

1 cup heavy cream, whipped

GARNISH
Tiny leaves of fresh mint

2 cups mixed berries, such as
blueberries, raspberries, and
blackberries

Tip

....

You can serve this dessert warm, in individual gratin or small baking dishes: Sprinkle the top of each portion with granulated brown sugar and run under the broiler until just caramelized.

A t r u l y ripe, sweet pineapple is often my spring choice for a simple dessert, sometimes teamed with Lime Caramel (page 290) or Strawberry and Red Currant Sauce (page 291). But for those times when I can't get the perfect fresh fruit, I reach for the frozen concentrate, and in a matter of minutes, I can whip up this refreshing mousse that is equally good warm or slightly chilled.

....

1. Trim, peel, and core the pineapple. Cut the pulp into 1-inch cubes. Combine with 2 tablespoons of the kirsch and 2 tablespoons of the sugar and macerate for 1 hour.

2. Combine the egg yolks and remaining ½ cup sugar and whisk until pale yellow. Add the pineapple concentrate, the remaining 2 tablespoons kirsch, and the Sauternes and whisk until well blended. Transfer to the top of a double boiler, set over simmering water, and whisk constantly until the mixture heavily coats a spoon. Immediately transfer to a bowl and refrigerate until completely cool.

3. Fold the whipped cream into the mousse and chill.

4. To serve, place the pineapple cubes in shallow serving dishes. Top each portion with a dollop of mousse and garnish with mint and a sprinkling of berries.

Espresso Mascarpone Mousse with Coffee-Soaked Biscuits

To prepare: 10 minutes
plus 2 to 4 hours to chill
To cook: 4 minutes
Serves 6

....

6 savoiardi or biscotti all'uovo
(crisp ladyfingers), cut in half

½ cup strong prepared coffee

MOUSSE
1 teaspoon instant espresso

⅓ cup strong prepared coffee

½ cup granulated sugar

1 teaspoon unflavored gelatin

8 ounces mascarpone

1 cup heavy cream, whipped

GARNISH
Dusting of cocoa

Tip

....

Biscotti all'uovo (biscotti means "twice baked") are very crisp Italian ladyfingers. Also called "savoiardi," they are available in some supermarkets and in specialty stores.

H e r e is a terrific light weekend dessert that is reminiscent of the ever-so-popular tiramisù. If you use fresh or soft ladyfingers, toast them first in a 200°F oven and let them dry before soaking them in the coffee. That way, they will be more intensely flavored and will not become soggy.

....

1. Dip the savoiardi quickly into the coffee and place 2 halves in the bottom of each of six 4-ounce ramekins. Set aside.

2. Prepare the mousse: Combine the instant coffee, prepared coffee, and sugar in a saucepan. Add the gelatin and simmer, stirring constantly, until the gelatin and sugar are completely dissolved. Transfer to a large bowl and cool completely.

3. Whisk in the mascarpone and gently but thoroughly fold in the whipped cream. Do not overmix. Divide among the prepared ramekins, cover, and chill for 2 to 4 hours. Serve chilled, with a heavy dusting of cocoa.

Vanilla-Scented Pots de Crème

To prepare: 10 minutes
plus 2 to 4 hours to chill
To cook: 15 minutes
Serves 6

....

¾ cup whole milk

½ cup heavy cream

2 extra-large eggs

2 extra-large egg yolks

⅓ cup granulated sugar

1 teaspoon pure vanilla extract or
   ¼ teaspoon fresh scraped
   vanilla seeds (see Tip)

TOPPINGS

Fresh raspberries or other spring
   berries, such as blueberries,
   or sliced strawberries, or
   sautéed apples or pears

Tip

....

To achieve the best possible vanilla flavor, use a fresh vanilla bean. Take a piece of bean about 3 to 4 inches long: Slice it in half lengthwise and then scrape the tiny black seeds into the milk and cream mixture. Each tiny black seed is full of delicious vanilla flavor and the lightly speckled custard will be both appealing and "authentic" tasting.

When I was growing up, pots de crème were a familiar weekday dessert at our house. The little custards, flavored with coffee, chocolate, or vanilla, were made in decorative porcelain ramekins especially designed for the dessert. Today, I still love making these custards, but simply bake them in ordinary four-ounce ramekins. The toppings vary according to what I see fresh in the market, but I usually opt for some kind of seasonal berry. Strawberries, raspberries, and blueberries work best, but you can also choose a pantry basic, such as instant coffee, vanilla, or candied ginger.

....

1. Preheat the oven to 350°F.

2. Heat the milk and cream together in a saucepan and keep warm.

3. Combine the eggs, egg yolks, sugar, and vanilla in a mixing bowl and whisk until fluffy and pale yellow. Add the warm milk/cream mixture and whisk until well blended. Strain the mixture into six 4-ounce ramekins.

4. Place the ramekins in a heavy baking dish, and fill the dish with boiling water to come halfway up the sides of the ramekins. Bake for 15 minutes or until the tip of a knife comes out clean; do not overcook. Remove from the water bath and cool completely. Refrigerate for 2 to 4 hours before serving.

5. Garnish with the topping of your choice, and serve lightly chilled.

Buttery Pine Nut and Brown Sugar Tart

To prepare: 15 minutes
To cook: 50 minutes
Serves 6 to 8

....

¼ cup granulated sugar

¾ cup dark brown sugar

2 extra-large eggs, lightly beaten

1½ teaspoons pure vanilla extract

1 tablespoon all-purpose flour

1 tablespoon heavy cream

8 tablespoons unsalted butter, melted

¾ cup pine nuts

One 9-inch unbaked ready-made tart shell in a removable-bottom pan (see Tip)

A nutty tart made with only butter, dark brown sugar, and pecans is a delicious classic American dessert well worth the calories. This version is made with pine nuts and can be assembled quickly, using store-bought pie dough. If you like, add a touch of rum, cognac, or Grand Marnier to the filling, but the best addition is a large dollop of whipped cream.

....

1. Preheat the oven to 350°F.

2. Combine the sugars, eggs, vanilla, flour, cream, and butter in a large bowl and whisk until well blended. Fold in the pine nuts, pour evenly into the tart shell, and bake for 50 minutes.

3. Remove the tart from the oven and let cool. Serve at room temperature, cut into wedges, with whipped cream or good-quality vanilla ice cream.

Ready-Made Pie Dough

*B*uy the dough that comes folded in boxes in the refrigerator case in the supermarket, not the frozen kind. Remove 1 sheet of dough from the box, place on a lightly floured surface, and let stand for 10 minutes. Roll to a thickness of ⅛ inch. Carefully ease into a 9-inch tart pan with a removable bottom and gently press into the bottom and up the sides of the pan. Trim off all but 1 inch of the excess. Fold the overhang back into the pan and press firmly against sides; this will create a double layer of dough, which will reinforce the sides of the shell. Prick the bottom of the shell with a fork and place in the freezer for at least 30 minutes, or until completely frozen, before baking.

Brown Sugar-Ginger Ice Cream

To prepare: 5 minutes
plus time for freezing
To cook: 5 minutes
Serves 6 to 8

....

6 extra-large egg yolks

1 cup dark brown sugar

⅓ cup granulated sugar

2 teaspoons pure vanilla extract

1 quart warm half-and-half or light cream

One 1½-inch piece fresh ginger, pressed through a garlic press

1 to 1½ teaspoons powdered ginger

T i p

....

Ice cream may crystallize after a day or two in the freezer. When that happens, let the ice cream melt completely and then refreeze in the ice cream machine. It will be as good as fresh.

N o w that I have an ice cream machine, the store-brought stuff just does not appeal to me anymore. Here is an ice cream that calls on your pantry and dairy basics, and the result is a rich and velvety dessert well worth the calories. This ice cream is particularly good with sautéed pears or with a peach cobbler, baked nectarines, or apple brown Betty.

....

1.   Combine the egg yolks, sugars, and vanilla in a mixing bowl and whisk until fluffy and pale yellow. Add the warm half-and-half or cream, the ginger, and powdered ginger and whisk until well blended. Transfer to a heavy 3-quart saucepan and whisk constantly over medium-low heat until the custard lightly coats a spoon; do not let come to a boil. Immediately transfer to a mixing bowl and chill for at least 6 hours, or overnight.

2.   Place the ice cream base in an ice cream machine and freeze according to the manufacturer's directions. If you feel the ice cream is a little soft, transfer to the freezer until it reaches the desired consistency.

Toasted Almond and Prune Tart

To prepare: 15 minutes
To cook: 45 to 50
minutes
Serves 6

....

¾ cup slivered almonds, toasted

½ cup granulated sugar

1 extra-large egg

1 tablespoon grated orange zest

⅛ teaspoon pure almond extract

1 tablespoon unsalted butter,
melted

½ cup heavy cream

6 ounces pitted large prunes
(about 20)

One 9-inch unbaked ready-made
tart shell in a removable-
bottom pan (see page 283)

T i p

....

*When I poach prunes for this tart,
I usually double the amount I
need and steep them for a day or
two in sweetened Earl Grey or
Irish tea, using 2 tea bags for the
poaching liquid. The tea highly
enhances the flavor of the prunes.
I serve the extra prunes for dessert
with some whipped cream flavored
with a few drops of Scotch and a
couple of tablespoons of honey.*

Does it make sense to build a menu around a dessert? Well, come Italian plum season, that is exactly what I do. I love everything about this short-seasoned fruit: its color, shape, taste, and wonderful texture. But good prunes, one of my "pantry musts," make it possible to make this tart year-round. A bowl of sweetened crème fraîche on the side is another must.

....

1.   Preheat the oven to 350°F.

2.   Process the almonds with the sugar in a food processor until finely ground. Add the egg, orange zest, almond extract, butter, and cream and process until smooth. Reserve.

3.   Place the prunes in a saucepan and add water to cover. Simmer for 2 minutes, and drain well.

4.   Cut the prunes in half and place in the bottom of the tart shell. Top with the almond mixture, and bake for 45 to 50 minutes, or until nicely browned. Serve warm or at room temperature with sugared crème fraîche (see page 31) or good-quality ice cream.

Compote of Dried Fruit with Ginger and Cinnamon

To prepare: 10 minutes

To cook: 20 minutes

Serves 4 to 6

....

4 cups mixed dried fruit, consisting of equal amounts of dried cranberries, cherries, apricots, pears, peaches, figs, prunes, and/or raisins

1 vanilla bean, split

2 tablespoons finely minced fresh ginger

2 cups dry red wine *or* 1 cup wine plus 1 cup water

One 3-inch cinnamon stick

¼ cup pure honey

¼ cup granulated sugar

2 lemon slices

Grated zest of 1 large orange

Tip

....

Look for dried fruits that do not contain any preservatives. These are usually sun-dried and may not be as sweet or look as glossy as supermarket brands, but they taste much better. You will find sun-dried fruit at most health food stores. They will last for a very long time if refrigerated in a well-sealed jar or a Ziploc bag.

C o m e winter, I prefer using dried fruit to unripe fresh fruit that lacks sweetness or flavor. Here you can use a combination of more "exotic" fruit such as dried cranberries or cherries and supermarket basics like prunes, apricots, and raisins. Stewed in a cinnamon-and-ginger red wine syrup, these fruits produce a quick and easy compote that makes for a delicious finale to any meal.

....

1. Cut the large fruits into strips; leave the small fruits whole.

2. Combine all the ingredients in a medium saucepan and simmer for 20 minutes. Remove the vanilla bean, cinnamon stick, and lemon slices and let cool. Serve at room temperature with yogurt or frozen yogurt.

Remarks: Use as many different fruits as possible — the more the better.

This is also a delicious accompaniment to roast or grilled turkey.

Oven-Baked Rice Pudding with Lemon and Raisins

To prepare: 5 minutes
To cook: 2 hours and 30 minutes

Serves 6

3½ cups whole milk

1 cup granulated sugar

½ cup long-grain rice

Zest of 1 lemon, cut into a fine julienne

¼ cup golden raisins

3 extra-large eggs, separated

1 teaspoon pure vanilla extract

GARNISH
Ground cinnamon or grated nutmeg

Tip

Do not use converted rice when making a rice pudding since it will not give the desired creaminess to the dessert. My first choice is Arborio rice, but a medium-grain Carolina rice or River Brand rice will produce good and very creamy rice puddings.

F o r an easy and satisfying weekend dessert, few recipes are as delicious and homey as rice pudding. You can put it together in a matter of minutes and bake it at your leisure without further attention. Dried cherries or cranberries are good substitutes for the raisins, and the strawberry and red currant sauce on page 291 makes for a terrific finishing touch.

1. Preheat the oven to 325°F.

2. Combine the milk and all but 2 tablespoons of the sugar in a large heatproof casserole and stir until the sugar has dissolved. Add the rice, lemon zest, and raisins. Cover loosely with foil and bake for 2 hours to 2 hours and 30 minutes, stirring once or twice. The rice should be quite tender and all the milk absorbed.

3. Remove from the oven, whisk in the yolks and vanilla, and set aside.

4. Beat the whites with the remaining 2 tablespoons sugar until they hold firm peaks. Fold into the rice, and transfer to a serving dish. Serve at room temperature or slightly chilled, sprinkled with cinnamon or nutmeg.

Kiwi Yogurt Sorbet

To prepare: 10 minutes
plus time for freezing
Serves 6

....

1½ cups plain yogurt

8 kiwis, peeled

3 tablespoons fresh lemon juice

⅔ cup granulated sugar

2 tablespoons Grand Marnier

T i p

....

Sprinkling peeled kiwis with granulated sugar and letting them stand for 20 minutes to absorb the sugar will turn their light green color into a brilliant green and intensify their taste.

Few desserts are as refreshing or as intensely flavorful as a fruit sorbet. Now that you can pick up a simple ice cream machine relatively cheaply, it is well worth keeping this cool and light dessert in mind. Other fruits such as blueberries, mangoes, and strawberries work equally well.

....

Combine all the ingredients in a food processor and puree until smooth. Transfer to an electric ice cream machine and freeze according to the manufacturer's directions. If you feel the sorbet is a little soft, transfer to the freezer until it reaches the desired consistency.

Catalan Bittersweet Chocolate, Orange, and Pine Nut Tart

~~~

To prepare: 10 minutes

To cook: 25 to 30 minutes

Serves 4 to 6

....

4 ounces bittersweet chocolate, chopped

One 9-inch unbaked ready-made tart shell in a removable-bottom pan (see page 283)

2 ounces pine nuts

2 tablespoons finely grated orange zest

3 extra-large eggs

½ cup granulated sugar

1 tablespoon Grand Marnier

¾ cup heavy cream

GARNISH
¼ cup orange marmalade

Sprigs of fresh mint

O n l y recently have pine nuts been used in America to lend their subtle taste to preparations other than pesto. They are a favorite of mine, and in Catalan cooking they have always been used with great creativity, often teamed with chocolate, oranges, pears, or apples.

....

1. Preheat the oven to 400°F.

2. Sprinkle the chocolate evenly over the bottom of the tart shell. Sprinkle with the pine nuts and set aside.

3. Combine the orange zest, eggs, sugar, and Grand Marnier in a large bowl and whisk until well blended. Add the cream and whisk until thoroughly combined. Pour into the tart shell and bake for 25 to 30 minutes, or until just set. Transfer to a rack to cool slightly.

4. Melt the marmalade in a small saucepan over low heat, pass it through a fine strainer, and pour over the surface of the tart, covering it completely.

5. When the tart is completely cool, carefully remove from the pan and transfer to a serving plate. Garnish with sprigs of fresh mint. Serve at room temperature.

Sweet Sauces

All serve 4 to 6

CARAMEL CREAM

Combine ½ cup granulated sugar and 2 tablespoons water in a heavy 3-quart saucepan and bring to a boil, stirring once to dissolve the sugar. Then continue to boil without stirring until the mixture turns hazelnut brown. Immediately remove from the heat and carefully add ¾ cup hot heavy cream, averting your face; the caramel will bubble violently. Return to very low heat and stir until well blended and smooth. Serve warm over sautéed sliced apples or pears.

MAPLE CARAMEL CREAM

Combine 1 cup granulated sugar and ¼ cup water in a heavy 3-quart saucepan and bring to a boil, stirring once to dissolve the sugar. Then continue to boil without stirring until the mixture turns hazelnut brown. Immediately remove from the heat and carefully add 1 cup hot heavy cream, averting your face; the caramel will bubble violently. Return to very low heat and stir until well blended and smooth. Add ⅓ cup pure maple syrup and simmer for 2 minutes longer, stirring constantly, until slightly thickened. Serve warm over sliced sautéed or baked apples or sliced sautéed bananas.

LIME CARAMEL

Combine ¾ cup granulated sugar and 2 tablespoons water in a deep 3-quart saucepan and bring to a boil, stirring once to dissolve the sugar. Then continue to boil without stirring until the mixture turns hazelnut brown. Remove from the heat and immediately add ¼ cup hot water, averting your face; the caramel will bubble violently. Return to low heat and stir until smooth. Transfer to a bowl and stir in the juice of 2 limes, ¼ cup dark rum, and 1 cup fresh peppermint leaves. Cover and chill until needed. Strain and serve over sliced or cubed melons or sliced bananas.

GRAND MARNIER SABAYON

Combine ⅓ cup Grand Marnier, ⅓ cup water, ⅓ cup granulated sugar, and 5 extra-large egg yolks in the top of a double boiler and whisk until well blended. Set over simmering water and cook, whisking constantly, until thick and smooth. Transfer to a stainless steel bowl and refrigerate until completely cool. Fold in 1 cup heavy cream, whipped; cover and refrigerate. (You can substitute Cointreau, rum, or cognac for the Grand Marnier according to your personal taste.)

RED WINE AND TANGERINE SYRUP

Combine 2½ cups red Bordeaux, 1 cup granulated sugar, and a cinnamon stick in a large saucepan and simmer until reduced by one third. Remove from the heat and add the juice of 1 tangerine or ½ orange, with 1 tablespoon finely grated tangerine or orange zest. Let cool completely. Serve over sliced strawberries or oranges.

STRAWBERRY AND RED CURRANT SAUCE

Drain two 12-ounce packages thawed, frozen strawberries in heavy syrup, reserving half the drained juices. Puree the strawberries with the juice in a food processor until smooth. Transfer to a bowl. Melt ¾ cup red currant jelly in a small saucepan over low heat, stirring constantly. Add to the strawberry sauce together with the juice of ½ lemon and 2 tablespoons kirsch or Grand Marnier (optional). Strain the sauce if desired, and add 2 cups thinly sliced fresh strawberries (optional). Cover and chill until serving.

White Chocolate Mocha Sauce

Combine 12 ounces good-quality white chocolate, broken into pieces, 1½ cups heavy cream, and 2 teaspoons instant espresso in a medium saucepan. Place over low heat and whisk until the chocolate has melted. Transfer to a large bowl and let cool to room temperature, whisking often. When completely cool, gently but thoroughly fold in 1 cup whipped heavy cream. Serve with chocolate desserts.

Remark: For a different flavor, omit the coffee and add a ¾-inch piece of fresh ginger mashed through a garlic press.

Or, omit the coffee. Add 1 cup chopped fresh mint and let steep in the cream for 15 minutes before you prepare the sauce. Strain the cooled sauce before you add the whipped cream.

Fresh Blueberry Sauce with Cassis

Combine 2 pints fresh blueberries, ¾ to 1 cup granulated sugar (depending on the sweetness of the berries), and the finely grated zest of 1 large orange in a medium saucepan and cook for 5 minutes over medium heat, stirring often, until the berries begin to exude their juices. Remove from the heat and let cool. Stir in 2 to 3 tablespoons Cassis. You can puree the sauce in a blender if you prefer a smoother texture. Serve with poached peaches, Peach Gratin with Creamy Pecan Crumble (page 279), good-quality ice cream, or cut-up melons or berries.

$\mathcal{I}$ndex

Corn *(continued)*
　　mango, and bacon medley, caramelized,
　　　　250
　　and shellfish chowder, 52–53
　　sweet yellow pudding, 263
Cornish hens:
　　grilled in tangy lime and onion marinade,
　　　　166–167
　　ragoût with potatoes, onions, and thyme,
　　　　227
　　roast, in rosemary-lemon essence, 230–231
Cornmeal, 16
　　see also Polenta
Corn oil, 13–14
Coulis, roasted pepper and chive, 192
Couscous, 16
　　carrot, raisin, and pine nut, 159
　　in cumin vinaigrette, charred red peppers
　　　　filled with, 180–181
　　curry-and-cumin-scented, with toasted
　　　　walnuts, 157
　　with melted scallions, 160
　　saffron, with spinach and red peppers, 158
　　tomatoes stuffed with, 157
Crab, green chili, and bacon chowder, 51
Cream:
　　caramel, 290
　　chèvre herb, 117
　　garlic, caper, and anchovy, 86–87
　　Gorgonzola, 131
　　heavy, 29
　　herb, risotto with smoked trout, tomatoes
　　　　and, 144–145
　　maple caramel, 290
　　mascarpone yogurt, with grated orange
　　　　and spring berries, 277
　　mustard, 208
　　porcini, 130
　　of roasted vegetable soup, 39
　　Roquefort, 205
　　sour, *see* Sour cream
　　tarragon, 114
　　tarragon and lemon, 204
Cream cheese and herb johnnycakes, 102–
　　　　103
Crème fraîche, 30–31, 74
　　and chive fritters, 74
　　jar for, 259
　　lemon, oven-braised salmon fillets in,
　　　　238–239
　　scrambled eggs with smoked salmon,
　　　　herbs and, 101
　　shallot, and chive sauce, 186

　　shallot, and herb essence, 85
　　sour cream vs., 30, 265, 267
　　spicy, fricassee of peppers in, 259
Cremini mushrooms, penne with broccoli,
　　　　tomato fondue and, 108–109
Cucumber(s), 27
　　cool soup with lime, shrimp, and cilantro,
　　　　54
　　glazed, fricassee of salmon with, 212
　　Mediterranean salad of radishes, feta and,
　　　　62
　　and tomato vinaigrette, 187
Cumin:
　　-and-curry-scented couscous with toasted
　　　　walnuts, 157
　　-lemon marinade, 165
　　roasted, vinaigrette, 63
　　-scented tomato fondue, 210
　　seeds, toasting of, 63
　　vinaigrette, 180
Cupboard, 10–25
Curry, curried:
　　crust with spinach and pine nuts, pan-
　　　　seared shrimp in, 207
　　-and-cumin-scented couscous with toasted
　　　　walnuts, 157
　　ginger-lemon vinaigrette, 76–77
　　leek and raisin chutney, 257
　　roast chicken salad, 65

Dairy shelf, 29–31
Desserts, 271–291
　　brown sugar–ginger ice cream, 284
　　buttery pine nut and brown sugar tart,
　　　　283
　　Catalan bittersweet chocolate, orange, and
　　　　pine nut tart, 289
　　compote of dried fruit with ginger and
　　　　cinnamon, 286
　　compote of gingered blueberries and
　　　　nectarines, 278
　　crisp almond phyllo cookies, 275
　　espresso mascarpone mousse with coffee-
　　　　soaked biscuits, 281
　　gratin of roasted cherries in red wine, 274
　　kiwi yogurt sorbet, 288
　　mascarpone yogurt cream with grated
　　　　orange and spring berries, 277
　　oven-baked rice pudding with lemon and
　　　　raisins, 287
　　peach gratin with creamy pecan crumble,
　　　　279

Provençal potato and garlic galette, 71
Prune(s):
   and bacon clafoutis, savory, 104
   as dessert, 285
   drunken, ragoût of pork with onions and, 220–221
   and toasted almond tart, 285
Pudding:
   rice, with lemon and raisins, oven-baked, 287
   sweet yellow corn, 263

Radishes, 29
   Mediterranean salad of cucumbers, feta and, 62
Ragoûts:
   braised halibut with pinto beans and saffron sofrito, 240
   of calamari with tubettini and onion-tomato compote, 234–235
   Cornish hens with potatoes, onions, and thyme, 227
   oxtail, in onion compote, 223
   pork with drunken prunes and onions, 220–221
   shrimp, bacon, spinach, and mushroom, with penne, 112–113
   stew of knockwurst and summer vegetables, 222
Raisin(s):
   carrot, and pine nut couscous, 159
   chutney, 232–233
   and leek chutney, curried, 257
   oven-baked rice pudding with lemon and, 287
   plumping of, 159
Red currant and strawberry sauce, 291
Refrigerator, 26–32
Rice, 16
   Arborio, soup with spring vegetables, 49
   caramelized onion pilaf, 139
   piquant parsley and lemon pilaf, 136
   pudding with lemon and raisins, oven-baked, 287
   risotto with smoked trout, tomatoes, and herb cream, 144–145
   shrimp, tomato, and red onion pilaf à la Catalane, 137
   skillet-braised shrimp, zucchini, and pepper paella, 140–141
   spicy Basque smoked chicken paella, 142–143
   tomatillo, cilantro, and green chili pilaf, 138
   zucchini and basil risotto with Parmigiano, 148–149
Rice vinegar, 19
Risotto:
   Al Porto's, with basil, rosemary, and mascarpone, 146–147
   with smoked trout, tomatoes, and herb cream, 144–145
   stock for, 149
   zucchini and basil, with Parmigiano, 148–149
Roasts, 217–240
   Catalan bluefish with gratin of new potatoes and onions, 236–237
   chicken legs with chili and cinnamon rub, 226
   Cornish hens in rosemary-lemon essence, 230–231
   garlic-roasted chicken with fennel and onions, 228–229
   leg of lamb with fricassee of beans "en persillade," 224–225
   oven-braised salmon fillets in lemon crème fraîche, 238–239
   turkey with golden raisin chutney, 232–233
Roquefort:
   cream, 205
   toasts with cabbage, potato, and turnip soup, 55
Rosemary:
   Al Porto's risotto with basil, mascarpone and, 146–147
   -lemon essence, roast Cornish hens in, 230–231
   semolina gnocchi with anchovies, garlic and, 154–155
   wild mushrooms roasted with thyme and, 262

Sabayon:
   Grand Marnier, 291
   pink grapefruit with strawberry sauce, 276
Saffron:
   couscous with spinach and red peppers, 158
   -infused fettuccine with braised leeks, 118
   powdered, 118, 158

Sautés and skillet cooking *(continued)*
    fillet of beef in tomato, caper, and
        anchovy sauce, 203
    flank steak in spicy ginger marinade, 202
    fricassee of mako with tomatoes, capers,
        and lemon, 216
    fricassee of salmon with glazed
        cucumbers, 212
    lamb chops with mustard, balsamic
        vinegar, and herb marinade, 200
    pan-seared chicken breasts in asparagus
        and dill sauce, 196
    pan-seared salmon with melted leeks and
        dill, 211
    pan-seared shrimp in curry crust with
        spinach and pine nuts, 207
    pepper-coated tuna with caviar aïoli,
        213
    scallops in cumin-scented tomato fondue,
        210
    scallops with root vegetables in mustard
        cream, 208
    scaloppine of turkey with chanterelles,
        tarragon, and tomato concassée, 197–
        198
    seared scallops with asparagus and wilted
        lettuce, 209
    seared swordfish with puree of sweet-and-
        spicy peppers, 214
    shallot and herb-infused lamb chops,
        199
    shrimp with roasted red pepper and
        shallot puree, 206
    steak in tarragon and green peppercorn
        sauce, 201
    swordfish with anchovies, garlic, and
        tomato fondue, 215
    veal chops in Roquefort cream, 205
    veal scaloppine in tarragon and lemon
        cream, 204
    zucchini Milanese, 254
Savoiardi, coffee-soaked, espresso
        mascarpone mousse with, 281
Scallion(s):
    and dill vinaigrette, creamy, 89
    -lemon mayonnaise, 183
    melted, couscous with, 160
    tangy lemon orzo with red peppers and,
        150
Scallops:
    and calamari salad with avocado in lime-
        ginger vinaigrette, 67
    cooking of, 209

    sautéed, in cumin-scented tomato fondue,
        210
    sautéed, with root vegetables in mustard
        cream, 208
    seared, with asparagus and wilted lettuce,
        209
Scaloppine:
    of turkey with chanterelles, tarragon, and
        tomato concassée, 197–198
    veal, in tarragon and lemon cream, 204
Semolina gnocchi with anchovies, garlic,
        and rosemary, 154–155
Sesame marinade, 176
Sesame seed oil, 14
Shallot(s), 29
    and balsamic vinegar dressing, 90
    crème fraîche, and chive sauce, 186
    crème fraîche, and herb essence, 85
    and herb-infused lamb chops, 199
    lemon, and sherry vinegar dressing, 90
    minced, 206
    and parsley butter, 252
    and roasted red pepper puree, 206
Shellfish:
    and corn chowder, farm stand, 52–53
    grilled, sauces for, 186–187
    see also specific shellfish
Sherry vinegar, 14
    lemon, and shallot dressing, 90
    and walnut oil dressing, 91
Shiitake, roasted, mixed green salad with
        Parmesan shavings and, 70
Shrimp:
    bacon, spinach, and mushroom ragoût
        with penne, 112–113
    cool cucumber soup with lime, cilantro
        and, 54
    farm stand shellfish and corn chowder,
        52–53
    and ginger fritters, spicy, 84
    grilled brochettes in sesame marinade, 176
    marinating time for, 176
    pan-seared, in curry crust with spinach
        and pine nuts, 207
    sauté of, with roasted red pepper and
        shallot puree, 206
    spicy al'ajillo, linguine with, 124
    spicy lime and lemon grass bouillon with
        avocado and, 43
    tomato, and red onion pilaf à la Catalane,
        137
    zucchini, and pepper paella, skillet-
        braised, 140–141

Wine, white:
   champagne vinegar, 14, 267
   mustard and champagne vinaigrette,
      267
   pineapple custard mousse with Sauternes,
      280
   sherry vinegar, 14
Woods, for smoking, 168

Yogurt, 30
   dressing, 62
   -and-ginger-marinated smoked chicken
      wings, 168
   kiwi sorbet, 288
   mascarpone cream with grated orange
      and spring berries, 277

Ziti:
   in roasted onion, fennel, and tomato
      compote, 111
   with smoked bluefish and summer squash
      in tarragon cream, 114
Zucchini:
   and basil risotto with Parmigiano, 148–
      149
   bell pepper, and smoked salmon salad, 66
   frittata with Parmesan, 95
   golden, and yellow pepper soup, 57
   and orzo soup with pesto, Mediterranean,
      50
   sauté Milanese, 254
   shrimp, and pepper paella, skillet-braised,
      140–141
   and tomatoes in pesto sour cream, 265